THE
PASSING
OF THE
ABORIGINES

*A Lifetime Spent among
the Natives of Australia*

DAISY BATES

With a Foreword by
Alan Moorehead
and an Introduction by
Arthur Mee

PUBLISHED BY POCKET BOOKS NEW YORK

THE PASSING OF THE ABORIGINES:

A Lifetime Spent Among the Natives of Australia

Praeger edition published February, 1967

POCKET BOOK edition published March, 1973

This POCKET BOOK edition includes every word
contained in the original, higher-priced edition. It is printed
from brand-new plates made from completely reset, clear, easy-to-read
type. POCKET BOOK editions are published by POCKET BOOKS, a division
of Simon & Schuster, Inc., 630 Fifth Avenue, New York, N.Y. 10020.
Trademarks registered in the United States and other countries.

                                                                    L

Standard Book Number: 671-78276-2.
Library of Congress Catalog Card Number: 67-12002.
First published by John Murray, London, 1938. Second edition
(with Foreword by Alan Moorehead and photograph by Douglas Glass),
1966. Foreword copyright, ©, 1966, by Alan Moorehead. All rights
reserved. This POCKET BOOK edition is published by arrangement
with Praeger Publishers, Inc.

Printed in the U.S.A.   Cover art by Alan Magee.

Contents

*A sixteen-page photo insert appears
between pages 102 and 103*

Foreword

A glance at the photograph and one feels one knows her pretty well—the eccentric, voyaging, Victorian spinster, pert and indestructible, the missionary figure: Florence Nightingale or perhaps the lady who went off to the court of the King of Siam. She is one's well-loved maiden aunt.

Yet I am not sure that any of these labels sticks. The more you know about Daisy Bates the less she is what she seems. She was no missionary. As far as I can make out she never tried to teach the Australian aborigines anything or convert them to any faith. She preferred them to stay as they were and live out the last of their days in peace. She doctored them a little but she was not really a female Dr. Schweitzer; she simply wanted to make her home with the tribes, and to take part in their customs and ancestral ceremonies—which was not at all "going native," those gloves and button-up boots were proof against that.

She was rather an egocentric woman. Clearly her Australian husband bored her, for she soon left him and there is not much evidence that she took any lively interest in her son.

One rather tends, on reflection, to liken her to Mary Kingsley since (as the reader of this book will discover) she wrote extremely well and she had, in the beginning, the Irish nose for polemical politics; and socially she was what one likes to think of as a "lady." Yet none of this will really do: she wrote very little, the politics were soon forgotten and her good manners were wasted in the desert air.

So we return inevitably to the fact that one thing dominated her life to the exclusion of all else—her passion for the aborigines—and it is something of a marvel that she never for one moment in anything she said or did became a bore about them. She illuminated them. She was not an anthropologist but she knew them better than anyone else who ever lived; and she made them interesting not only to herself but to us as well.

And because of this absorption of hers I am inclined, in the end, to think that she was really a mystic. Living in the most arid bush, surrounded by the most primitive people, she found a revelation, a version of the true nature of things, that was far clearer to her than the normal life we know. It was not so much a return to primitivism as an act of faith—or a belief in mankind itself. She was content. She woke each morning to a valid world which she understood and loved and did not want to alter. It is this air of completeness that makes her such a remarkable woman— such a lovable woman. Whenever one thinks about her one smiles inwardly a little—that get-up in the desert really was extraordinary—and somehow one's temper is improved, the day is brighter. How much one would have liked to have met her and talked to her. But at least we have this book.

ALAN MOOREHEAD

Kabbarli

ON THE FRINGE OF THE VAST ISLAND CONTINENT OF AUS-
tralia live a few millions of white people; in the vast desert
regions far from the coast live a few thousands of black
people, the remnant of the first inhabitants of Australia.

The race on the fringe of the continent has been there
about a hundred years, and stands for Civilization; the
race in the interior has been there no man knows how long,
and stands for Barbarism. Between them a woman has
lived in a little white tent for more than twenty years,
watching over these people for the sake of the Flag, a
woman alone, the solitary spectator of a vanishing race.
She is Daisy Bates, one of the least known and one of the
most romantic figures in the British Empire.

She has left these poor people whom she counts as her
children and has come back to civilization for a little while
to write this story of her life among the aborigines on the
rim of the great Nullarbor Plain. She has given her life and
her heart to this dying race, the first people of our southern
Dominion. She has done it for the love of humanity and
for England. She has neither sought fame nor found it. She
has made no money by her long life's work. Through all
these years she has been alone, cut off from the world, with
only these strange, backward, hopeless people to give her a
little human society now and then. There is in her life
something of the spirit of service that moved Florence
Nightingale, and something of the spirit of sacrifice that
filled the heart of Father Damien. She would not put it
so, for she has loved her life and made a joy of her labour,
but it is right that this tribute should be paid to Mrs.
Daisy Bates.

She was the daughter of an Irish family, and came over to London in those far-away days when journalism was a noble business and Fleet Street was excited by the doings of a young man named Stead. Daisy Bates joined his staff. She was a keen observer, a woman with scientific knowledge and a gift for languages, and she began her working life in the glow of that great spirit who stirred and entertained all London in his day. He lies in the bed of the Atlantic with the ruins of the *Titanic* about him, while the Irish lady on his staff sits in her tent on the banks of the Murray River, looking back on those few years at the hub of the world and her long years alone in the Australian wilderness.

She went out to her aborigines in the first years of this century. She found them decreasing in numbers with the coming of the white man, their root-foods ploughed up, the tracks to their water-holes disappearing. She wrote a history of them which still remains in manuscript. When the century was ten years old she went out to two islands on a Commission to study the hospital treatment of these poor people, and while there she set up a post office so that the patients could communicate with their families on the mainland. One of the first services she rendered to them was to conduct a mail with notched sticks, conveying messages to their friends. She had forty patients on her hands and pulled every one through. She kept them tranquil and cheerful in their bush shelters, sat by their sick beds listening to their tribal stories, joined with them in praying to their totems when they wanted rain. They had never known anyone like her. They named her Kabbarli, grandmother.

It happened that her husband died, and Mrs. Bates, left with a cattle station and thousands of cattle, decided to dispose of her property and to interest herself in these people. She decided that the only way to help this dying race was to live with them, and she travelled wherever she heard of natives gathering. She made herself known to all these wandering tribes. Five times she pitched her camp along the edge of the Plain which none of these aborigines had dared to cross till Edward John Eyre crossed it in

1840; and her fifth camp was in the sand-hills of Ooldea, which she reached when the Great War was raging in Europe. There she stayed, living a mile from the transcontinental railway in a tent and a shed made of boughs, ringed round by a high breakwind. Here she passed from her prime to old age, walking a mile every day when she was over seventy years old to get water, and carrying it back to her tent, where she would spare it for the birds though the thermometer was 112.

Sitting at her tent she would receive these wandering tribes, little regiments of them coming one day from nowhere to nowhere, another day in search of revenge for some blow struck at them by another tribe ahead. She would greet the little ragged procession (ragged or naked as the case might be) as the one friend they had in the great world beyond their reach. They would come to her with the confidence of a child in its mother, yet like creatures from another world than ours. I shall never forget her writing to me that a woman she had had for tea at her tent had eaten her own child. Dramatic and terrible as such a thing is to us, it was no new experience for Daisy Bates, for cannibalism has never died out among these wandering tribes. They will kill and eat from revenge, or from primeval motives beyond our understanding.

More than once the last number of one of these tribes has died in the arms of Daisy Bates. "Where am I going?" asked one of these pathetic dying people, and we may wonder if anything could be better than Kabbarli's answer: "My Father is where you are going." All fear was gone. "Your Father, Kabbarli? Then I shall be safe," and the poor tired Jeera fell asleep, her warm hand growing cold as Kabbarli held it.

Between her mind and theirs was the gulf that only many generations can bridge—she with a deep love of humanity, a mind filled with dreams, and her heart stirred with a passion for England; they with the primeval emotions of mankind, to whom the railway train puffing steam is the great white snake, in whom the spirit of the cannibal is not yet dead. To her the most pathetic memories of her life are the sights and sounds of England, the primroses and the church bells, the green fields and the song of birds, the wild rose in the hedgerow, the little church at the end of a country lane, and the harvest field; but for a generation she has not seen these things, and will not now. She has chosen, instead, to be the last friend of the last remnant of this dying race. The last friendly hand, the last kindly word, that will come to them will be hers.

She knows them as they know themselves. She knows their languages, their rituals, their traditions, their capacities and their incapacities, as no white man or woman on the earth knows them. She can talk to them in 188 dialects. They have invited her to ceremonies which their own women may not attend, and have admitted her into their tribes and put their sacred totems in her keeping. She is a magical figure to them. She can quell a squabble with a word or a look. They come to her hungry and she feeds them. They come to her naked and she clothes them. They come to her sick and she heals them. She belongs to no church, no mission, no creed; she has been a woman alone befriending these poor people, ruling them not by law but by the simple directness of character, the power of a personality which has no room for selfishness and seeks no end but the happiness of others.

If we ask what it is that she has had in view through all these years it is the thought that England, with these people in the shelter of the Flag, owes something to them. Their race is bound to disappear—it is about 60,000 strong and does not grow like the proud Maori race of New Zealand. It has been her idea that their lives should be controlled and cared for with that fact in view. They should be left as free as possible, to pass from existence as happily as may be. She has wanted to save them from the worst effects of casual contact with the fringe of civilization. In their way they are pure and simple folk, and she has come to love them. She has a strong belief in British administration, and has always wanted a King's Man to look after these people.

It is for this end that she has lived the life of a heroic woman, labouring in solitude in a climate often parching and only rarely bursting into beauty, seeking to succour a noisome race, melancholy in outlook and terrible in habits. For a little while she has left them. She left them for three enchanting weeks in 1933 when the Government invited her to Canberra to discuss the aborigines. A surprising figure she must have been in the streets of the capital, this white-haired old lady from the uncivilized world, wearing the shirt blouse, the high collar and the long skirt of the early years of our century. For her there are no changing fashions. For a little while, again, she returned to civilization to set down this story, and, tiring of city streets, she has set up her tent once more on the banks of the great Murray River where years ago these people made their home. She has found their old haunts deserted, with not a native left.

Perhaps she may return to them; perhaps not; but still she dreams that the Empire will not fail this human remnant in its keeping. Still she is buoyed up by the belief that a man, the right man, a King's Man, will some day be appointed by Australia to take charge of these children of a race which inhabited Australia before the white man heard of it, and are dying out not knowing how wonderful life is.

To us she is Daisy Bates, Commander of the Order of the British Empire, the most remarkable woman in Australia. To them she is the magical Kabbarli, whose word is love and law, and whose life is swayed by the spirit of the Master whom she serves.

ARTHUR MEE.

Prologue

A VANISHED PEOPLE

PERTH FROM KING'S PARK. I CAN NEVER LOOK DOWN ON the panorama of that young and lovely city from the natural parkland on the crest of Mount Eliza that is its crowning glory without a vision of the past, the dim and timeless past when a sylvan people wandered its woods untrammelled, with no care or thought for yesterday or tomorrow, or of a world other than their own. Scarcely a hundred years have passed since that symmetry of streets and suburbs was a pathless bushland, a tangle of trees and scrub and swamp with the broad blue ribbon of river running through it, widening from a thread of silver at the foot of the ranges to the estuary marshes and the sea.

Through it all, a kangaroo skin slung carelessly over his shoulders, a few spears in his hand, strode the first landlord, catching fish in the river-shallows, spearing the emu and the kangaroo, and finding the roots and fruits that were his daily bread. His women and children meekly followed, carrying his spare weapons, their own household gods, and perhaps a baby swung in the kangaroo-skin bag. Every spring and gully, every quaintly distorted tree, every patch of red ochre or white pipe-clay was his landmark, and every point, hill, valley, slope or flat from the river's source to its mouth had its name. Simple in his needs in a land of plenty, knowing none other than the age-old laws of life, and mating, and death, that have been his through the unreasoning centuries, he was a barbarian, but his lot was happy. As far as humans can, he lived in perfect amity with his fellows.

For hundreds of miles about him the people of the country were all his kindred, and the camp-fires dotting the river-flats, and the ranges, and the sea-coasts, and the great timber-forests were fires of friendliness.

As I dream, the red glow of those fires of fancy grows hard and cold and yellow, regular as the street-lights of a city, and the ranges beyond them are lost in the shadow— even as the last of their people. Of the songs that rang to the stars in the far-off time there is no echo. The black man survived the coming of the white for little more than one lifetime. When Captain Stirling landed on the coast in 1829, he computed the aboriginal population of what he had marked out as the metropolitan area at 1,500 natives. In 1907 we buried Joobaitch, last of the Perth tribe.

N

TIMOR
SEA

PORT DARWIN • DARWIN

NORT

TER

Baadu
Tribe

Nyool-nyool
Tribe

BROOME

EDA L.

FITZROY R.

HALL'S
CREEK

LAGRANGE BAY

ROEBUCK
PLAINS

Eighty Mile

PORT
HEDLAND

WESTERN

• ETHEL C

Fortescue R.

• MARBLE BAR

Ashburton R.

OPHTHALMIA
RANGES

SOU

Gascoyne R.

Ngalli-a
Tribe

BOUNDARY
DAM

CARNARVON
BERNIER I.
DORRE I.

AUSTRALIA

DARLOT L.

Wong-gai-i
Tribe

Murchison R.
• GERALDTON

JURIEN BAY

Monger's L.

COOLGARDIE

• KALGOORLIE

NULLABOR A
PLAIN
JEEGALA

• Oc
HA

EUCLA

GREAT
AUSTRAL
BIGHT

NEW NORCIA

FRASER RANGE

GUILDFORD
PERTH

YORK

AVON R.

ESPERANCE

ARID CAPE

BUNBURY
BUSSELTON
BRIDGETOWN

Salt R.

BREMER BAY

ESPERANCE BAY

DARLING RANGES

ALBANY

KING GEORGE'S
SOUND

SOUT

100   0   100   200   300   400

Scale of Miles

The positions of the tribes as shown on this map are only approximate.

Chapter I

MEETING WITH THE ABORIGINES

As I dream over the orphaned land of the Bib-bulmun,[1] my thoughts fly back, too, to the events which brought me on a second visit to Australia after a period of journalism in London with W. T. Stead, on the *Review of Reviews,* back to the stone-age nomads whom I had but glimpsed on my first visit to Australia, but among whom the rest of my life was to be cast. It was in 1899 that circumstances made possible my return to Australia.

Just before I left London a letter had been published in *The Times* containing strong allegations of cruelty to Western Australian aborigines by the white settlers of the North-West. I called upon *The Times,* stated that I was going to Western Australia and offered to make full investigation of the charges, and to write them the results. The offer was accepted.

While friends were bidding me farewell, one of them espied a kindly old Roman Catholic padre on deck, and asked him to "keep an eye" on me on the voyage out. The priest was an Italian named Martelli, and on the deck the first evening we embarked on a delightful friendship that lasted till his death. I studied Italian under his tutelage, until one day I mentioned the subject of the Australian natives, and showed Dean Martelli the letter in *The Times*. Italian grammars were promptly put aside as I gained my first knowledge of the remnants of a fading race, and the problem they afforded the Government and the missions in the Western State. I learned also of the Beagle Bay Mission, away in the wilds of the North-West, where the

---

[1] See Chapter VII.

Trappist fathers had come from their beautiful old home monasteries among the vineyards of Sept Fons in France in rigours and difficulties to minister to the aborigines in the vicinity of Broome.

Shortly after I landed in Perth, I obtained a buggy and horses and camp-gear, and journeyed by sea to Port Hedland. Arrived at that remote port, I stayed at a licensed shanty with earthen floors and blue blankets, where the hermit crabs from the seashore nibbled my feet every time I put them to the floor. I then traversed in my buggy eight hundred miles of country, taking six months to accomplish it. I could not prove one charge of cruelty, except that of "giving offal to natives instead of good meat," and "sending them away from the stations without food when work was slack." So far as these were concerned, I found that the favourite parts of any animal, large or small, were the entrails, which were torn out of the beast and eaten half raw. Later, on my own station, I discovered that the blacks insisted on a "pink-hi" or walkabout season —they could not live without it—and that they would not carry flour and tea, preferring their own bush tucker. Once in my inexperience, I myself packed up a plenitude of provisions for them, tied neatly in bundles on their heads, with new shirts and trousers and medicines and other conveniences I thought they might need. A few days after they had gone, riding to an outlying windmill, I came across a snow-storm of the flour that they had playfully thrown at each other. The tea and sugar had been consumed at this first well, and the trousers and sundries were deposited in a tree-fork.

Care-free and unclad, gathering their native foods and bending to drink at the soaks and water-holes, the natives had taken a hundred-mile trail to anywhere, to call on their friends and relations, where they could play and quarrel till the desire for damper and tea saw them homing to the station again. So much for the allegations that awakened my interest in the Australian aborigines, and which were the beginning of my life's work among them. *The Times* published the result of my investigations and the matter dropped for a decade.

It was while I rested at Sherlock River Station, near Roebourne, in 1900, that I gained my first knowledge of the natives' social organization, and the classes into which they were divided, and was myself entered into one of these classes. The white people of the station, the well-known pioneering families of Withnells and Meares, were West Australians, and father, mother and children had all been classed by the natives according to their aboriginal relationships. I was so much interested in the systems of these primitive people that I inquired if I also had been classified.

"Oh yes," Mrs. Meares told me. "You belong to my husband's class, and you are his sister and my sister-in-law, the paternal aunt of my children."

Before I left Sherlock River, I had discovered the fundamental simplicity of the system. Later, at Beagle Bay, I found myself entered in exactly the same class division. This was enlightening and good news to me, and I utilized it later among the Broome groups, with excellent results.

It suffices to say that in every group throughout all Western Australia, and passing from group to group in South and Central Australia, I assumed as a matter of course my proper relationship. Even when I went to my camp in the desert at Ooldea, I found the natives there in touch with those of the west a thousand miles away across the border, and the western class divisions remembered.

On my return to Perth, Dean Martelli invited me to the Bishop's Palace to meet Bishop Gibney, Roman Catholic Bishop of the State of Western Australia. Bishop Gibney and the Dean were about to pay a visit to Beagle Bay. I was invited to go down with them and see this Mission for myself, and to tell of its benefits, or otherwise, to the natives. I was told that the fate of the Mission hung on the report of the government valuator, who would make a patrol almost immediately to see if the scheduled improvements that would entitle the Mission authorities to a fee-simple over 10,000 acres had been carried out. These improvements must total £5,000, otherwise the grazing lease must be forfeited. I accepted with alacrity, and made my preparations with stores of clothing, food and sweets for distribution.

In July, the two priests and I were under way for the port of Broome, from which we were to tranship to Beagle Bay. At Broome the *Sree pas Sair,* at once time the yacht of Rajah Brooke, was placed at our disposal. It had been stripped of every comfort. Cleanliness there was none, as it was the "feeding-lugger" of the pearling-boats owned by a Manilaman, and brought back the shell from the luggers. After an interesting voyage round the fleets in the *Sree pas Sair,* we returned to Broome, and with three of the Trappists waiting there, loaded up the yacht. I learned that not only was there no accommodation for a woman at the monastery, with all its rigid poverty and simplicity, but, according to Trappist principles, no woman except a queen could be allowed within its walls. However, there I was, and the dear little acting abbot took it upon himself to grant a dispensation, and went out to see what furniture he could buy for me, making wild guesses at what a female might need. His bewildered and exaggerated idea of hospitality filled me with astonishment.

We all worked hard at the loading and packing of the lugger, and in the beginning of August the *Sree pas Sair* set out northward. There were eight of us on board—the Bishop, the Dean, the acting abbot, two brothers, Xavier and Sebastian, the owner and helmsman, his Malay uncle and a small Malay child. We reached Beagle Bay on the high tide that rises thirty feet in a few hours, and the whaleboats took us, and eventually the stores, to land. Just near the beach was a primitive turtle-soup factory and in the fenced-in enclosure an unfortunate turtle awaited transformation into eighty tins of soup. We inspected the factory, but were not impressed by the dirty native women and girls loafing about it, so we did not accept the turtle soup.

Mounting from the ship's deck on horseback, we set out, the Bishop and I, across the nine miles of bleak flat that lay between the beach and the Mission, Dean Martelli and the brothers following with the bullock-team which had been sent in for the stores. I rode side-saddle on a stride-saddle—a painful ordeal. A few half-clad natives straggled along behind us. As we jogged on through the heat and flies and blankness, the Bishop intoned the rosary, and the natives joined in when they knew the words. The horses were Trappists, too, skin and bone in their poverty. They stopped so often for their meditations and devotions that the bullock-team arrived before us.

At last in the early moonlight we pulled in to a few tin buildings in a clearing. About 150 natives, men, women and children, shouted a welcome to us from the shadows. None of us had eaten anything to speak of for three days on the *Sree pas Sair,* and the lay brother had set about unloading the stores and preparing a meal.

Beagle Bay had been founded by Bishop Gibney ten years before, when, with two exiles of Spanish priests, he had taken a long pilgrimage through the bush from Derby, at last finding suitable country with ten precious acres of wonderful springs, natural wells and extensive swamps, the best water in the North-West. He had secured a lease, under certain conditions, of 10,000 acres, and the native reserve which extended for 600,000 acres about it. The Trappists there established the first Mission in the far North-West. Unable to speak English and quite unused to Australian conditions, the two little pioneer priests and the sixteen ordained men who had followed them from the old French monastery had endured years of unbelievable hardships in a remote wilderness. Some had died there, under the saddest conditions. Others, blind and emaciated, had been rescued from their fate and invalided home.

When I arrived, the Mission was but a collection of tumble-down, paper-bark monastery cells, a little bark chapel and a community room of corrugated iron, which had been repeatedly destroyed in bush fires and hurricanes. There were four monks left on the station. They were Abbot Nicholas, a Catalonian Spaniard, father confessor, doctor, teacher and overseer; Brother Sebastian, a Manilaman who was the cook; Brother Xavier, a Broome constable who had laid down his baton for the rosary-beads on the Bishop's first visit, and was gardner, storekeeper and handyman, and Frère Jean, stockman.

Frère Jean had been dedicated to the service of God at Sept Fons in his early childhood. I was the first white woman, other than his mother, he had seen or looked at in his life. As I came into the community room, which had been set aside for our living-place, eager for my supper, Frère Jean fled from the world, the flesh and the devil that I represented, but before I left Beagle Bay he had so far overcome his religious horror of me that he made and fitted me with a neat little pair of kangaroo-skin shoes, and even slept trustfully in my company when we all camped out on our survey expedition.

The Trappists led a life of rigorous poverty, intensified in this barren remote land to the point of starvation. There were cattle on the station, but meat was excluded for religious reasons, and the monks existed on one meal a day of pumpkin and rice, and a little beer that they had made from sorghum grown in the garden. Rising at 2 a.m. they kept vigil in the dark chapel till dawn, then worked till daylight's end, speaking no word save in necessity, and closing the day with some hours on their knees on the bare earth. I was the first white woman to appear among them at the Mission, and the first that the natives of the region had seen.

From the newly arrived stores, Brother Sebastian had provided a strange and varied meal for us according to his lights, extraordinary stews and puddings served in any order and all strongly flavoured with garlic, milkless tea in a huge jug that was both teapot and cups for us all. Poor Brother Sebastian may have been a paragon of piety, but he was no cook. In my keeping to-day is a fragment of petrified bread roll he made for me in 1900! It has been mistaken for a geological specimen, and, always carried with me in loving memory, it has survived, without losing a crumb, thousands of miles of rough transport.

Perhaps the first woman in history to sleep in a Trappist bed, I was allotted the abbot's bag bed and seaweed pillow, and the sawn-off log for my chair or table. I woke to hear the natives singing a Gregorian chant in the little chapel near by. Half clothed and, for all the untiring work of the missioners, still but half-civilized, they comprised the

Nyool-nyool tribe, of the totem of a local species of snake. Most of the women and men had their two front teeth knocked out, and some still wore bones through their noses. Infant cannibalism was practised, where it could not be prevented—as it still is among all circumcised groups. One of the old men, Bullybulluma, having been an epic meat-hunter in his day, had eight wives. Another, Goodowel, was dressed in trousers and shirt, one stocking, his face painted red with white stripes from each corner of his mouth in broad lines. A red band was around his head, the hair drawn back to form a tight knob, and stuck in the knob was a tuft of white cockatoo feathers and a small wooden emblem. I know now that he was in the sixth degree of initiation.

Although they had tried their hardest, with prayer and precept, to teach these natives cleanliness and Christian living, giving their very lives to the work in torture and privation, those Spanish priests could hope for little headway in the first generation. There was one terrible manifestation of savagery that I can never forget.

A man had been found dying of spear-wounds out in the bush, and carried to the Mission as he was breathing his last. I watched two of the lay brothers bearing the stretcher to one of the huts, a horde of natives following. I noticed that they held their burden curiously in the air. Suddenly, as it was lowered for entry to a doorway, the natives crowding round, to my horror, fell upon the body of the dying man, and put their lips to his in a brutal eagerness to inhale the last breath. They believed that in so doing they were absorbing his strength and virtue, and his very vital spark, and all the warnings of the "white father" would not keep them from it. The man was of course dead when we extricated him, and it was a ghastly sight to see the lucky "breath catcher" scoop in his cheeks as he swallowed the "spirit breath" that gave him double hunting power.

Chapter II

IN A TRAPPIST MONASTERY

I WAS AWAKENED BY THE SOUND OF THE CONCH SHELL which did duty for a monastery bell in that primitive spot, and when I went out into the open I was surrounded by all the women and children, a bright, pleasant little crowd, but oh! how dirty! Although the monks for some years had issued the dictum "No bath, no breakfast," the natives preferred the lesser of two evils, and went hungry until the ban was lifted. Shack dormitories had been erected for the unmarried girls and men, but most of the natives came in from the camps in the bush where they slept under the trees. Their beds were hollows scooped in the sand where a fire had been burning, the sand and the stones sometimes so hot that they left raw wounds in the flesh. Father Nicholas told us that they ate dirt in handfuls, and that the women sometimes ate their new-born babies, but that since the advent of the Mission, with its admonitions and its daily distribution of pumpkin and rice and tea and flour, cannibalism was not nearly so much in evidence.

Immediately after our monastic breakfast of coffee and Brother Sebastian's rolls, we started off to inspect the Mission property and set it shipshape for the valuator's visit. A survey of the whole lease was to follow. Although I had come up merely as a "child taking notes," I started on the very practical manual labour necessary to improve the appearance of the place, sharing the toil with the brothers and the blacks, and the Bishop in his shirt-sleeves. The four months that I spent there were nothing but the sheerest hard work under the most trying conditions.

Manual labour has been the keynote of all my work for the aborigines. I have never made servants or attendants

8

of them. I have waited upon the sick and old, and carried their burdens, fed the blind and the babies, sewed for the women and buried the dead—only in quiet hours gleaning, gathering, learning, always hastening, as one by one the tribe dwindled out of existence, knowing how soon it would be too late.

At Beagle Bay, the Spanish priests and monks had performed almost incredible labours in their ten years' isolation, but there was little to show for it. Willie-willies and fires and tropic conditions had taken constant toll. When houses and crops and gardens were burnt, they had to start all over again. When their horses were lost, or died from eating poisonous weed, they harnessed themselves to carts and logs, yet the conditions of the Mission seemed hopeless. The bark huts were dilapidated, the gardens smothered in growth of saplings and suckers, and some of the wells had fallen in.

I was sent in charge of some native women to do some "scrubbing"—that is, hoeing up the small shoots, or saplings, of uprooted trees, and to open up the fallen wells, of which the flooring was as shaky as an Irish bog. I worked like a Trojan, but the force of my example failed dismally. Day after day those women played with the babies, and laughed both with and at me, full of merriment and good feeling. Now and again, a few of them took up the spade or the hoe in a stirring of conscience, but not for long, and all my efforts to make it an interesting game failed to produce results. I tried to gather the babies and children and play with them, and let their mothers do a little manual labour, and I started "Ring-a-ring-a-roses." No sooner had we got into the swing of the game than every woman and girl "downed tools" to join in. I compromised. We adults must work, and when the rest time came at hot midday or evening, we would have games. The little plan worked, and so we worked and played merrily throughout. As I worked they talked to me, and told me a little of their laws. Curiously enough, they had entered both the Bishop and me, believing him my brother, into one of their four-class divisions, the abbot and the monks belonging to another. The women quite frankly admitted to me that they had killed and eaten some of their children—they liked "baby meat."

There was a fight, apparently to the death, between two of these women one day, one of them heavily pregnant and the other an aged creature, nothing but skin and bone. It was the old story, an eternal triangle. Some time before, a boy had come down from Sunday Island, and being of good conduct and a fair worker, had been duly married to one of the unallotted girls of the station, which was what he had come down for. All went happily until, with another batch of visitors from the northern land, there arrived an old lady with prior claims, and maledictions and a yam-stick to prove them. The women fought steadily, blow for blow alternately, each blow well-timed and aimed for the direct centre of the skull. As each one took her turn the other passively submitted. At length the younger woman fell unconscious, and the fight was over.

When these purely personal quarrels took place, the Trappists found it best to let them run their course, so that there would be no subsequent ill-feeling. In this case the old woman lovingly attended the other, and stayed with her peacefully in the camp until she returned home, minus the husband, but quite satisfied. This was another "law" universal throughout the groups. Twins were born to the young woman shortly after, and the Trappists named them Matthew and Daisy, in honour of the Bishop and myself—a doubtful compliment, but appreciated.

So far as the safety of the missioners was concerned, there had never been any trouble at Beagle Bay, but at every laying-up season, when the pearling ships were offshore, practically every boy who had a woman took her down to trade her with the Asiatics. These women returned dying and diseased, after the boats had resumed pearling. It was an iniquitous thing, but it could not be prevented. Some boats laid up at Beagle Bay during our stay, and to keep the women and girls away from them, the Bishop told Father Nicholas to lock them in the store for the night. There was only one small opening high up in the wall, fifteen or twenty feet above ground, and no ladder. Even so, at daybreak when we went to the store there was not a woman there. They had piled up the store cases and climbed to the little window, dropping without hurt on the soft sand. The Bishop hurried down to the seashore to reclaim the girls, and ordered the coloured men away. Next night the blacks and their women joined them at another anchorage.

The association of the Australian native with the Asiatic is definitely evil. There were four Manilamen at Beagle Bay married to native women. By tribal custom the women had all been betrothed in infancy to their rightful tribal husbands. They were therefore merely on hire by their own men to the Asiatics, and, in spite of the church marriage, remained, not only their husband's property, but that of all his brothers, and all the Manila husband's brothers who paid for the accommodation. It was hard to convince the Bishop and the little abbot of this fact and of the terrible cruelty to the women and girls of such a system, and I had to show the two priests a poignant example. I had visited the Manila quarters in Broome, and in one house found a poor aboriginal woman, the "wife" of a Manilaman, with five of his "brothers" waiting to have and pay for intercourse with her. The poor soul told me that this happened daily. A few day afterwards I took the two priests to the hovel, choosing the Manila rest hour of the day for our inspection. I knew the terrible shock this would be to the little abbot and the Bishop to realize what Manila-Aboriginal marriage meant for the native woman: but with these facts the Bishop gave his direct veto on the dreadful system, and in future such marriages were prohibited.

For three months, and more, we had worked on the reclamation of the place, and the valuator arrived just as we had cleared the last corner. He was surprised to see a thriving property where he had expected ruin and decay. Every screw and post, every fruit and vegetable, buildings, wells, trenches and implements were meticulously valued, and with the livestock on the run, the supplies in the store, the sorghum and sugar-cane fields, the tomato and cucumber patches, and the orange, banana and coco-nut and pomegranate groves, the sum reached over £6,000. Even one Cape gooseberry bush and one grape-vine had to be valued. The Mission was saved for the natives. All together and in much jubilation we made the first brick of sand and loam and clay for the new convent and monastery, of which I laid the foundation brick.

I had then, and have now in retrospect, the greatest admiration for the Trappist missionaries, and nothing I may say about the sometimes incongruous results of their self-sacrificial work implies any inability to understand its sacred purpose. Although I am an Anglican, I attended all religious ceremonies, morning and evening, during my stay, and loved to listen to the natives, with their sweet voices, intoning the Latin chants and responses as much as I loved to listen to their own weird music. There were innumerable baptisms and weddings. On one occasion a little wisp of a girl about 12 years old was married to a man old enough to be her grandfather, who had always been lucky in the allotment of wives. He was a good hunter, and the unborn babies were betrothed to him to excite his generosity. If they happened to be boys they became his brothers-in-law. I spoke to the child-bride, Angelique, intending to rescue her from unwilling bondage, but she told me that she "likim that old man all right."

The wearing of a wreath and veil at religious ceremonies is an old Spanish custom, and the Trappist fathers kept wreath and veil in stock. All of the newly baptized and the brides wore it in turn, a delightfully ludicrous touch it seemed to me, worn above wild hair and matted beards, and no respectable clothing to speak of.

Knowing that he would probably never pay another visit to the Mission, the Bishop announced his intention of making confirmed Christians of all the natives in the district, and I shall never forget the occasion. Dean Martelli and the brothers rounded up the mob. Crowded into that little bark chapel, and smelling to high heaven, sixty-five wild men and women and babies of the Nyool-nyool stood before a prelate of the Roman Church, in all his ceremonial robes of lace and purple and mitre, to be anointed with the holy oils and receive the papal blessing and the little blow on the cheek of the "Pax tecum." Some of the men wore nothing but a vest or a red handkerchief, some a rag of a shirt, and the fraction of a pair of trousers. They had been told to keep their hands piously joined together, and their eyes shut—and the flies were bad.

Standing behind them, close to the door for a breath of air, I tried in vain to maintain a solemn countenance and a reverent mien, only to explode at least once in choking laughter at the antics of one boy. Knowing that I was behind him, he was at the same time desperately trying to keep his hands clasped in prayer, and a rag of decency well pulled down over his rear elevation. A frown of disapproval from under the dazzling mitre and an impatient jerk of the sacred crook in my direction sobered me up, but that afternoon, hearing a succession of loud shrieks of laughter from the camp, I went along to see how the newly-confirmed Christians were progressing.

Imagine my mingled horror and delight to find Goodowel, one of the corroboree comedians, sitting on a tree-trunk with a red-ochred billy-can on his head, and a tattered and filthy old rug around his shoulders. In front of him pranced every member of the tribe, all in a line, and each wearing a wreath and veil that were a bit of twisted paperbark and a fragment of somebody's discarded shirt. As they passed Goodowel, each received a sounding smack under the ear with a shout of "Bag take um!" Hilarious and ear-piercing shrieks of laughter followed each sally. I went back in glee to tell the Bishop. He shook his head. "Ah, the poor craytures!" was all he said.

There was yet another ordeal before us, a never-ending ordeal it seemed. In a few days' time, we set out again, with the natives and the bullock-dray, to survey the whole leasehold of 10,000 acres. Our only surveying instruments were the compass of an old lugger and a chain. The Bishop and I were the chainmen, and we walked in a steamy heat, of 106 degrees at times, sometimes twelve miles in the day. Over marsh and through the *pindan,* now lame from the stones and prickles, now up to our thighs in bog, we plodded on, the Bishop in the lead, throwing down a small peg to mark the chain limit, the brothers and the blacks and I behind him. I was always in difficulties owing to my small stride and high-heeled footwear, and many a time, seeing me perched perilously on the edge of a bog, the Bishop would give a mischievous twitch to his end of the chain, and land me deep in it.

We were all always hungry. Brother Xavier, in charge of the commissariat, was very good so far as he went, but he never seemed to come as far as we did, and we were always faint from lack of food. In the simplest meal— and they were all simple meals, of bread and beef—he would forget the salt, or the bread or the meat, or the place where he had arranged to meet us, or that we existed at all, but in hunger and hardship we managed to keep our good humour throughout our whole long stay, strange companions in the solitude of the bush.

On the night-walkings, rosaries were chanted all the way home, the natives and brothers responding. I often stumbled and fell in the dark, but that rosary never stopped. Sometimes we washed our faces in water from a bottle-tree. Felix, the native guide, chose his tree, chopped at a spot with his tomahawk, left the axe sticking in the cut, and the water came out clean and sparkling like a miniature waterfall. One morning, just before dawn, we came to Argomand Water—a glorious pool of still silver, where there was a sudden whirr of myriad wings to greet us, and thousands of birds of brilliant plumage rose in a cloud, screaming. That was the happiest circumstance of the long and arduous circuit. I compiled all the survey notes at night. Those survey notes were later a source of great amusement to the Bishop and his staff, but the Bishop received the title-deeds of his ten thousand acres, so the mud-stains and blots scarcely mattered. Later, in Perth, he presented me with an inscribed gold watch, in memory of our survey work, and the saving of the Mission for the natives.

The valuation was satisfactory, and the valuator departed. Travelling with the bullock-dray our next journey was to Disaster Bay, twenty-five miles north, to bring the consolations of religion to those not yet converted. The Bishop and I rode ahead, with two native women, the bullock team, Father Nicholas and the boys bringing up the rear.

It was a two-days' journey, and on the first we outdistanced the bullock-dray, camped in a good spot, and hobbled out the horses. Hour after hour we waited in the moonlight, but no dray appeared. At length we made back on foot to meet it. We found it three miles behind, all its party settled down for the night and fast alseep. The bullocks refused to move on after that day of blazing heat. Coffee and damper improved our spirits, and then we too settled down.

In the morning, Father Nicholas made some coffee of the last little supply of water left on the wagon, and we were on our way before the sun was up. It rose hot and fiery. There was no more water, and no water-hole until we reached Disaster Bay. We had been able to find neither drum, keg, nor water-bag at the Mission. We tried to hurry, but our horses were bad-tempered and thirsty. Now and again we dismounted to let the black women ride. Lake Flora we found to be a hard, dry clay-pan, which would not yield to spade or shovel. We went on as quickly as we could, the black women leading, the Bishop keeping them in sight, and I vainly trying to keep the Bishop in sight.

That night again found us far from our haven, as we had been zigzagging to try and find water. The Bishop suffered greatly from thirst, but he was a good bushman, and plucking a gum-leaf held it between his teeth to stimulate the saliva. At length one of the women cried "Ngooroo!"—fire or camp—and in a few minutes we were beside the water. Everybody rushed to the open well. It was sweet magnesium water, but they drank and drank, insatiable. I wisely waited for the boiling of the billy and the making of tea. During the night, or what was left of it, the whole party was convulsed with sickness and pain, and I produced my flask of brandy, that I have always carried throughout my travels, to accord each of them, Bishop and monks, a little relief.

I camped in the hut that the previous missioners had erected at Disaster Bay, and the others camped outside it in the moonlight. I had scarcely snatched an hour of sleep in one of the four dust-bag bunks that hung to the walls when I was rudely awakened by the presence of thirty naked women, of all sizes, giggling at me. From the neighbouring camps the natives had been rounded up by one of the Beagle Bay boys for the Bishop's visit. Being quite unsophisticated they were as much amused by my appearance as I at theirs. I have always preserved a scrupulous neatness, and all the little trappings and accoutrements of my own very particular mode of dress, sometimes under difficulties, but I think I never made a more laughable toilet than that one. Every motion of mine, as I laced my corsets and eased my shoes on with a shoe-horn, brushed my hair and adjusted my high collar and waist-belt, was greeted with long-drawn squeals of laughter and mirrored in action, though the slim black daughters of Eve about me had not even a strand of hair string between the whole thirty.

We could not spend more than a few days at the outpost, and next morning my Lord the Bishop baptized and confirmed every man, woman and child that could be gathered in, including babies in arms. Father Nicholas dutifully had brought along the wreath and veil, and there it was, the only article of wearing apparel in evidence. Vividly I can see again the spectacle of a hairy savage with a bone through his nose, a wreath and veil, and nothing else whatever.

Food was given to the natives from the bullock-dray, also the rest of the clothing I had brought for them from Perth, but they had in mind the tail of a " 'gator" they had seen in a nearby creek, so, eager for my first sight of a crocodile, while the priests were attending to their plans and duties, I rambled away with them. Wading barefooted in the shallow waters of the mangrove flats, now deeply embedded in the grey mud, now scratched by the shells and suckers, my feet immediately swelled with some swift poison, until I could fit them into nothing smaller than two sugar-bags. There was little pain but much inconvenience as, with my poor nether limbs like hills in front of me. I endured the carriage in the dray back to the Mission at Beagle Bay.

The valuator with Dean Martelli, an aged man worn out with his exertions, had made overland with the only horse vehicle, to Broome, but the ship was again waiting for us. So the Bishop and I, and the four natives carrying our luggage, set out to walk the nine miles to the Bay, anxious to catch the tide as the ship's captain Roderiguez, was eager to be off. After a last meal of grimly abstemious Trappist fare, we bade farewell to the heroic little brothers, and began our journey at 2 p.m. on a day of century heat in November. We talked as we walked, of the work done and the joy of its successful accomplishment. But presently the Bishop, who had never lagged before, showed signs of collapse. He laid his hand, and then his increasing weight, upon my shoulder, and so we crept on.

The journey would ordinarily have taken three hours, but we had only reached the five-mile well when darkness came. The Bishop showed signs of slight delirium, calling me "Margaret," the name of a beloved sister in Ireland. It must have been ten o'clock when the natives whispered to me that we were at the beach, where he sank down unconscious. We straightened his weary body, the natives and I, with part of my rug-strap under his head. There we camped, unable to see the ship offshore, and I quite ignorant of our surroundings. The only sound I heard was the tide sucking at the mangroves. To make matters worse, the natives came, in frightened whispers, to tell me that "big pindana (inland) mob blackfellows come up" close by, strangers from the inland bush. I said "Don't be afraid. Eebala (father) and I will take care of you." Then I placed two of them lying one at each side of the Bishop, and I lay down with my head on the rug-strap and my feet in the opposite direction, the other two natives on either side of me.

The Bishop slept in utter exhaustion, and I not a wink. Stamping of feet and wild cries came to us clearly. Now and again a black form between me and the stars told me that our natives were listening, and in terror they would whisper to me of these bad *pindana-womba* who sometimes hung about the outskirts of the Mission to steal their women and to fight. I changed the subject to the stars and

the sky, and they told me of the dark place in the Milky
Way which was once a native road to the sky country,
until one day some women on the way lighted a fire and
burned the road, which was really a sacred wooden emblem. Our heads were together as we whispered, the
Bishop's white unconscious face beside us. Then a fiercer
chant and the mound-beating of the pindana men would
send us all noiselessly on our backs again. Through the
false dawn we were particularly watchful, but nothing
happened.

Broad daylight brought a boat from the *Sree pas Sair,*
four months dirtier than when we boarded it at Broome in
August. The Bishop was laid on deck. Only Manilamen
were on board, and I sat near the Bishop through the
hundred-mile journey. An uncle of the Manila owner there
was, a naked cheerful old man, who sang one tune the
whole way down. That lilting little tune always brings the
scene vividly to my mind—the filthy boat that was once
a miniature floating palace, the sleeping Bishop lying on a
sail-cloth, and the Manila helmsman looking up at a sort
of calico cornucopia which, when filled with the winds, was
his steering compass.

Just before we entered Broome waters the Bishop
opened his eyes and looking round wearily, saw the old
Manilaman lying naked and unashamed near by.

"Go and put your clothes on!" he called to the poor old
fellow, who had neither clothes nor need of them in his
rough life on the sea.

A typically Irish ending to a difficult work accomplished.

Chapter III

SOJOURN IN THE DREAMTIME

So FAR, MY ASSOCIATION WITH THE NATIVES HAD BEEN cursory, and purely practical. I had caught nothing but a few stray glimpses, and those through other eyes, of the strange hidden life of this last remnant of palæolithic man. The next eight months were spent among the Koolarra-bulloo tribes of Broome, and it was there that my first attempts at systematic study of aboriginal beliefs and customs were rewarded with the most unexpected results, results which I have never made public, until now.

Broome was a quaint and prosperous pearling port in the 1900's with a polygot population living out on the ships and along the foreshore—Chinese, Japanese, Malays, Manilamen, and a score of European races. I believe there was actually an Eskimo among them. The hotels were full of pearl-dealers and traders, white and coloured, and night-time was a continuous revelry. At one period, so fast and furious was the racket that I was locked in my room from danger of unpleasantness.

Even in those days the tribes of the place were but a remnant. My interest in the town natives was confined to those in gaol. They were chained to each other by the neck, and there was discussion as to the humanity of this procedure. The natives themselves told me that it gave them more freedom than handcuffs, and that a piece of cloth wrapped round the collar relieved the weight and the heat of the iron, and left their hands free to play cards and deal with the flies and mosquitoes.

From Broome, I took up my residence at Roebuck Plains, the property of Messrs. Streeter and Male, an out-lying cattle-station. There was a comfortable homestead with good outbuildings. A housekeeper simplified my domestic problems, so that my time was free. Aju, the Japanese cook, was the only disturbing circumstance. He was an excellent cook, but was not normal, and developed the habit of running amok at unexpected moments. Sometimes, as I sat reading in the garden, his grinning gargoyle of a face would appear out of the foliage, or upside down from the roof of a nearby shed, and following my sudden start of fright, "Missie like a cuppa tea?" he would inquire pleasantly, or "Lunch I been make him quick-time now, you come?"

The black house-women were efficient enough in their lazy way, trailing about the garden and their domestic duties in the bright dresses I made for them, but try as I would, watching them with an eagle eye, I could instil no morality into them so far as Aju was concerned. Within his own tribal laws, the aboriginal is bound hand and foot by tradition; beyond them, he knows no ethics. My only recourse was to frighten Aju with the threat of instant dismissal if any of the girls were found at night near his quarters.

Riding and roaming in the *pindan,* always accompanied by the boys and women of the station, and any nomad visitors that came along, I would camp out sometimes for days, sharing my food, and making friends with the old men. Thus I extended and verified my knowledge by gradual degrees until I gained a unique insight into the whole northern aboriginal social system, and its life-story from babyhood to age. Every moment of my spare time was given to this self-imposed and fascinating study. Not a word nor a gesture passed me by without opening up an avenue of inquiry, tactfully and methodically pursued.

I realized that the Australian native was not so much deliberately secretive as inarticulate. He looked upon his "black life" as a life apart from his association with the whites, few of whom had shown any interest in it. I also realized that to glean anything of value, I must think with his mentality and talk in his language. By the wells and the creeks, sitting in the camps in the firelight, on horseback and on foot, my notebook and pencil were always with me. I began by compiling a Broome dictionary, of several dialects and 2,000 words and sentences, with notes of innumerable legends and myths.

The natives I found at first amused, and then stimulated to further confidence by my obviously eager and sustained interest. I pretended that my native name was Kallower, and that I was a *mirruroo-jandu,* or magic woman who had been one of the twenty-two wives of Leeberr, a patriarchal or "dreamtime" father. After that, the way was clear. They accepted me as a kindred spirit, and with the utmost patience elucidated the seeming tangle of relationships and class-groups, the marriage laws, the tribal tabus, the traditional songs and dances. They even allowed me free access to the sacred places and the sacred ceremonies of the initiations of men, which their own women must never see under penalty of death.

The abstruse "matronymics" and "patronymics" of native marriage laws as expounded in the hieroglyphics of the anthropologists, through which I have vainly floundered many times before and since with no clear conception of their exact meaning, the natives could simplify for me—a definition of the four group classes, and the cross-cousin marriage of paternal aunts' children to the maternal uncles' children, the only lawful marriage between the groups.[1] I have found these four groups and relationships, under different names, identical in every tribe in Western Australia, east, north, south and southwest among the great Bibbulmun people of the white cockatoo and crow moieties. Aboriginal genealogies go no further back than grandmother, and the cycle is thus limited to three generations.

I have always been placed in the same class-group, corresponding with that of Pooroongoo, my place in the

---

[1] In Broome district, these were Pooroongoo, male, fair, and Pannunga, dark; Karrimarra, male, fair, and Parrajer, dark. Pooroongoo man marries Pannunga, and their children are Karrimarra. Pannunga man marries Pooroongoo, and their children are Parrajer; Karrimarra man marries Parrajer, and their children are Pooroongoo; Parrajer man marries Karrimarra and their children are Pannunga, and so on throughout all generations.

family being among the father's sisters, but from this
period, right through my thirty-five years of journeying,
and including the twenty years in Central Australia, I
was believed to be not so much a woman as an age-old
spirit of *Yamminga* (Broome district term), the dreamtime, and keeper of all the totems.

Once I had grasped their relationships, the lives of the
natives soon became easier to understand, and the poetry
of their ceremonies and legends and rituals an enchanting
study. At the men's hidden corroborees, far from my own
people in the heart of the bush, because I showed no
quiver of timidity, or of revulsion of feeling, or of levity,
because I was thinking with my "black man's mind," I
have never been a stranger.

Sitting in a neighbouring creek-bed, or boiling the billy
by an old tank out on the plain, the men would gather
round me, taking infinite pains to tutor me in the rippling
inflexions and the difficult double vowels of their language
—a series of vocal gymnastics quite impossible to the
average white linguist, and which, I am perfectly sure, in
all my years of juggling with them, have altered the formation of my larynx. They explained in detail the purpose
of all their weapons and implements, why the boomerang
and the shield and the spear-thrower were curved or
hooked just so; they let me watch their making and the
chipping of stone tools, and told me the half-legendary
stories of their origin. Dances and songs were explained
to me at symbolic and play-corroborees, and so we pro-
gressed naturally from the world of actuality to the dream
world. At last, with the utmost simplicity and frankness
the old men disclosed to me little by little their most
secret rites and initiations, without fear of ridicule or
objection, just as they disclosed the mythologies and
allegories of the mind of the primeval black man as
mystical in their beauty as the sagas of the old Norse
gods.

Unique in Australia, I believe, and perhaps unique in
the world, is the legend of the dream-child, *ngargalulla,*
as told me by the Broome tribes, comparable only with

Mæterlinck's delightful fantasy, *The Kingdom of the Future,* and its parallel in many respects.

Whereas the general aboriginal belief is that children are dreamed by the mother, made pregnant by a spirit baby from the rocks and springs and other traditional haunts of the baby spirits of birth and re-birth, among the Koolarrabulloo it was the father who dreamed the child that was to be born to him. They believed that below the surface of the ground, and at the bottom of the sea, was a country called Jimbin, home of the spirit babies of the unborn, and the young of all the totems. In Jimbin there was never a shadow of trouble or strife or toil, or death, only the happy laughter of the little people at play. Sometimes these spirit babies were to be seen by the *jalngangooroo*—the witch-doctors—in the dancing spray and sunlight of the beaches, under the guardianship of old Koolibal, the mother-turtle, or tumbling and somersaulting in the blue waters with Pajjalburra, the porpoise.

When the time came for a *ngargalulla* to be a human baby, it appeared not to its mother, but to its father. Perhaps a Karrimarra man had fished and eaten his catch, and settled in the shade to sleep. Then would the *ngargalulla* baby appear to him, with all the signs of its own ground and its own totem, calling upon him in the name of *eebala,* father. That night it entered the body of his wife. The *ngargalulla* is seen only by the men, and only by those men, I learned, who possess a "ranji," a subconscious spiritual gift, a spirit, or mind, as far as I could make out, corresponding to a soul. The woman is sometimes told that her husband has dreamed the *ngargalulla.* She does not know until she is conscious of it within her.

The *ngargalulla* has its *booroo,* or ground, which is always beneath the surface of its father's ground, but it is not a reincarnation of any who may be buried in that ground, or of any dead ancestor, even of those who went into the ground in *Yamminga,* the dreamtime. Their disappearance is marked by some unusual feature, red cliff, stone emblem, etc. The live totems go back to the sea and the land of Jimbin when their season is over, but the spirits of the human dead are carried away to the island

of Loomurn, which lies over the western sea. The man is
so familiar with every feature of creek and rock and tree
in his country that he can immediately locate the ground
of his dream, and no matter where the baby is born, that
dreamed ground is its *ngargalulla* country. Its individual
totems are those *ngargalulla* totems which appeared with
it, its inherited totems are those of its father.

So firm was the belief in the *ngargalulla* that no man
who had not seen it in his sleeping hours would claim the
paternity of a child born to him. In one case that came
under my observation, a man who had been absent for
nearly five years in Perth proudly acknowledged a child
born in his absence, because he had seen the *ngargalulla,*
and in another, though husband and wife had been separated not a day, the man refused absolutely to admit
paternity. He had not dreamed the *ngargalulla.* Should a
boy arrive when a girl came in the dream, or should the
ngargalulla not have appeared to its rightful father, the
mother must find the man who has dreamed it correctly,
and he is ever after deemed to be the father of that child.

The *ngargalulla* is still a spirit in the first months of its
existence, but when it begins to laugh and cry, to touch
and talk, and to manifest its personality as a little human
being, its link with the dream world is gone, and it becomes *coba-jeera*—in other words, a normal baby.
Thenceforward, through its whole life, the fathers who
have dreamed its existence are the controllers of its des-
tinies, within the relentless circle of tribal law. There is no
glorification of maternity, no reverence of woman as
woman, in the dark mind of the aboriginal. Apart from
the natural affection between mother and son, sister and
brother, and apart from her physical fulfilment of certain
dominant needs, a woman is less than the dust. Her in-
feriority is recognized by the very youngest of the tribe.
Many a time I have seen a toddler throw sand in his
mother's eyes, and jeer at her and injure her, should she
attempt to control him. The secrets of life, the laws of
life, are in the hands of men.

As soon as I began living among the natives I came up
against those weird rituals of the initiations of the Aus-

tralian aborigine, unchanged through thousands of years, the novitiate of youth to manhood—a sacrament of sex, a communion of blood, and a Black Mass of witchcraft and savagery, yet instinct with a pure poetry of symbolism that goes back to the blind beginnings of all religions, and throbs with the beating pulse of the primeval.

Each successive initiation marks a vital stage in a man's development, and the rites connected therewith are age-old and uncanny. No white man has ever seen them as I have seen them, because I have attended them day-long and night-long, camped sometimes for weeks alone with the natives in the bush, through the whole western half of Australia, among the circumcised and the uncircumcised, and through the centre of South Australia, where the old marriage laws have totally declined in the passing centuries.

So important are these initiation rites towards an understanding of life and belief in those primitive lands and for appreciation of what follows that some account of them is essential.

Chapter IV

THE BEGINNING OF INITIATION

THE TRIBES OF AUSTRALIA MAY ROUGHLY BE CLASSED AS circumcised and uncircumcised. So far as their origin is concerned, that, too, belongs to the dreamtime. I am doubtful that it will ever be established, except in theory. I do not regard them as a race apart, but as a mixture, a nomad people picking up scraps of racial character in their different environments, and at last, in primitive Australia, gravitating to the primitive life that they have led here for centuries.

I can follow only a boomerang clue of these wanderings,

a geographical curve back to Egypt, cradle of the human race—from Thebes, where the boomerang is to be found in mural paintings and carvings, to Kattywar in India, on to Celebes, and a step across to Australia. In the very heart of this continent, and among the Bibbulmun of the South-West, I have traced the Kas, Egyptian spirit of the newly dead, and the Central Australian aboriginal cry of mourning, a word identical in meaning and pronunciation, the graves that ever face the rising sun, and the Serpent Cult of all groups.

Certain it is that all tribes came from northward, and that the uncircumcised were the first hordes, later driven down south, east or west by the encroachment of the circumcised. So rapid was this encroachment of recent years that the whole of black Australia would have been circumcised. Thirty years ago the practice embraced the north and centre of Western Australia, save for a narrow irregular line from Balla-Balla to Geraldton, skirting the sea, and thence a line cutting off the south-west in a triangle to Cape Arid, on the rim of the Great Australian Bight. Even with my own later experience, some of these outlying tribes were drawn in, in the course of a few years, by intermarriage and association.

The tribes of Broome were, therefore, among the circumcised, and still are, unless contaminated by Asiatic influences and by the influx of the whites, as I believe they have been. In the sequence of the ceremonies here described, I adhere rigidly to their practices and use the words of their language, but the initiations are similar, throughout the circumcised groups of Western Australia and the Centre.

The aborigine serves his apprenticeship to manhood from early childhood to old age, and the degrees through which he must pass before he is entitled to marry occupy many years. We left the newly-arrived *ngargalulla* on the threshold of its babyhood sleeping in the bush shelter of his own father and mother, playing with other camp-babies, never smacked and rarely scolded, with a rotund little stomach so visibly swelling in girth that, to a white man's inexperienced eye, it flouts the possibility of digestion. However, a few years of quick growth solve the problem, and at the age of about eight years or so comes the first step in the march of manhood, the separation of the sexes.

As *nimma-nimma,* the boy then joins the camp of the younger men, bachelors all, in various stages of initiation, their quarters being generally in front of the married men's huts, and a little to leeward. There follows what is probably the happiest period in the boy's life. He goes out with his young companions, honey-seeking and hunting for small game. Toy spears and boomerangs and shields are made for him, and he is taught their manufacture and their use. He learns to dance in the play-corroborees and begins to sense the significance of the totems; in short, he goes to school. His elder brothers in a tribal sense are his monitors, his guardians being his father and his father's brothers and his grandfathers. From the outset, an older man known as the *yagoo* is appointed to his especial charge. The *yagoo* is usually a brother-in-law to be, a man to whom the tribal elders have betrothed one of his sisters, who may still be an infant, or as yet unborn. He will be playfully decorated, each decoration being explained to him in a childish way easy of understanding.

When the time comes for him to enter upon the first definite stage of initiation, usually when he is eleven or twelve years old, plans and preparations are made. The women are sent far afield to collect quantities of vegetable food, while the old men inspect the sacred ceremonial and totem boards, in their place of hiding, the *beegardain-ngooroo,* or *beega.* This is usually a bush-shelter, rock-hole or large shady hollow tree. Should women or children intrude upon this secret place, either intentionally or unintentionally, they are immediately killed. Should they unknowingly walk beneath the shade of its tree, it is believed that they will lose the use of their limbs. The sacred boards must never be disclosed to the eyes of women. I know of one instance, on a north-west station, where a white girl visitor came into possession of these boards, presented to her as a curio by a white man who had found them. One afternoon she carelessly exhibited them to some friends in the presence of three of the natives, two women and a little girl. All three were dead by the end of the week. If the boards should be eaten by white ants, or damaged beyond repair, they are burnt or buried and new ones made.

The second stage of initiation is *nimma-mu,* the nose-piercing. The *yagoo* takes the boy apart, fashions a string of opossum fur and places it about his waist, then sits him in a cleared space some distance from the camp, with meat, fish and vegetable food piled beside him. The men sit round in a circle while the *yagoo* puts one of the smaller bones from the forepaw of a kangaroo through the septum, leaving it there through the night. Foods are then shared. Next morning a turkey bone replaces the kangaroo bone. Strict avoidance of all women and girls begins from this period. *Nimma-mu* extends for some months, from autumn to spring. At the beginning of the summer wet season, secret preparations are made for the fourth and one of the most vital stages of initiation—*balleli,* the circumcision itself.

The *yagoo* anoints the boy's body all over with charcoal and grease, places a band of opossum string on his head, and the boy becomes *balgai.* This is the third stage. Amongst the Beagle Bay people, the two upper front teeth are knocked out at this time, but this is not often done by the Koolarrabulloo of Broome. Early in the afternoon, the boy (now *balgai*) starts on a journey, accompanied by his *yagoo* and other guardians, to collect relatives and friends within a certain radius to assist at his initiation. They travel in one direction only, north, south, or east, at the rate of about ten miles a day, and may cover 130 miles or so in the full journey. If there are two or three *balgai* boys, each one travels in a different direction. Among the primitive people with no mathematics, there is a very ingenious method of regulating days and distances by means of the finger-joints, the right hand for the outward journey, the left for the return.

The boy is a great favourite wherever he goes, and as he approaches a camp is greeted from afar with shouts of *"Balgai! Balgai!"* There is singing and dancing to celebrate his arrival. On the return journey each camp sends its representatives to the coming ceremony, with gifts of vegetables and meat food, until, nearing home, the gathering swells to a very large one, heavily burdened with food and presents in anticipation of the feast.

The *balgai* is now placed in charge of those who are to take the chief part in his circumcision ceremonial, the *waiung-arree,* chosen from among his principal relatives in all surrounding camps, with perhaps a newly-selected *yagoo.* Escorted *balgais* from every direction approach the appointed spot. The assembled party makes a halt some distance from the home-camp to decorate. Here the *balgai* is ceremonially painted by his *yagoo* with fat, charcoal, and an insignia of red ochre on forehead, cheeks and chest.

At last the great day dawns. A *wallang-arree,* or double circle, is cleared some distance from the boy's camp. Among the visitors are usually a number of young men in later stages of apprenticeship, who have come to undergo certain other initiations. Every man taking part in these is distinguished from the *balgai* group by having his legs covered with blood. No youth is ever allowed to be present at an initiation higher than that he himself has reached. The *balgai* have no blood sprinkled upon them, nor have any of the group in charge of them, their decorations being red ochre, white pipeclay, charcoal and dark yellow ochre.

The afternoon is the time of the *balgai's* expected arrival in camp. No sooner is the sun below the meridian than the fathers take their place in the centre of the *wallang-arree,* and with their boomerangs raised in welcome await the visitors. As the first group approaches, there is a ringing shout of *"Aie! Kaie! Kaie! R-r-r-r-r-r-r-r-r-r!"*

The *balgai* is brought to the circle. The *yagoo* takes hold of the boy's hands from behind, and shows him first to his father's uncles, and then to his female relatives, who may look upon him only from a distance, and through a veil of their hair. The boy is then held aloft and shown to all his people assembled, while those standing within

the circle sing the following song with their faces turned
to the north-east:

> Waiung-arree ngow, waiung-arree ngow,
> Jandoo ngarrie ngaiee
> Waiung-arree ngow!

This song continues while the *waiung-arree* leader takes
his men round the inner circle.

All of the *waiung-arree* dancers are fully armed with
spear and spear-thrower. They wear the insignia of their
various stages of initiation, and faces and bodies are
painted in highly original and symbolic design that lend
them an aspect fiendish and fantastic. Entering from the
right, they make a circuit of the *wallang-arree* and depart
from the left, taking the *balgai* with them and leaving
room for the others, the groups of the various *balgai* at
last forming coils without intermingling. Then all groups
join together and arrange themselves in several broken
concentric circles, each alternate group rotating in a
different direction—a maze of painted black bodies that
stamp and wheel and swing to a strident accompaniment
of loud shrill singing. The women keep their own circle on
the outskirts, and must never come near enough to touch
the men.

When the dance is ended, a double row of men lies flat
on the ground with their heads in opposite directions. Another double row lies on top of them and another, and
another, until they become a human stack several feet
high which, with the *balgai* seated aloft in the centre, begins to rock and sway from side to side. At a given signal,
the men spring to their feet, and the *balgai* falls gently in
the midst of them.

Each row, catching hands, swings again into the *wallang-arree,* alternate rows going in opposite directions, the
boys and the old men always in the centre. This ceremony
is called *moorooboyn,* and is accompanied throughout by
a spirited high chanting and a stamping of feet. At the
close of it, the boy is taken out of the circle for a brief

respite, then brought back into it on the shoulders of his *yagoo*. As soon as he reaches the centre, he throws himself backwards into the arms of his mother's brothers, and, clasping his hands behind his head and stiffening his legs, is thrown into the air again and again by four or five men. The *yagoo* takes charge of the *balgai* and all adjourn for supper.

At this time all licence is allowed, and the laws relating to persons who at other times are forbidden to look at each other are suspended. Mothers-in-law may even approach or address their sons-in-law, and at the supper, the *thaloo,* as the mother-in-law is called, makes the best of it. A whole year of grievances is stored up, and the son-in-law has no right of reply. She can touch him, taunt him, pull away his weapons and decorations, and make him a public mockery. Her delight is to worry and annoy, and he must keep a poker face through it all, unaware, as it were, of her presence.

Now she tempts him with a hollow scoop of vegetable food—"You hungry? Here is food. If you don't take it, I will hit you. All right, watch me eat it!"—and she snatches it away. She tears off his arm-band, head-band and other ornaments, and knocks his boomerang out of his grasp. As provider for the family, he pays the price of his betrothal in meat food, and she has much to say about this. "This meat no good!" she tells him, "why don't you bring up a tadpole?" or, "Watch me, everybody, I'm going to kill a fish," and she snatches his spear and aims it dangerously near him. The *wallang-arree* is the crowded hour of glorious life for the mother-in-law, and the whole tribe, with the exception of the son-in-law, enjoys her sallies to the full.

In the early dawn, the men rise from their camps and go again to the circle. If the mothers-in-law are awake, they throw insults after injuries as their sons-in-law go by. The older men sit in the centre of the circle and sing. When the sun is high overhead, the *balgai* is placed a little apart. A spear is stuck into the ground in front of him and the men return to the circle. The women now approach the boy with weeping. He holds the spear with both hands, and looks upon his mothers and sisters, but he may not speak to them. A mute farewell, and they are hurried away.

The *yagoo* appears, a fearsome figure, painted with jet-black charcoal with stripes of yellow ochre down the front of face and body, red ochre across forehead, nose and chin, feathers on arms and head, and hair hanging loose below the hair-belt. He takes the boy to the forbidden ground. The *waiung-arree* men approach, and again form a circle. The *yagoo* presses the boy close to his breast for a moment, then turns him with his back facing him, and holds him in a vice-like grip. An older brother-in-law, with a small stone knife, swiftly performs the operation of circumcision. The flow of blood is stopped with warm ashes.

The boy, who is now *balleli,* is seated on the ground. A small fire may be lighted close between his thighs, supposedly to lessen the pain and dry the flow of blood. His *yagoo* immediately takes off the head-ring and other *balgai* decorations, replacing them with a flat forehead band and a chignon made of human hair or opossum fur-string, a belt, and a tassel, or perhaps two or three attached to it. Fresh red ochre is put across his forehead, nose and cheeks, and then his fathers, uncles, and brothers pay him a visit of congratulation. His true father brings to him a little vegetable food, that has been specially prepared by his mother. The ceremony is over, and the whole camp settles down to a feast, with usually a fight or two to follow, the avenging of grievances new or old, rarely with fatal effects. Later the visitors return to their own country.

The *balleli,* if there is only one, remains apart, his brothers feeding him and attending to him. He may walk about, but not within the sight of the women. If there is more than one, the seclusion is not so trying. The period is fixed by the older men. When it is over, the boy's own mother, his father's sisters, and his own elder sister, make a bark bed near the camp, upon which he is placed. His closest female relatives may not touch him but they place vegetable food on the bark bed. The boy now takes his place among the young men, sharing their quarrels and joining in their evening songs, but he is kept entirely apart from the women, as are all of the other young men who have passed through various higher initiations. Should any woman, wilfully or accidentally, follow their tracks at that time, she is killed. One child, Nganga-gooroo, thus followed a boy, who threw his spear and killed her. The tracks were carefully examined by the old men, who, finding that the boy had not allowed the girl to approach, exonerated him and praised him. It is the law.

While they are in the bush, the youths subsist on flesh food only, and their faces and bodies are coloured with charcoal, so that any woman may see them from afar and know that they are "forbidden." A fire is lighted, upon which thick green boughs are placed, causing a thick smoke and the young men, arming themselves with hunting weapons, go by relays into the middle of the smoke, to smoke the magic of the ceremonies from their bodies and restore their strength. Weapons are frequently smoked to ensure success in hunting, and make their aim true. In my many years among the blacks, I myself have been smoked by my thoughtful friends more than once. During this process the smoke song is repeated till the last man has trodden it, and the smoke dies away.

When the morning star rises, they sing the Morning Star song, and the song of the Kingfisher, which belongs to young initiates only.

A little later, a meeting is appointed with the old men, in the cleared space at the foot of a big *gooneroo,* a species of gum tree. When all are arrived, the boys climb the tree, using no native tomahawks but only their hands and toes, and swing on the branches. Then a man in an advanced stage of initiation—*maam-boongana*—sits close to the foot of the tree with his legs at either side of the trunk. An old man comes close and hits the tree with a club, whereupon the young men slide down one by one and fall into the lap of the *maam-boongana* man, making a pile of human bodies. The old man cries, "Aie! Aie!" and the *maam-boongana* slides from under the heap, the rest separating in the same manner.

This little ceremony, it was disclosed to me, harks back in its turn to the dreamtime, when men were birds and when birds were men. The songs sung throughout the stages emphasize this dreamtime belief.

Chapter V

THE END OF INITIATION, THE BLOOD-DRINKING

AS THE YOUNG MEN[1] COME IN TO CAMP FROM THE TREE ceremony they are received by a capering jester, called *mami ngarring wombanoo,* who sings as they approach:

> Balnga, marrinday, balnga, marrinday,
> Lingoorambaa, lingooraa.

When they hear the jester's song, they pretend to be greatly frightened, and shouting "Wo! Wo! Wo!" surge into a closely-packed crowd.

Then the clown, bedizened with pipeclay and red ochre, comes closer and repeats his song, dancing about them. All sit down and partake of meat food, and there is dancing and singing by the old men's fires throughout the night, the Morning Star and Kingfisher's songs being sung alternately. The *balleli* are separated from the *weerganju* during the more advanced ceremonies that follow.

The old men obtain some of the inner bark of the *woordoola,* or paper-bark, and this is doubled into about six inches in width, and fastened at each end with opossum fur string, forming a wide belt called after the *woordoola.* This belt the older men tie round the *weerganju's* waists. Logs are placed end to end by the old men, with bushes

---

[1] During this stage they are called *weerganju.*

laid upon them. All the *weerganju* lie down with their
heads resting on the logs, then the older, fully-initiated
men, each of whom will be guardian to a younger man,
tie their lower arms, and, piercing the vein, hold the arm
over the young man until both the bark and his face and
body are covered with blood. The blood dries quickly
and blackens the *woordoola*. The guardian flicks away the
dried blood from the boy's eyelids, nose and chin, puts a
little red ochre on his breast, and a headband round his
forehead. Over the *woordoola* three belts are placed, the
upper and lower being of opossum string, light in colour,
and the middle belt of black human hair. Attached to the
lower are two or more pubic tassels of opossum fur.

The *balleli* are now brought forward, and dressed by
their *yagoo* with string-belts, hair-belts and tassels, with
red ochre across their faces. All journey towards the
women's camps, where bark beds have been made ready
in a long row. The *weerganju* sit on the bark beds and are
cried over by their female relations. No woman must ever
touch a *weerganju* over whom the blood has been poured,
else she will die, or the young man will die, or the part
touched will wither and become useless. Next day the
belts of string and hair are placed in charge of father's
sisters or mother's brothers' wives. The *woordoola* is
worn until the old men see that it is getting broken, when
it is buried by one of the fathers, or by its wearer. When
this is done, the *balleli* puts his belt aside and wears only
the forehead band, chignon and the tassel which hangs by
a single string.

Balleli lasts a year or so, and the next stage of initiation
is *jamung-ungur,* the blood-drinking. This ceremony is
called *walla-wallong.* When the fathers think it is time for
the *balleli* to become *jamung-ungur,* a message is sent to
camps to collect all those whose presence is desired. When
these are assembled, the *yagoo* calls the boy aside, and
tells him *"Moogula baaloo!"* (Put your string on!) At
sundown, the *balleli* approaches the men's camp, and
someone shouts to him *"Wamba Jeeoo!"* (Man coming for
you, run!) He runs, but must quickly allow himself to be

caught or his mother will die. He is then taken to the secret place.

In the evening, the men come and take their places according to tribal precedence. Uncles and brothers are seated in the inner circle, and the boy in the centre, lying with his head on his own father's thighs. Presently the blood-relations, younger fathers and older brothers, come within the circle. Standing over the boy, with one leg on either side of them, they begin a step dance, lifting their feet quickly in time to the *joorrga* song, sung by the men in the circle. Two men may dance above him at one time, and then others take their places until all the blood-relations have danced above him.

This is the eve of the blood-drinking, and while the men sleep a *yagoo* keeps night-long vigil with the boy. In the morning, all gather at the secret place. The boy again lies with his head on his father's thigh. He must make no movement, or he will die. The father blindfolds the boy with his hands, as if he should witness the following proceedings it is believed that his father and mother will both die.

A wooden vessel or a bark vessel is placed near one of the boy's mother's brothers, who, having tied his arm tightly, pierces the upper part with a nose-bone and holds the arm over the vessel until a certain amount of blood has been taken. Then the man next to him pierces his arm, and so on, until the vessel is filled. It may hold two quarts or so.

The vessel is brought to where the boy is lying. The father takes his hands from the boy's eyes, though they remain closed while the rude bark chalice is lifted to his lips. The boy then takes a long draught of the blood. Should his stomach rebel, the father holds his throat to prevent his ejecting it, as if that happened his father, mother, sisters and brothers would all die. The remainder of the blood is thrown over him.

From this time the boy is allowed no other food than human blood, Yamminga, the mythical ancestors, having made this law. After the blood-drinking, he is left either by himself or in charge of a *yagoo,* and the others go back to the camp to eat. In the afternoon, they return and the boy again lies with his head on his father's thighs and closes his eyes, and the men take the pieces of opossum string which they have used as ligatures, holding them taut between their hands. The father cries to the boy to open his eyes and look upon the string. While he is silently looking, the men chant the blood song, one single monotonous note of pulsing rhythm:

Warrboo jool-jool baa naa!
Warrboo jool-jool baa naa!

Each man ties his own arm again with the string, pierces the swollen vein with the nose-bone, and fills the vessel for a second blood-drinking. When the boy has taken a certain quantity, old men and younger men drink also, and the remainder is thrown over the boy. Sometimes the blood is dried in the vessel, and then the *yagoo* cuts it in sections with the nose-bone, and it is eaten by the boy, the two end sections first eaten. These sections must be regularly divided, or the boy will die. The threat of death, in all of these instances, is not from the spears of the old men but of the supernatural powers, which exercise such dominance over the minds of the natives that invariably and swiftly they do die.

On this night there is no singing.

Next day, the boy is taken again to the sacred place, guarded by his *yagoo,* and the men go hunting, coming back in the afternoon with meat food, which he is not allowed to share. Before they eat, more blood is drawn from their arms, and the boy is given his draught. A single string or rope belt, to which a tassel is attached, is round his waist, a forehead band above his brow, and his body is caked with human blood.

In the afternoon, some of the men slip away into the bush to swing the sacred bull-roarer, *kalligooroo.* The boy is frightened. Those who are with him add to his fears, saying it is the voice of Nalja. *"Nalja ee nganggal"* (Nalja is talking!), chant the old men. Nalja is the spirit of an old, old man with white hair, and his voice comes from the hair beneath his arm-pits. The word *"kalligooroo"* is never spoken in the hearing of women or children or the uninitiated, but the voice of Nalja is known to them all. He is a spirit whom to look upon would be death.

The sound of the *kalligooroo* comes nearer and nearer, booming weirdly across the twilight. Should the bull-roarer touch a tree in its rotations, "Nalja is throwing his boomerang!" the boy is told. The men rise to their feet in expectancy. The boy shivers with fear and draws close to his *yagoo*. Before the swingers have reached the circle, one of the mother's brothers hides an old *mirruroo-kalligooroo,* or magic bull-roarer, almost at the boy's feet, the string and the hole through which it is passed left above the earth. While he is doing this, the voice of Nalja is silent.

An uncle now asks the boy did he cook any meat or roots, or has he eaten any. The boy does not answer. His *yagoo* points to the spot where the *kalligooroo* is hidden, and says, "Your *kalligooroo!*" The *yagoo* stoops, takes it out of the ground and swings it. The boy cannot yet swing it himself till other initiations have passed. His father then tells him that the noise he has heard was made by that *kalligooroo,* and not by Nalja, but he must never tell the women and children, or he will die. He is given temporary possession of the sacred bull-roarer, and sleeps with it under his head. There may be only two or three old *kalligooroo* in the camp, but they are highly prized and carefully hidden after each blood-drinking ceremony. The older and more frail, the greater their magic, and they are carefully preserved with grease and fresh ochre from time to time.

On that day, and for many days following the boy again drinks blood. Sometimes it is a whole moon before the blood-drinking period is finished, and blood is poured over him daily. The length of time the visitors stay depends upon the food supply. On the last night of the ceremony, the women and children move their camp still farther away from the *beega,* and all night long the savage rites go on, to the roar of the *kalligooroo* and the chanting of songs. When the morning star rises, the men make preparation for a move to the women's camp. Hearing the noise approaching, the women hide in terror, secreting themselves under the bushes which they have gathered for the purpose. As the older men come in, the advance guard, they cry, "Don't look! Shut your eyes! Sleep!"

The men come into a cleared space near the camp, and the boy, who is covered with blood, half sits, half kneels on the ground and holds in his arms the vessel from which he has been drinking, darkened and dyed with blood. As soon as he has taken up this position, an attitude of sheer sacrificial devotion, the old men rapidly cry, "Did! Did! Did! Did! Did! Dee, Dee, Dee, Dee, Dee" and the women come from their hiding places. All behold the boy. His mother and sisters and father's sisters come to wail over him, and then he is taken away.

The ceremonies conclude with the totemic dances of the turtle, snake, and other ancestral fathers, and a general orgy.

Returning to their homes through the bush, the visitors sound their bull-roarer as they travel, and the women and children breathe a sigh of relief as Nalja goes back to his own country.

The boy now sets out on a journey. His brothers-in-law and uncles make several nose-bones for him, and these he places in front of his forehead band. Thus "labelled," and having a club stuck in his belt, he starts with his *yagoo* for the next camp. When his relations in that camp see him, they know the purpose of the visit, and they do not rise to receive him. He goes towards the married men's camp, and when he reaches the men, either touches their feet with his or taps them lightly with the club. He then goes to the sacred place, and the men, after a time, follow him. Taking a nose-bone from his head-band, they prepare their arms and presently fill a bowl, which is always kept there. The boy may drink their blood two or three times, but there is no ceremony. Next day he moves on to another camp. He may cover 150 miles in the journey, and always he returns by the same route. The blood rites are indulged in throughout. When he returns to his home-ground, blood-drinking again takes place, but for the first time he is allowed to eat a little vegetable food, gathered and prepared by his mother.

Both before and during his travels, he is not allowed to touch a honey-tree, nor must he remain in the vicinity of one. As soon, however, as his father has removed the restriction of vegetable food, a father, uncle, or *yagoo* brother-in-law will one day find a honey-tree when the boy is with them. Telling the boy to approach, one of the men rubs his breast or mouth with the bees' wax, and gives him permission to find honey for himself. He may not eat flesh flood until the last of the blood has caked, dried and fallen from his body, and he has been anointed with fat.

During all this period the boy must never speak to, or be touched by, women and children. Only the most necessary words may be spoken between him and his *yagoo*. To talk or laugh at this period would mean death to the boy's mother. His father's uncle or his *yagoo* can impose or break silence. *Jamung-ungur* approaches its final stage in the first sub-incision, an operation performed while the boy is lying on the backs of his brothers-in-law.

At the next degree, two *yagoos* obtain opossum fur string and, twisting two strands of this, each ties up an arm of the young man. They make two or three rounds, then carry it underneath the arm, over the opposite shoulder, and diagonally across the back, fastening it in the waist-belt. Each *yagoo* attends to his own string only, and the young man sits with folded arms. Sometimes the string is wound so tightly that he rolls over and over in an agony of strained muscles, but he must make no sound. After a day or so the string is replaced by lesser, lighter bonds, and the man becomes *jallooroo*, or *kambil*. He may now wear the forehead-band and feather plumes, face-markings of red and white ochre, and the belt and tassel on festive occasions. He may also swing the bull-roarer at *walla-wallong* time, and contribute his share of the blood in the making of *jamung-ungur*.

A few moons, and his *yagoo* obtains a pearl shell which he gives to the oldest fathers and uncles, to be covered with *yamminga* markings, crude or symbolic drawings of birds and animals that are his totems and the totemic fathers of the race. This is prepared in readiness for the "honey-eating" degree, in which the man is again incised in the same manner as before. The pearl shell is attached to his belt in front, with the tassel worn over it. A little later, his father and uncle command him to bring to them the fat of two species of sting-ray and the blowfish, a quest which may occupy him for days or weeks. He puts a little charcoal on chest and face at this time, and when the fat is obtained, is anointed with it, lying on a bark bed that his mother has made, near to his uncle and father's own ground. The next day the bark bed is moved to a spot between the married men's and the bachelors' camps. The chignon has been removed, and his long hair streams over his shoulders. A long time elapses before he can dispense with this bark bed, as the sacred fat and ochre on his back must not touch the earth.

The man is now *boongana*—honey-eating. A new name is given to him by father or guardian. It may be a change of name with some *yagoo,* but it is not a secret name. In the morning, he goes to the bachelors' camp, and taking his boomerang, throws it some distance. His *yagoo,* uncle or father, reclaims it for him. He throws it again, and this time he himself must bring it back. This act apparently ends the general services of the *yagoo.* Henceforth he stands alone. At this stage, he adds to his ornaments and insignia necklaces fashioned of pieces of pearl shell and of kangaroo teeth, the pendant of each at the back of his neck.

After three days, a second anointing makes him *maam-boongana* or *talloor,* free from all restrictions as to food. He may eat the *wy-ooloo* and the *walga-walga*—fish that have been forbidden him all his life—and he may take his wife, if one or more have been betrothed to him in infancy.

The period of these nine degrees covers many years. Not infrequently a white hair or two will be observed in his beard when he comes, fully initiated, without any ceremony whatever, to claim his bride or brides.

Chapter VI

THREE THOUSAND MILES
IN A SIDE-SADDLE

THE WONDERFUL CEREMONIES OF INITIATION WERE ended, and with the corroboree-season over, the natives went back to their work on the stations and in the township. I could understand now the reason of their swift passing from a world in which they were an anachronism and of their withering from contact with the white man's civilization, which can find no place for the primitive. The year's work with the cattle began, and the desire came to stock up my own run of 183,600 acres on Ethel Creek in the Windell area of north Central West Australia.

The frightening names of the locality—Ophthalmia Ranges, Dead Man's Hill, Grave Creek, and so on, had hitherto deterred other pastoralists from contemplating settlement there, but they appealed to me, and on my previous journey by buggy, 1899–1900, I had found that far-out area an encouraging proposition. I named the property Glen Carrick, in affectionate remembrance of a dear friend in England, and set about the purchase of the cattle to stock it.

To watch my mob of 770 well-fed Herefords placidly browsing round the fringe of Lake Eda, some forty miles east of Broome, brought back vividly to my mind the inspired lines of Adam Lindsay Gordon, Banjo Paterson and other Australian poets, whose stirring verses lift droving to the realms of high adventure. How little I knew! Today I detest even the picture of a Hereford cow. I loathe their whitewashed faces, for I have ridden behind them with eight of my own drovers, for six months, 1,000 miles as the route went but some 3,000 as I rode it, zigzagging behind the mob at six or eight or ten miles a day, and every one of the 770 surpassing the Irish pig in contrariness.

This great mob was, perhaps, the largest number that had travelled down from the West Kimberleys in a single herd. Stores and equipment I obtained from Broome, also a cook who was a Maori half-caste, for Broome was mostly "breed" in those days, with just a few decent whites to leaven the mass. Sundry droving hands were also engaged, whose knowledge of the gentle art about equalled mine. We all armed ourselves with a long stock-whip and, while the head drover and his lieutenant were mustering and branding, tried to flourish them in true stockman style. After much climbing into the trees to disentangle the lash, the stock-whips were quietly rolled up and hidden in the dray, a humble buggy-whip or less ambitious instrument of sapling and twine taking their place.

My equipment was a good English pig-skin side-saddle with ordinary stirrup; three pairs of laced wallaby-skin shoes; three habits, a felt hat, three pairs of riding gloves, and plenty of fly veiling. A compact hold-all and portmanteau carried all necessaries, and was easily accessible on the dray, which also carried the stores for the trip and the drovers' swags.

I undertook the purchase of the "plant" myself. Besides the four fine draught-horses, there were some thirty-six riding horses for the use of the drovers, myself, and my son, aged 12. There were a few good stock horses in the mob, but not one of the drovers owned a cattle dog, a most necessary adjunct to droving.

On a golden day in the Australian April we lifted the big mob from Lake Eda and started off behind them. The head drover assigned each one his position and duties. Some guarded the flanks, the leader and his second headed the mob; the Maori cook, Davy, took complete charge of the dray, provisions and spare horses, and the others became the "tailing" hands.

A travelling mob of cows usually shapes itself in the form of a triangle, the strongest beasts forming the apex, while the stragglers make an ever-widening line at the rear in their efforts to find food, as the leaders and flankers consume almost every blade as they go along. All the cattle had been accustomed to surface water, and while the going was over the claypan and well-grassed country south of Broome, the big mob travelled easily. My place and that of my boy, which we retained throughout the journey, were the base of the triangle, zigzagging to and fro behind the "tailers."

There is no eight-hour day in a droving camp. All hands are roused at peep of dawn. Davy had breakfast ready and steaming, horses were brought in and saddled, and the mob was waked and started. At each night camp, many of the mothers hid their calves, hoping to make back to them later. To watch a cow hide its calf behind a four-inch tussock is a lesson in wild mothercraft. Sunrise generally saw us on the move, the leaders grazing and the stragglers finding their places at the tail. Back and forth along this ever-widening tail of cows and calves we rode, with eyes alert for break-backs. Meanwhile the head man went on to find a night camp. Davy followed the horse-track and only twice failed to turn up in time—but even so, he incurred my extreme displeasure on one occasion. The only greenstuff I had had to eat for weeks, a fresh young lettuce presented as a gift of grace at one of the stations, he took away and boiled!

All went well until the Eighty-Mile beach was reached; here the surface waters ceased, and the wells began. Six canvas buckets, each with a twenty-gallon capacity, with pulleys and gear, were brought for emergencies. Most of the wells along the Eighty-Mile were in a bad state, owing to the disuse of the stock-route, and there was hefty work for all at the end of each day's droving. The long-disused windlasses, timbering, and platform more than once gave way, burying bucket and gear and effectually closing the wells, so there was nothing for it but to move the thirsty mob onward. The wells were far apart, and cows in calf are slow walkers.

At Whistler's Creek, near Lagrange Bay, the sea became visible and with a "Hurrah swing" of waving tail, the beasts rushed into the bay. Fortunately the water was shallow at that point, and they were soon on the road again. Nambeet Well, half-way along the Eighty-Mile, was the first good well struck, a shallow soak with beautiful and abundant water. Beside the well was a corrugated iron tombstone, telling of the murder of a white man named Hourigan by his native boy, for a few ends of tobacco. The boy was caught and hanged.

Old breakwinds on the slopes surrounding the valley of Nambeet Well showed that the place was once a favourite camping-ground, but after the murder no natives would camp there. Some poisonous or stupefying herbage laid a score or so of our cattle apparently dead there, but we heard later that they all recovered and returned to their own ground.

The coastline along the beach is only ten to twelve feet above sea-level, and in all the long stretch of plain only two little pinnacles—Barn and Church Hills—raise their heads above the level. These little hills were beacons for the schooners and luggers along the Eighty-Mile beach. A species of bloated rat, with a thick tail, makes shallow burrows on the plain, and these pitfalls added to the difficulty of manœuvring the thirsty mob. Along the whole length of the beach, we had to carry our firewood in the dray. There was but one tree, an unburnable "thorny sand-paper," left standing, covered with axe chops, and impregnable still.

The first stampede occurred at Barn Hill, and standing on the little knob, I looked down on a sea of horns and tails and dust as the whole mob suddenly started back for home and water. At last the galloping drovers "headed" them again, the sea of dust subsided, and the runaways were under control.

All along the coast, and right out in the bays are fresh springs bubbling up through the mud, and at low tide one can see and taste the beautiful fresh water. Smoke signals of the natives could be seen on the horizon every day, messages carried on for many miles. The signals were all identical—a long spiral drifting away to the south. The inlanders were even in those years coming to the coast from ever-increasing distances to replace the coast groups that had died out, until they, in their turn, succumbed to the new conditions. Practically all the coastal natives are now dead, those frequenting the townships and beaches being far inland "relatives" of the dead tribes.

The long day's tailing made riding very wearisome, and I frequently changed to the off-side. I noticed that many of the drovers rode side-saddle now and then, but generally the quick and arduous work of the wells relieved the weariness of the saddle.

Gradually the Herefords became used to the wells and our only trouble was the rush to the troughs. We had hoped to reach Glen Carrick before any calves were dropped, so no lorry had been brought along for day-old calves. Many had to be killed, owing to forced marches, and their mothers gave endless trouble, and made night hideous with their bellowing. Night-long watches, with great fires at various points, became the rule. More men were needed, and I had to go back to Lagrange Bay to telegraph for extra hands and horses. The way lay over a wide plain, sparsely dotted with high ant-hills. I was cantering easily, eyes and thoughts on the scenery, when my mount began to "pig-jump" and threw me. His trouble was a slipping saddle-cloth. I caught the reins, and held them, through all the play that followed, though now and then the flying hoofs came nearer to my head than was pleasant. At last he quietened down. A twisted ankle and no mounting block baffled me for a moment, but the horse had had enough play, and came along to an ant-hill, from the top of which I mounted and proceeded on the journey.

As we trailed along over the Eighty-Mile, prodding a sturdy little calf or clubbing a day-old weakling, those of us who were at the base of the great moving triangle were surprised one morning to see the mob suddenly split in two, leaving a narrow lane along the centre, and along the lane quietly walked a Jew pedlar with his huge pack strapped on his back. Drovers and horses stood like statues as Moses passed through the Red Sea, never once hastening. The head drovers were waiting for him—fortunately out of earshot. All that he remarked at the close of their tirade was, "Who iss the lady mit the veil?"

At Wallal we came to the end of the dreadful Eighty-

Mile, good herbage, good water, and a blessed spell. At the time of our passing, there were six white men and over a hundred natives at this isolated station. Supplies were brought to it quarterly by schooner, and though they were always depleted by travellers long before the schooner was due, the white men bravely carried on in good times and lean. The new country was better for the cattle, but the size of the mob necessitated our reaching water always in good time. The station-owners showed us every courtesy in free paddocks and water rights, and we, on our part, paid due attention to time-limit rules.

One night we camped at a beautiful waterhole called Jalliung. Native legend made Jalliung a bottomless pool, and the home of a magic snake who devoured any strange black fellow who drank of it.

At Balla-Balla, we replenished our supplies at the little tin store of a bare-footed and bearded gentleman who told me that he was a brother of Tiffany, the millionaire-jeweller of New York. Such was the adventurous and polyglot population of the north-west at that time that he may have been.

We were accorded a great welcome at the stations. Pardu had suffered a willie-willie a few weeks before our visit, but the roofless house was covered by the hospitality of its owners. At the de Grey the finest four-in-hand of greys that I had seen in West Australia drove out to greet and take me back for a day's "spell."

In the saddle for eighteen hours a day, from dawn till the sharing of the night watches, we plodded on. The drovers and cattle stopped for a siesta at midday, in the worst of the blazing heat. Never able to sleep in the daytime, I seized this opportunity for explorations and collections of botanical and geological novelties, which I later forwarded to the museums.

Marble Bar, which received its name from the mottled bar of quartz which crosses the Coongan River, is 130 miles from Port Hedland, and Nullagine, 80 miles south of Marble Bar—all mineral-bearing and good pastoral country. We kept well west of both these townships. It was a dry year, but the feed was splendid. The mob spread itself out on the flats, wading knee-deep in lush herbage, grazing leisurely along the wide swathe of their going. Ashburton pea made a green carpet in the river-beds, so that the river-beds sometimes became the stock-route. At last we came to the Shaw Hills, denuded masses of granite, silent and sombre. No sound greeted us as we climbed hill after hill; the songs of birds are never heard. Mine was the first dray that ever passed through the Shaw Gorge, where flood-marks showed some sixty feet above the river-bed. Our last night there was a nightmare. The rain came down with the darkness. We were all in a cul-de-sac, cattle, men and horses, our only outlet the river-bed, along which the flood waters would run. Everyone had had some experience of the quick rise of these rivers. No one slept, and we all watched anxiously from our shelters under the rocks. Happily the rain was light and local but there had been catastrophic floods many times in this area, and we were deemed fortunate.

In a lonely part of the Shaw, I came upon a native with his two women, three children and some dogs, all very emaciated. I made them follow to the camp, and two young calves about a fortnight old were killed and given to them. Each calf weighed about sixty pounds, but when I rode to the camp at dawn there was not a bone left to tell the tale—only six human stomachs incredibly distended, and six happy faces grinning greeting and farewell.

We crossed the Divide, and so came to the Fortescue River and Roy Hill, with excellent fodder to fatten our herd, now increased to nearly 1,000 head. Day after day we travelled a land of plenty, thick mulga scrub, succulent salt bush and Mitchell grass. The pioneer of Roy Hill was Peter MacKay. A few miles from the homestead is a knobby rise where, in the early days, he was once assailed by a horde of savages. He had his gun and ammunition, and he was a dead shot, as they well knew. There he re-mained for two days without sleep, eking out his portion of damper and mutton, and keeping the crowd of canni-bals at bay. They hurled their spears and clubs at him. but he had learned to dodge these weapons. On the third day help came from the station.

Our worst stampede occurred on Roy Hill property, on one of the station wells in a fenced paddock. The cattle had had a long and trying day, the tired calves reluctant to move, and their mothers half maddened with thirst and distracted with mother love. Horses and men were down and out with watching and guiding the troublesome beasts, and it was dark when they had all been safely passed through the fence.

Relying on the security of the mob and the safety of the fence, all hands immediately unsaddled for a drink of tea, when the cattle broke camp and rushed the fence, heading straight for Roy Hill and the pools there. The whole mob, except those too weak to travel, were away in a twinkling. About 400 tailers, cows and calves, were left to three of us to water—myself, my little son, and one droving hand, with Davy and the dray to look after our inner man. The other drovers headed back to many days of trouble before the stampeders were collected and brought on. Our mob was too tired to move, even when it heard the squeak of the windlass. My son and I shared work with the twenty-gallon buckets from early dawn till late at night, and managed to satisfy our charges by steady lifting and emptying. The paddock was full of feed, and with plenty of water there need be no anxiety.

We all divided the night-watch. Nights were still and cloudless. Hercules and Lyra, Aquila and Cygnus were my fellow-watchers in the silence, on their way to the mystical west. No sound was heard save the quiet breathing of the sleeping herd—the little calves snuggled up beside their mothers in full content. I was thankful that their hard times were over.

A chastened mob was brought back to the paddock, and after a few days' spell we moved on the last eighty miles to Glen Carrick. Pools were full and frequent in the many creeks and tributaries which rise in the Ophthalmia Ranges and form the head waters of the Ashburton and Fortescue. There was no dearth of good feed, and the last part of the journey was without event. In such good grass was my own little run that in three months' time the cattle had put on wonderful condition and it was possible for them to take the six weeks' trip to Peak Hill, there to be disposed of as "forward stores."

There was no homestead but a bough shade at Glen Carrick, but I remained there happily for a short period, waiting the opportunity to return to Port Hedland. At last I secured a passage with one "Black Johnson," a man who had been taking out a buggy-load of dynamite to a far distant mine. We arrived, without any trouble, at Port Hedland, within nine or ten days. I was in time to embark on the steamer *Sultan* on the downward journey to Perth.

Chapter VII

LAST OF THE BIBBULMUN RACE

PERTH BROUGHT SURCEASE FROM THE STRUGGLES AND crudeness of the North-West and refreshing contact with those of my own kin, but it was not to be for long. The call of the task to which my life had been dedicated was insistent. It drew me first to solacing the passing of the last of the Bibbulmun, that once great race which had roamed the fertile coastal plains on which Perth is set and the delectable uplands of the Darling Ranges.

The Bibbulmun race was the largest homogeneous group in all Australia. Their country extended for many hundreds of square miles, and comprised the extreme triangle of the south-west, its base drawn from about Jurien Bay, slightly south of Geraldton on the West Coast, to Esperance on the Great Australian Bight. The Perth groups occupied a wide area, towards Northam, Toodyay, Gin Gin and Southern Cross on the north, and south to Bunbury and The Vasse. The last of the uncircumcised hordes, gradually driven down by a lustier, fiercer people, and finding by chance the wealthiest and most fertile corner of the State, "sat down" in the forests by rivers and water-holes of rich flora and teeming fauna, sharing them with the birds and animals and reptiles that they believed to be their "elder brothers" or that became, in the passage of the centuries, their ancestor-gods.

The word *bibbulmun* signifies many breasts, a name derived, perhaps, from the fecundity of that region, or from the unusually great proportion of women and children among them. There were more than seventy groups in the Bibbulmun area linked by one language with local variations. They had neither chiefs or kings nor overlords, and although they were innocent of arts and crafts, they were by no means savage, and accorded their women more of initiative liberty than the circumcised. They were the finest groups in all West Australia.[1] The Manitchmat and Wordungmat, the fair and dark people of the White Cockatoo and Crow, always kept their marriages within the four class subdivisions of these two primary divisions, which I believe to be fundamental and Australia-wide. These tribes were not cannibals. Infanticide was rarely practised except in the case of twins and then only because of the magic of "two heads" coming where one was expected. Such was their simple philosophy that the facts of birth were unknown to them. Their only deity was a *woggal* or serpent-god, that dominated the earth, the sky, the sea, and punished evil-doers. They believed that the spirits of the dead were taken to Kur'an'nup, a land beyond the western sea.

The only raiment was a fur-skin cloak, made from the skins of seven kangaroos. Their tools were palæolithic, with a later intrusion of the neolithic scarcely evident—a *koja,* or stone axe with wooden handle fastened with wattle gum and a rough knife of serrated stone. It is a question whether to any great extent they used the boomerang, which I believe to have been an importation, as it was useless in such thickly-timbered country. They had no fighting-shields. The spear, miro, or spear-thrower, and the

---

[1] Probably their prototypes were to be found in the New South Wales and Victorian coastal tribes, which disappeared equally rapidly.

club, were their only weapons, and spear-dodging was a consummate art among them. The women carried a *wanna,* or digging stick, the usual bark or wooden scoop, and a kangaroo-skin bag. A camp-fire for winter warmth, and a bough shade for shelter from the sun were the only homes, fire being made by the friction of a stick applied drill fashion to the flower-stem of the resinous "black-boy" tree-fern.

These southern people had a sense of hereditary group ownership of their land, upon which no other tribe might trespass, but all were generously invited to share its special products in times of plenty, a hospitality unknown in the poverty-stricken wastes of the great north-west and centre. The sea-coasts, estuaries and rivers were full of fish, and the inlanders and hill-folk were always welcome visitors in the spawning and crabbing seasons. The tall timber country, of which the magnificent jarrah and kerri now occupy a pride of place among the world's hardwoods, was alive with bird and animal life, and rich with numerous fruits of shrub and vine, a meeting-place of tribes within hundreds of miles when the wild potato was in harvest there.

When I came upon the remnants of the Bibbulmun, they had been in contact with civilization for some seventy years, and in that short time it had reduced the native inhabitants of the city of Perth and its environs to one old man, Joobaitch, and an older-looking niece, Balbuk. On this old man's group area, at the foot of the Darling Ranges, the first reserve had been established by Lord (then Mr.) Forrest in the nineties, and here were gathered all that were left of the tribes.

The desire of the Government was that I should base my investigations upon history and existing data, and build upon the anthropological premises accumulated by cultured and well-informed men such as Sir George Grey, Bishop Salvado, G. F. Moore and others. For two years I studied every note of the bibliography at my disposal regarding the aboriginal tribes of West Australia, with augmented information from South Australia, Victoria and other states. I found that in many essentials these Western Australian authorities contradicted each other, and that it was difficult to come to a conclusion. So I made the suggestion that I should begin at the beginning, and seek the truth at the fountain-head.

My first camp was established on the Maamba Reserve near the present National Park, a few miles from Cannington, to-day an outer suburban area of great fertility, set with orchards and vineyards, but in the early years of this century a beautiful kingdom of bush still rich in native foods and fruits. The Bibbulmun race was represented by some thirty or forty stragglers, and these would gladly have gone back to their own various grounds; but their health and sight had failed.

It is saddening indeed to wander the vast expanse of hill and dale and cliff and grove, and find not one of its own people remaining. They have vanished from the face of earth as completely as the extinct sthenurus, of which their far-off ancestors were contemporaries.

The first landing of the white man was the beginning of the end. Often have I heard the story, a never-failing marvel to the three generations who survived it, of the landing on the banks of the Swan River in 1829. In his camp by a little spring called Goordandalup, a wilderness of bush that is now the metropolitan subdivision of Crawley on the highway of the Mount's Bay Road, Yalgunga lay dozing in the heat of mid-afternoon. He did not know that it was 1829, or hear the death-knell of his people. He knew only that the world was blue and smiling, and the rock-holes filling with fish in the incoming tide, and that the sun was good. Suddenly he heard a new sound on the river, a soft continuous sound, and coming closer. He rose to his feet and looked about instinctively for his spear. His women crouched round him, and his children ran to him afraid. Round the bend came an open boat, and the phenomenon of *jang-ga,* spirits of the dead who had come back as white men, borne upon the waters. Spears were useless. Yalgunga waited. Walking as other men, the strangers stepped ashore and came to him, speaking words that meant nothing. Then one of them put out a hand in greeting. Yalgunga grate-

fully clasped it in his own, and with his other hand made
a gesture to his camp and his spring—they were all he
had to offer. That evening he gathered his family, his
spears, and all his belongings, and wandered away to the
swamp at Goobabbilup, which is now Monger's Lake,
never to return to the leafy home and the curve of bush
and beach that had been his alone. So easily had the white
man won.

There must have been some tradition handed down
from Yalgunga's forefathers of Vlaming and other earlier
arrivals of *jang-ga* who moved over the waters in their
strange ships, and walked about unafraid, and returned
to Ku'ran'nup. Yalgunga did not know that these later
jang-ga had come to stay. The gazettes of the early thirties
made frequent reference to his peaceful and kindly disposition. It was Maiago, whose camp was where the Perth
Town Hall now stands, who later travelled with Stokes on
his exploration, and who introduced the white man's flour
and rice to the natives, the first instalment of payment for
their country. The rice they buried in the earth, but the
flour they appreciated, calling it always "barragood"—
the nearest they could get to the assurance of "very good"
with which it was given to them.

The belief of the Bibbulmun that the first white men
were the returned spirits of their own dead relatives, led to
friendly feeling towards the "spirits" from their first en-
counter.

A peculiarity of gait, a slight deformity, a scar, a missing
toe, finger, tooth, etc., singled out some white person for
special recognition and friendship. When Sir George Grey
was Governor, word came to him that the old woman
Delyungur had recognized in him her long-lost son, and
cried and wept unceasingly in that she could not see him
or touch him.

Grey appointed a day for a Native Levee on which all
the natives of the district came to the appointed place and
approached the spot where he and his staff were standing.

A great wailing was presently heard, and as the natives
opened their ranks along the cleared space came old
Delyungur, crying and peering to find the face of her long-

dead son. She walked slowly up until her eyes could see the Governor clearly. Her step became quicker, stronger. She looked at Sir George, who was looking kindly towards her, and in a moment she had him in her embrace, crying, *"Boondoo, boondoo! bala ngan-ya Kooling"* (True, true, he is my son), as she fondled the face and form of her long-lost son and wept for joy at their re-union.

Sir George Grey's gentle sufferance of her embraces strengthened immeasurably the friendly bond between the black and white in those early days. His kindly reception of old Delyungur, who was sister to Yalgunga's dead mother Windera, became known to every group throughout the metropolitan area.

What a surprise the fences, and the sheep and horses and cattle within their boundaries, and the telegraph line with its magic messages swifter and truer than smoke signals, and the ships sailing into the estuaries, and the jetties and wharves built out to meet them! Who shall say what vague despair and unrest entered these primitive minds as the natives beheld one after another of their cherished homing spots ruthlessly swept away in the resistless march of civilization, and the winding tracks to their various food grounds obliterated by houses and streets?

They could no longer seek for the *goonoks* in their season, their *mungaitch* honey-groves were cut down to make way for flocks and herds. Could they hunt for the *bai-yoo* nuts of the Zamia, the *warrain,* and the *joobok* roots on the slopes, when the white men had fenced them in, and driven their old friends beyond the pale? On their own country they were trespassers. There was no more happy wandering in the interchange of hospitality. Sources of food supply slowly but surely disappeared, and they were sent away to unfamiliar places, compelled to change completely their mode of life, to clothe themselves in the attire of the strangers, to eat foods unfitted for them, to live within walls.

Their age-old laws were set aside for laws they could not understand. The younger generations, always wilful, now openly flouted the old, and defied them, and haunted the white man's homes, protected by his policeman. A little while, and they resorted to thieving—where theft had been unknown—and sycophancy, and sold their young wives to the depraved and foreign element. Half-castes came among them, a being neither black nor white, whom they detested. They died in their numbers of the white man's diseases, measles, whooping-cough, influenza, and the results of their own wrong-doing.

Change of food, environment, outlook, the burying of the old traditions and customs, inhibitions and the break-down of the laws all conspired to bring degeneration, first to the individual and then to the race. Can we wonder that they faded so swiftly? Can we blame them for the sudden reactions that found vent in violence in certain instances few and far between, punished sometimes with terrible reprisals on the part of the white man?

The pioneers of Western Australia were noble men and women, and nearly all of them were above reproach and more than kindly in their treatment of the aboriginal. There is evidence that they did everything in their power for the preservation and betterment of the race. Schools were established as early as 1831, and reserve sanctuaries, with interpreters and ration-givers and government inspectors. There were innumerable systematic schemes on the part of religious organizations, and social organizations and private persons, from King George's Sound north to Geraldton, with no encouraging results. Missions of all kinds were established throughout the Bibbulmun area. The most out-standing of these was undoubtedly the great Benedictine Mission of New Norcia, 80 miles north of Perth, founded by Don Salvado in 1846, among the dingo-totem tribes of the Victoria Plain.

As a young and earnest evangelist, Bishop Salvado journeyed into this then remote country, camped with the natives at a water-hole to gain their confidence, then gathered them to him in the name of Christianity. In a fertile valley he established his church and his colony, later sponsored by the Queen of Spain, and destined to become the great Spanish monastery it is to-day, a seat of the arts and sciences with its colleges of secular and religious educa-tion, a railway-town of considerable importance with its far-flung and prosperous agricultural and pastoral estates, a jewel of the South-West.

Bishop Salvado fed and clothed the natives. He built a tidy little Continental village of stone houses, twenty-eight in all, laid out in streets, and induced them to live in them. He saw that each man had his own allotment of land. For the preliminary work done upon it the Bishop paid him, and put the money in the bank, and purchased implements for further development, and educated his children. He taught them handicrafts and stockwork and telegraphy and accountancy and music and languages, every one of which they could absorb and absorb well. He went further. He selected five promising young aboriginal boys, and took them with him to Rome to study for the priesthood in a Benedictine seminary there. Among them were two who received the names of John and Francis Xavier, and the habit of the Order from the Pope himself. All died in Europe, with the exception of one, who returned to New Norcia, promptly flung away his habit, made for the bush, and died there.

Children of the woodland, dwelling in a squalor that could not be avoided in their stone-walled houses, closed in from the air that was their breath of life, in the heat of summer and the dank cold of winter, they lost all touch with their native earth. They slept on beds—but they could not learn cleanliness. They wore clothing, and developed chest complaints and fevers. They died, and the dead were carried out of the little houses, and others sent to live in them—a superstitious people with a horror of the dead, there they too died. Alas for the poor "little brothers of the dingo"—civilization was a cloak that they donned easily enough, but they could not wear it and live. Bishop Salvado had counted 250 members of the Victoria Plains group in 1864. The last of these, Monnup, died in 1913.

It was the same story everywhere, a kindness that killed as surely and as swiftly as cruelty would have done. The Australian native can withstand all the reverses of nature, fiendish droughts and sweeping floods, horrors of thirst and enforced starvation—but he cannot withstand civilization. In 1883, a commission was appointed in West Australia to control native conditions of living and employment, and in 1886 all aborigines of the State were brought directly under the guardianship of the Government. In the early nineteen-hundreds a special Aborigines' Department was created, with protectors travelling throughout West Australia, and a Chief Protector in authority in Perth.

There is no hope of protecting the Stone Age from the twentieth century! When the native's little group area is gone, he loses the will to live, and when the will to live is gone, he dies.

The West Australian Government treated the natives generously, each fortnight sending them liberal rations of flour, tea, sugar and tobacco, with meat and jam added, and provided them with little wooden huts, each with a fireplace, a bed, a spring-mattress, warm cosy blankets and even crockery. There was a well in the centre of the reserve which was fenced into individual areas that they might grow flowers and vegetables and keep goats. The natives were intensely proud and even jealous of their little villas and built themselves *mias* (bush shelters) outside them, where they slept with the dogs. They broke through the fences for a shorter route when they went to visit each other. Every now and then, those who were able wandered restlessly away to their own *kelleep* (group area and "home" land), in the seasons of its fruitfulness and old-time ceremonies, and finding no friendly fires, and the houses and fences of the white man everywhere, they fled in panic back to the city to sell clothes-props or to beg, to pick up scraps of charity and vices and disease. Too often the white man's sympathy was expressed in beer and whisky, and so they drifted in and out of gaol, and back to the reserve again.

A circular tent, 14 ft. in diameter, sagging about me in the wet and ballooning in the wind, was my home for two years in that little patch of bushland bright with wild flowers, overlooking the beautiful valley of Guildford and the winding river. There by a camp-fire when the dampers were cooking, or in the winter sitting on the ground by a fire inside their *mia,* I would be on duty from night till morning, collecting scraps of language, old

legends, old customs, trying to conjure a nation of the past
from these few and homeless derelicts, always in haste, as
they died about me one by one, in fear lest I should be
too late.

Dirty and degraded as they all were, they were very
human. Joobaitch of the kangaroo tribe of Perth, a
Wordungmat or dark-type crowman, had been born in
Stirling's time, and was the son of that Yalgunga who
ceded his spring on the banks of the Swan to Lieutenant
Irwin. Joobaitch, who was then nearly 50 years of age, was
a protégé of Bishop Hale and at one time a native trooper.
He had had contact with only the best of the white families,
neither drank nor smoked, and had no affinity with the
poor depraved and drink-sodden old men and women who
"sat down" at Maamba.

There was Baaburgurt, blind and feeble. Once a
"brother" of the Kalda (sea mullet) in the Capel River,
he would sit all day long, the tears streaming from his
sightless eyes, singing songs of his lost country. There
were Woolberr, last of the Kuljak (black swan) of Gin
Gin; Monnop, last of the dingo-totem of the Victoria
Plains; Moorangan, of Wagin's emu; Genburdong, of Kellerberrin's snake people; Nyalyert, a woman of the white-
bait of Pinjarra; and Ngilgi, of the kangaroo of Busselton;
Kajjaman, of the edible gum; and Dool, a Nanitchmat of
York. Other sad old pilgrims of the White Cockatoo and
Crow came and went. The only stranger among them was
Bimba, a member of one of the circumcised groups east of
Kellerberrin, but nobody ever wanted to hear about his
totem.

The last Perth woman, Balbuk, or Fanny Balbuk, as
she was called, was a comic, if tragic, character, and a
general nuisance of many years' standing. To the end of
her life she raged and stormed at the usurping of her beloved home ground. One of her favourite annoyances was
to stand at the gates of Government House, reviling all who
dwelt within, because the stone gates guarded by a sentry
enclosed her grandmother's burial ground. She would trail
the streets shouting her curses upon them, and impose on
all the members of the "first families" with whom she had

played as a child. Balbuk had been born in Huirison Island at the Causeway, and from there a straight track led to the place where once she had gathered *jilgies* and vegetable food with the women, in the swamp where Perth railway station now stands. Through fences and over them, Balbuk took the straight track to the end. When a house was built in the way, she broke its fence-palings with her digging stick and charged up the steps and through the rooms. Time and again she was arrested, but her childhood playmates, now in high positions, would pay the fine for her, and Balbuk would be free to get drunk again, and shout scandal and maledictions from the street corners.

To the end of her life, Balbuk would not have a half-caste near the place—she said they smelt worse than the white people.

Her matrimonial lapses evoked many a delighted grin, for Balbuk had a past. A Wordungmat, or Crow, in her young days, she had attached herself to another Crow, and when his sister resented the unlawful union and fought her, Balbuk's rage was so intense that she drove her digging stick through the woman's body, killing her instantly. She fled from justice to the boundary of the Bibbulmun and the circumcised tribes. There she saw human meat eaten, and was offered a thigh, which she refused. Being young and fat and possibly succulent, she promptly fled back to the Victorian plains. So attractive was her personality that in the ensuing seven years, wandering from group to group, she contracted seven marriages, most of them illegal, from the aboriginal point of view, though some were cele-brated in the chapel of New Norcia by unwitting priests, who did not remember that they had seen her before. The fame of her fury had travelled far, and none of the New Norcia natives dared to tell.

Her old crime forgotten, Balbuk at last returned to her own Perth country. Although she had broken every law of her group, she had broken none of the totem food-laws, and never failed to perform propitiatory services to the magic snake or the spirits in rocks and caves and hills. She knew every sacred totem spot, and all the devils that haunted them, from the mouth of the Swan to the ranges, and even when she was a fat old woman, and her seven husbands, and numerous lovers had long preceded her to the Bibbulmun heaven of Kur'an'nup, she assiduously avoided every "baby stone" from which a babe might come to her.

When she lay dying in her shelter at Maamba, a female kangaroo, her totem, suddenly made its appearance among the bushes some yards away. With dimmed eyes she looked upon it. "My *borunggur* has come for me; I go now," she said. She died a few days later in Perth Hospital. Just at the end the doctor came into the room. Balbuk recognized him. "Ninety-nine!" she hurled at him facetiously with her last breath.

Ngilgi was the rich widow of the camp. She had been born at Busselton, just at the moment when her mother was caught red-handed robbing a potato-patch, and her unexpected arrival made the potato-patch her ground thereafter, and she became an amusing protégée of the white people who owned it. At Maamba, she was the proud possessor of seven goats, twelve fowls and thirty-two dogs, incredible mongrels all. To watch the procession enter her house at night, in single file, with Ngilgi bringing up the rear, was a never-failing entertainment. The fowls roosted on the bed's head, the dogs and young kids formed a living blanket on the mattress, and goats filled the floor and the fire-place. In the morning they emerged in the same order, unless Ngilgi had a laundry appointment at Guildford. On those days the livestock were left closed in the little hut, where their howls and crowing made day hideous until her return.

Monnop, and Woolberr, Baaburgurt and Bimba were all suitors for her hand and possessions. Woolberr and Baaburgurt, being blind, could not fight. Monnop and Bimba were active rivals, and ribs and jaws were often broken. A half-caste named Jimmie, young enough to be her grandson, made his appearance with her one evening, and joined the livestock within the hut. The arrangement was that Ngilgi would be breadwinner while Jimmie acted as overseer. Next morning four raging suitors were on the doorstep waiting for Jimmie. Woolberr began to "sing magic" at him. Blind Baaburgurt raised his stick in readiness for the half-caste odour which would tell him Jimmie was near, and Monnop and Bimba presented a combined front of battle. Jimmie dodged, and did not stop running till he reached Guildford. Ngilgi shut up her shack and followed him. A few days later when she returned forlorn, Baaburgurt slily brought up the rear of the fowls and goats to console her. The three rivals again gathered to revile the union.

"Baaburgurt's Cockatoo, and so is Ngilgi. I am Crow, and her proper husband," said Monnop. "So am I!" said Woolberr. Both glared at Bimba, who was neither Bibbulmun nor Wordungmat, and a fight would have followed had not the door of Ngilgi's house at that moment violently opened, and from it emerged Baaburgurt closely followed by a bucket of cold water. Presently there came a shrill wailing—Ngilgi's lament for the faithless Jimmie. Next morning they were preparing to turn their backs on each other to eat, when the door opened again, and from it came a repentant Ngilgi, with damper and jam and tea for Baaburgurt.

"I don't want you for my husband," she said, "but I threw water at you, so I bring you food." Content with her flocks and herds, Ngilgi tried no further matrimonial experiments. Her dogs, in spite of their physical infirmities and mixed breeds, were notorious fowl-hunters of the Cannington district, but she could sense a policeman's visit well beforehand, huddled the motley pack into chaffbags, slung them over her shoulder, and betook herself to a cave in the hills when he came to Maamba. When she was caught at last, and the policeman mercifully destroyed all save the single whole specimen, she shook the dust of the reserve from her shapely feet and retired to the outskirts of Guildford, where she busied herself cleaning and washing for the white man.

Nyalyert and Kajjaman drank themselves to death. Woolberr made a valiant effort to reach his home at Gin Gin when the black swans were nesting, but following the track of the railway line, lost in memories of the distributions and ceremonies of long ago, he was struck by a train and killed. Baaburgurt, blind and feeble, continually cried and mourned for his *kalleep* at Wonnerup until at last some members of a well-known family in the South-West, whose father had been murdered in the early days by Baaburgurt's father, took pity on the poor old man, and cared for him till the end.

All of these natives had been in close contact with Christianity during most of their lives, but little it penetrated their consciousness. Joobaitch considered that the eagle on the lectern of St. George's Cathedral had been provided by the white man as a totem for him, a totem he accepted with amiability but no enthusiasm, while Monnop pinned his new-found faith to the dove in the Benedictine built chapel, now St. Mary's Cathedral in Perth.

As I sat at the feet of my first Bibbulmun teachers one of the most important lessons was communicated to me unconsciously, but so important and significant was it that I remembered and acted upon it through all the years. When I began my camp life at Maamba Reserve in the early 1900's Sir Frederick Bedford, the then Governor, and Lady Bedford honoured us with a visit. An old and fine sailor, Sir Frederick wished to see every detail of my camp life and walked through and into my living- and dressing-tents on his tour of inspection. The same evening as we were seated round a fire discussing the visit of our Queen's Representative, Ngilgi said: "The Governor is like the Great Queen's son, and the Queen can go everywhere and so can the Governor, but no man can go into your *mia* (tent, shelter) unless he is your husband *(korda)*. That is Bibbulmun law." I never forgot or ceased to obey that fundamental law. And, so, when Bishop White of Willochra visited me at my Ooldea camp in the late 1920's I received him outside my breakwind, and taking out three kerosene cases, we had tea and a friendly talk while sitting on our primitive stools. It was interesting to hear from the Bishop that this fundamental social "law" was not known either to himself or to any of the Missionaries in charge of his Native Missions in Queensland and elsewhere, but it is one of the most important "laws" in the whole native system; not a law having a moral founda-

tion in the native social system, but an economic foundation. The woman is an economic asset to the man who
owns her. He can lend her but in barter always. He can
exchange her for another woman, or for weapons or some
such as payment, and he may even dispose of her finally
for a price and scrupulously keep his agreement in that
transaction. She then ceases to be his economic asset, the
important fact that counted in native domestic relations
being that sexual jealousy was secondary to what might
be called economic jealousy.

It was always a part of my work amongst them to endeavour to give them a little insight into our own social
system, but to the end of their lives they failed to understand it.

The moment the low white entered their lives all native
social and sexual tabus were broken. When the first white
man took the young native woman he fancied, his status
in her family and group was adjusted according to native
law. He chose his woman and automatically became her
husband's brother with all the rights and obligations of the
husband's brother, son-in-law, etc. So long as the white
man took other women from among his new brothers'
wives he incurred no bodily risk, and the foods he gave
were distributed according to the food laws in this respect.
But when his lustful eyes fell upon women and girls who
were tabu to him in his new "native" relationship, he
committed a breach of native law punishable with death.
Many a white man has been killed for this offence, of
which he may have been ignorant or defiant.

When they saw the white man living in the same hut as
his mother, mother-in-law, grown-up sisters (grown-up
sisters and brothers were always tabu to each other); when
they perceived that every native law regarding tabus was
apparently set at naught by white people, the law-abiding
native groups attached the odium of group marriage and
promiscuity to the white people!

Among the Bibbulmun, who had kept their laws intact
until the coming of the white man, this apparent promiscuity of the whites had a disastrous effect. They broke
their age-old tabus, and no "magic" punishment resulting,

the young men took whom they willed and hugged the white settlements for safety. The elders of the groups lost their magic powers through the white man's drink; the evil example was set and the groups became like dingoes. But as in every human heart there is a sort of relative conscience, so every Bibbulmun who took his sister, mother or daughter to wife knew in his heart that he was committing a dreadful offence, and this feeling was no small factor in their quick extinction.

Joobaitch clung steadily to Maamba, his own ground, even when the doctors urged his removal to hospital. "No," said Joobaitch, "I shall die on my own ground, and not in a white man's house. When I die, I shall go down through the sea to Kur'an'nup, where all my people will be waiting on the shore with meat food, my mother and my woman, my father, and my brothers. Before it sets out on its journey, my spirit must be free to rest on the *kaanya* tree. Since *nyitting* (cold) times all Bibbulmun spirits have rested on this tree on their way to Kur'an'nup, and I have never broken a branch or flower, or sat in the shade of the tree, because it is the tree of the dead, the sacred tree."

One day the cart came to take Joobaitch to hospital. "Don't let them take me!" he pleaded. I said, "It is all right, Joobaitch. You will die before you pass the *kaanya* tree at Karragullen, and your soul will rest there before it goes to the sea." Joobaitch died as the cart crossed the little creek near Maamba, as he had wished it, still on his own ground, close to the *kaanya* tree.

So the last of the Perth tribe was buried in the aboriginal section of the old Guildford cemetery, which formed part of his people's home. He had had fifty years of Christianity, but he died in the faith of the Bibbulmun, looking westward to Kur'an'nup.

Chapter VIII

SOUTH-WEST PILGRIMAGE

FROM THE RESERVE AT MAAMBA, WITH MY OLD FRIENDS gone, I set out on a two years' pilgrimage of the South-West, through all the old camping grounds which had become railway cities and towns and centres of industry, pastoral and agricultural. In the whole Bibbulmun area I sought the living remnants of the various groups, the turkey-totem, mallee-hen, opossum, emu, fish, kangaroo. Many were completely extinct. Two or three old derelicts with women who were their unlawful wives according to aboriginal convention comprised the largest camps I could find, all of them Government pensioners or beggars.

As members of the groups died out, the ranks closed in, and men and women from east of the dividing ranges mixed with the river people *(beelgar)* and sea-coast people *(waddarn-gur)*. The birth of half-castes still further broke up the wandering families, for the half-caste fears and dislikes his mother's people, and objects to the communal food laws, while the natives despise the half-caste for his colour and his breed and his odour.

At Busselton the salmon trout group was represented by one old man, who sang for me the songs of the spawning season while he imitated the movements of the great spate, and told me the legend of huge cannibal dogs that daily hunted human flesh, carrying men in their mouths to the lair. This legend attained a curious significance when fossil bones of a flesh-eating sthenurus were discovered in the Margaret River caves in the vicinity. The last survivor of the Albany tribe, Kalgun or fish totem, was Wandin-yilmernong, a solitary White Cockatoo. From Albany I went to Bremer Bay, and then fifty miles inland to

Jerromunggup. There I found a five-generation family, but they were not all full-blood. Ngalbaitch, the matriarch, was a lively old woman, and might easily have survived to see the sixth successive branch of the family tree. As there can be no more than three generations in aboriginal genealogy, Ngalbaitch called her great-granddaughter "Mother" and her great-great-grandson "Brother." The girl was a Chinese half-caste, born with no eyelids, and Ngalbaitch's brother had performed a surgical operation with a skill and intelligence rare in a native. He had pulled out the skin covering of the eyes, held it vertically and slit it horizontally. As the cut edges healed, they had actually developed lashes.

At Ravensthorpe and Hopetown, the natives had almost completely died out. At Esperance there were but two old brothers, Deebungool and Dabungool, known as Dib and Dab. I rode a draught horse fifteen miles to interview Dib. He told me that the circumcised tribes had by this time encroached upon his home-ground. They had given him a woman, but had taken his little son Ro, and initiated him into their tribal practices. Between Esperance and Eucla, there were not half a dozen natives along the coast, but at Twilight Cove, where the explorer, Eyre, was rescued by an American ship, I found a true first cousin marriage, the only group of true first cousin lawful marriages that I could discover in the South-West. Another group also having true first cousin marriage laws was among the Roebourne area group of the North-West.

The mallee-hen group of the Palenup or Salt River area ended sadly. A special friendship called *babbingur* between certain brothers-in-law prevailed among the Bibbulmun, and two Palenup *babbingur* were the last of their group in the district. These men clung to each other in an extraordinary comradeship. In the passing of the years one became emaciated and listless from some disease—or it may have been the loss of the will to live. His *babbin* cared for him devotedly, worked for him, hunted for him, fed him. At some white man's farm or sheep-run he would find employment, but the white employer would tell the sick friend to work or get out. The moment his *babbin* heard the words, he would put down axe or spade and move on with his mate.

The wanderings circled their home ground, and one day the sick *babbin* lay down by the riverside and died. His friend dug the grave and buried him, lingered in the vicinity a little while in mourning, seeking no food, until he, too, became feeble and listless. He had lighted no spirit fire for the dead man, because there was no fear of the spirit of a friend so much beloved. All round the little area he walked with stumbling feet, and at last laid himself down near the new-made grave, and the two *kaanya* souls passed over to their heaven together.

I reached Bridgetown in the wet and windy wintry weather. Its fertile hills and valleys are among the finest fruit-growing districts in Australia, and, as Bibbulmun country, had provided unlimited food for the groups for countless centuries. Bridgetown yielded one old man, living in his beehive hut on the side of the new road. His dwelling was sheltered from the bleak winds and rains, and he preferred his freedom to the comfort of a hut offered by the Bridgetown municipality. He received Government rations, blankets and tobacco, and lived contentedly by his little *kalleep*. I came upon him on a rainy morning, and I sat beside him in the shelter, with a thermos of tea, cake and tobacco that I had brought for him, listening as he explored the memories of his life history, genealogy, dialect and myths. Another winter, and he was gone from the place for ever.

The wild cherry groups *(jeeuk)* between Esperance and Katanning were few. At Kojunup and Narrogin the same sad state of things prevailed, the few derelicts eking out an aimless existence with no interest in the new life or people. The totem either preceded or followed its human *borunggur*. Food was supplied to them, but they were all wanderers. I would sit with them for an hour, a day, a week, learning from them, pitying them, but unable to bring back the old condition. We parted always as "relations." I knew their simple social organization, and could speak to them as one of themselves, a blood-relation, and listen patiently to the old songs and stories. Many a time I found the end of a legend begun at Albany or Pinjarra, or the beginning of another whose end I never heard, but they were always comforted by company and understanding.

Everywhere I heard the plaint—*"Jangga meenya bomunggur"* (The smell of the white man is killing us).

The love for their own group area urged them to reach it and die on their own ground, but the spread of the white population sent them wandering ever farther and farther, so that they made superhuman efforts to reach their *kalleep* when they found themselves growing old and feeble, for fear that their spirit would be a trespasser upon strange country and lose the way to Kur'an'nup when the time came.

Old Yeebalan of Kendinup, a township east of Albany, found herself in the Dumbleyung district when palsy and blindness came upon her. Her white protectors tried to dissuade her, but she promised them she would go back to the Hassals of Kendinup whose sheep run had been her father's group area, and who had been good to her in her young days. They gave her food and money for the journey, and she immediately handed it over to the derelicts in camp in return for their hospitality, as in their primitive sense of honour every native must. Months later, after a solitary journey through the white settlements, she crawled towards the old Kendinup homestead where she had so often sought and found food and clothing. It was empty and deserted. Yeebalan made her last camp in the gully, and died a few days later.

There was a native reserve in the Katanning area, where it was hoped the Bibbulmun relicts would find rest in the evening of life, with their own shelters and fires that no institution could give them. I put up my tent near by, and made friends with my new "blood-relations," gathered from near and far Mungail, the oldest, of Ravensthorpe, a mallee-hen, had a grievance against the world, and in his moments of dementia would sing his woes the whole night through, in the shrill monotone of the *joolgoo-kening* of the forgotten corroborees. Among the Australian aborigines, as among the southern Irish peasantry, there is a curious sympathy and compassion for the mentally afflicted, so Mungail's ravings were patiently listened to in silence.

Some half-castes were there, one, Henry Penny, with white complexion and blue eyes, who easily passed as a white man at every hotel in Katanning.

A poor consumptive girl, Ngungalari, was one day brought in to me from Kojunup, carried in a stretcher by her father and sister for twenty-five miles. She had been reared by kindly and gentle white people, and had become used to their ways and refinements. While she lay dying, I took her a lace-covered tray and all the little appurtenances of afternoon tea. Although she was in the last stages of disease, she loved to handle the thin slices and dainty cups as she had seen her white girl companions do. She died very quietly a week after she arrived.

It was through the patriotic desire of Togur and Daddel to see the Coronation pictures, and the unlucky gratification of that desire, that brought the measles to the Katanning camp in the 1900's. There were some fourteen family shelters at the camp, besides two bachelors' huts, the total of inhabitants being between forty and fifty occupants. Togur and Daddel had come to my camp the morning after the visit to the pictures, to tell me in their own way what they had seen, and myself and the rest of the children who had gathered to hear the account, were treated to a dramatic recital of the wonderful things seen and heard, the mimicked play of the various musical instruments; the manager's high-toned announcement of the various pictures; the clapping; the crowd; the native comments on this or that series of films, and the sigh of regret when the wonderful sights were over. All these were presented with strong dramatic force, and we listened and applauded heartily. It was the last merry day at the camp.

The second morning after the visit to the pictures, they came to tell me that Togur and Daddel were sick, and would I come over and see them. I went over, and knowing that measles was rife in Katanning, I turned down their lips—the easiest way to tell when a native has got measles —and found of course what I looked for. It seemed to me a case of doctor and hospital, so I sent a messenger post-haste to town, and on the heels of the messenger came the doctor.

"Yes, it's measles," he announced, "and Daddel has got it rather badly."

"When will it be convenient to take them to the hospital, Doctor?"

"Can't do it. The hospital is full to overflowing with measles and other patients; they'll have to remain in camp, and I'll come out daily to see them. You'll have to do the best you can, and I hope it won't spread amongst them. Give them gruel, milk, soup, tea, any liquid food for a few days," and the busy doctor hurried away, leaving me stranded with two measles patients.

To begin with, I can't cook. I had never made gruel. I had, however, either heard or read somewhere that properly made gruel took four hours in the making. I wish I could put all the native magic I possess into the fiend who made that statement! My fire was an open one, and the winter winds of Katanning are not faithful. I sat down by the fire on a kerosene case to make my first billy-can of gruel, the billy being a two-gallon one. There was an east wind when I began, and I sat to the eastward of the fire and commenced to stir the oatmeal into the cold water. The wind shifted suddenly, and the fire caught a handful of my hair and singed it. I changed my seat, but the wind changed too, and blew smoke and flames against my scorched face. I stirred the gruel steadily, discarded the kerosene case, and walked round the fire and billy-can to the forty-eight points of the compass with which the wind was flirting that dreadful afternoon. I had started the gruel-making at 2 p.m., and at six exactly I took it off the fire. By that time I had recited Fitzgerald's Omar at least six times, each time with increasing vehemence, the while I monotonously stirred the gruel. It wasn't the words of the poem that brought the relief to my feelings, but the way they could be uttered that helped. There are times when *Bajjeejinnajugga* suffices, but that afternoon was not one of them, and after repeating it about ten times I fell back on Omar. Neither quite filled the bill, however, and I found out afterwards that gruel took at most only half an hour to cook.

Togur proved an excellent little patient, taking the medicine, gruel, or anything I gave him obediently. Daddel was a horror to nurse. The measles touched him rather heavily, and he became too "slack" to lift even the spoon, so I had to spoon-feed him four times daily, and coax him to take the necessary nourishment and medicine, and even when he was recovering he would hide the food I brought him rather then sit up to eat it, and so I had to sit beside him until he had finished the last bit.

On the top of nursing there came Nung'ian from Kojunup, a poor girl in the last stage of consumption. She also had to be kept in camp and ministered to, though one could only tempt her with a few "white" delicacies, for the poor girl—she was only 26—had gone beyond the coarse damper and black tea; indeed she only ate a few trifles I brought her out of regard for me. On the evening of the sixth day she died in her sleep.

Meanwhile Togur and Daddel became convalescent, and just when I was in sight of a little rest from nursing and cooking, Daddel's own mother, and his "second" mother, and his seven brothers and sisters all caught the infection, and the real work of nursing and cooking began. Baiungan, the older wife, got the measles very badly and lay absolutely helpless for days. Her little baby, Muilyian, was also very ill, and not having been weaned, there was the added trouble of special baby food. Baiungan and her five children occupied her half of a beehive shelter, a space not more than five feet in diameter holding the family! They lay with their heads within the shelter, their feet towards the open fire-place between the two huts, and to reach one I had to lean over the others, who were huddled up at either side. They lay like peas in a rounded pod, in that dreadful hut, with the smoke blowing in upon them at every gust of wind.

Dillungan, the younger mother, whose attack was not nearly so severe as Baiungan's, did nothing but grunt and groan, and open her mouth to be fed, and resume her groaning. Her two little children, the baby and his brother, howled and roared, and refused to take nourishment and medicine without endless coaxing. Their mother, scarcely more than seventeen years old, paid no heed to them. She suckled her baby by fits and starts, but the disease had dried both her breasts and Baiungan's and the poor children suffered greatly from the sudden stoppage of their natural food.

Dillungan had slightly more room in her tent, there being but three of them in it, and so the feeding of her and her two little ones was not such a hard task, except that the closeness of the fire, the difficulty of getting the babies to eat artificial food, and the coaxing and pleading necessary to induce them to accept some nourishment, often resulted in my forgetting that the fire was close, and boots and clothes suffered now and then from burning. There came a time, however, when children and mothers took all and everything I gave them, medicine or food or whatever it might be. A little variety was added to the nursing of these two mothers and children by old Mungail going temporarily off his head and making the nights hideous with his monologues. In those temporary aberrations, Mungail harked back to his early days, and in a recitative that lasted one night for three hours, he harangued all the members who, now long dead, had once been his companions and his kindred. He hunted and fought with the young men of those long-past years; he made love to their women; he ranted his prowess in the hunting field, in the fights—in the hundred and one affairs of gallantry in which he was the moving figure, and old sinner that he was, within the last few years he had captured a Balladonia woman who was shepherding at Ravensthorpe and carried her away with him to places far removed from any possible revenging husband. This woman bore him two children, the younger not four years old. Mungail was approaching the seventies and his woman was not much past twenty. In his non-lucid moments he was obsessed with the idea that she wanted to kill him, and he often rose in the night and ran away from her, either wandering off into the bush, or taking refuge in some of our camps. To keep watch and ward over Mungail was no light task.

Before Baiungan and Dillungan and their families had got rid of the measles, Mungail's wife, Warinyan, and her two children were down with it, but they were good little patients and gave no trouble. Then Kaiar, his wife Wirijan, and their four grandchildren, Wenyil, Genujan, Florrie, and Bobbie, caught the infection, and after them came Derdingburt, his woman, Yoolbian, and their little adopted child Win-ngur-man. All these at once, and in the rain and cold they claimed my services. At 7.30 a.m. I took them some food, bread and milk, tea and toast, an egg here, a few sardines there, and so on, till all were satisfied. Then at 11.45 bread and soup—tinned something and bread and jam and tea. Then afternoon tea for all—then evening gruel, and to bed. I believe it was about this time that all of them got it into their heads that it was good to have the measles and have their mother, sister, auntie, granny, or whatever relation I was to each one, to wait upon them, and bring them their food in nice clean mugs and cups and saucers and plates.

I had improvised a wooden tray out of the side of a kerosene case, and this I carried to and fro four times daily to each family. Now and again I essayed to hold an umbrella to keep myself and the food dry, but at those times I generally bumped my toe against a stump or rut, upsetting tray and contents, and had to return to camp and do some fresh cooking. And my patients had their fads, as sick white people have, and their wants multiplied as they became convalescent and hungry. I frequently felt like the old woman who lived in a shoe, for these people were children in every sense of the term. But their little fads and fancies were gratified as much as possible. And they were patient and willing, and obedient, and everything that one could wish for in sick nursing. The older patients would laugh with me when I announced fresh cases, and the new ones would settle themselves comfortably to go through the ordeal, taking medicine and foods with equal readiness. Barderuk—a woman of many husbands—and her latest conquest Yiner, and their son Roy, wandered from sick camp to sick camp, seeking infection. They caught it at last, to their great delight, and I used to see Barderuk, when she got better, go over to the other camps and play cards and talk gossip, until she saw me coming over with a meal, when she would return to her camp and pretend she had never left it, lying down, and assuming all the airs of the pampered invalid. Their little tricks to gain special attention were so palpable, so transparent, that I quite enjoyed falling into the humour of the thing, and being their victim.

My fame as a nurse and healer—for although the kindly doctor visited them daily during the progress of the epidemic, they looked to me for their condition, and I always treated their attack lightly—spread amongst them, and two cases came up from Broome Hill, sick with the complaint, and Daiamirt and his wife and child came in from their camp some twenty miles away, where they had been bark stripping, and Nellungan and many others. I enjoyed the task, and revelled in the gratitude and affection of those poor people who considered themselves my kindred, and who were so proud of their relative, and although I had to chop and carry home my own wood and buy my own water—for only once did Kaiar bring me two big logs—I could not ask or compel them to do work for me, if the offer did not come spontaneously from them.

When all were convalescent, and everyone was inordinately hungry, the trouble with the children was the impossibility of my being able to feed them all at once. At the double camp, as soon as I arrived with the food, every child began to howl for its share, and while I was feeding one the other six were bawling at the top of their voices. I tried letting them feed themselves, but the poor little things had not the strength to hold the mugs or cups—they have little real vitality—and I found it easier to spoon-feed all, and resign myself to the howling chorus, which rose to Wagnerian pitch at times.

And those awful huts! How we all escaped fever I don't know. They lived, ate, slept in, and never moved out of these huts for days, and in all that stench one had to lean over to the patients, who might be huddled in their farthest corners, and inhale the germs of every filth-producing disease. Bending over them to cleanse them and give them food, I was so sorry for them that I would not be sick. I believe that in Heaven, in 40,000 years' time, if somebody uncorks a bottle of native odour, I shall be able to tell them the tribe it comes from.

During the whole of my stay at the Katanning camp, a "spirit" fire *(beemb)* was lighted every evening at a spot a little distance from the camp. The *beemb* was lighted to the south-east of the huts, and round it a low semi-circle of bushes was arranged, with the opening also facing the south-east. The *beemb* was placed there to warm the spirit of Nebinyan, the last remaining Two People Bay native, who had died at the Katanning camp. Nebinyan's shelter was to the north-west of Baiungan's hut, and it was Baiungan who lighted the fire nightly in order to intercept Nebinyan's spirit, which she said might return to his own fire, in which case he must go through her hut, and perhaps injure herself or her children, and so the fire was lighted so that the spirit on its way back would rest and warm itself beside it, and come no farther.

In my two years of constant travelling, by railway train, by coach and buggy, I followed the nomads, seeking for camps, learning and noting the legends and relationships, groups and totems and way of life, and compiling my scientific data hand in hand with the unwritten literature of the race, so far as I could elicit it from shreds of song and story.

Northam, Goomalling, Kellerberrin, Merredin, Toodyay and Moora; through all of these towns I wandered in search of the old home people, and found a few, living in armed neutrality with strangers from the North-West collected on station and farm as cattle men. Each feared the magic of the other, and when he felt it in his body the white man's tools were put down and wandering was resumed, so that neither reserve nor institution could hold for long the opposing elements.

In the streets of Geraldton I met a solitary old Bib-bulmun with a brass plate dangling from his neck—"King

Billy of Geraldton" inscribed thereon. He was dressed in an old frock-coat, trousers and top hat given him by John Forrest. We talked for a little while of the rites and true relationships, and then I touched the plate and asked:

"What is this, brother?"

"That is a lie," said Dongaluk, "but the *jangga* give me 'bacca and money for it when they laugh at me."

A little ashamed, he held it out to me. "No, Dongaluk," I said, "let the white men give you 'bacca and money. You can't tell the white men about our ancestors *(demma goomber)*."

To the end of his life he used it as a catch-penny. These plates should be preserved in our museums to demonstrate how little we could fathom the universal kinship and absence of lordship that mark the aboriginal, the true child of Nature, the great mother that knows no class distinction. John Forrest's bungalow in Hay Street gave shelter to Dongaluk whenever he visited Perth.

Southern Cross was the eastern border of Bibbulmun country. In 1909 all remaining members of its group had been drawn in to the circumcised tribes on their eastern boundary, the last natives of Merredin and Burracoppin also having been circumcised before they died out.

When I reached Kellerberrin in the early morning, some poor old derelicts were just being taken away by a good-natured farmer to his place. I came upon them near the Bank of Australasia, and we sat down on the doorstep and talked about family matters, quite oblivious of the curious crowd that collected. Throughout the whole of my Bibbulmun pilgrimage I found full and clear evidence of the kindliness of my British kin to the people they had inevitably supplanted, but—they could not understand.

Somewhere about this time, Perth held a carnival fortnight, and the Government lent my services to the committee to arrange native displays. Twenty Bibbulmun and twenty nor'-westers had to be collected and after much travel and trouble I camped with them on a vacant allotment in Hay Street West. The two factions were already eyeing each other with hostility. To keep drink from complicating the probem and derelict native and half-

caste women from the camp was a full-time task. The city
council gave them abundance of meat and bread and tea
and tobacco, and pannikins and billy-cans, but neither
spears nor clubs were allowed. When we needed them, we
obtained them from the Museum.

In full corroboree paint, the native marched mornings
and afternoons along Hay Street pavements, two abreast,
to the recreation oval. They were a great attraction, and
their progress drew dense crowds to the streets. At the
Oval, they threw their spears and boomerangs to shouts of
admiration, and danced a weird conglomeration of native
dances highly popular with the crowds. The itinerary was
drawn up by the Carnival Committee. I bought a red
umbrella and, when my charges had to appear at Oval or
park or suburb, walked on the opposite side with it unfurled.
The leaders were to keep an eye on the umbrella, and
follow its vagaries, and the white crowd invariably com-
mented upon their orderly rank and file, their apparent
familiarity with city traffic, and the "prodigious Mrs. Daisy
Bates who slapped and washed and put them through their
paces each morning!" And certainly I was with them day
and night, save for a few hours of sleep at the home of a
friend near by.

The last evening was a memorable one. Only through
unremitting watchfulness had I succeeded in keeping the
peace between the two factions. Just as I was congratu-
lating myself on an unexpected success, one of the nor'-
westers missed a new pannikin, and tracked it to the
Bibbulmun camp. War was declared on the spot. I was in
the act of returning the *casus belli,* without undue display,
when I met Wajji and his mates coming through the low
scrub, armed with shillelaghs they had rooted out of the
ground in just but exaggerated anger, intent on a little
"diversion." I temporized and turned them back, then
marched the whole crowd urgently out into Hay Street. I
had been making small collections among my pastoral
friends during the carnival, and carried the money visibly
with me in a little bag. They knew it was their own, and

eagerly anticipated the division, but for many reasons I did not wish to give it to them in the city.

I remained with them in the temporary camp all night, and just before the Bibbulmun were timed to leave for the southern train at daylight, obtained a candle, and seated the whole mob of forty in a circle about me. I sat in their midst, and made forty piles of silver, one for each, naming each pile. Forty pairs of dark eyes watched me closely, shining as the piles grew higher. Each native received his share gladly. Then the bundles were collected.

The natives had kept their paint and decorations fresh during their fortnight's exhibition, and wore nothing but loin cloths. We were a weird spectacle, delighting the early morning milk-men, as I moved the camp of Bibbulmun off to the railway station in the dimly-lit streets at 4 a.m., myself in the midst of the apparent horde of cannibals, which the Bibbulmun were not, leading an old blind corroboree-singer by a long staff.

I later received a letter of thanks from Police Commissioner Hare who told me that I had saved him the necessity of placing six constables in relays of two over the mob during the fortnight, as never before had two different tribes camped together without the breaking of heads.

Chapter IX

ISLES OF THE DEAD

IN 1910, TWO INTERNATIONAL EXPEDITIONS ARRIVED IN Perth to undertake field work among the West Australian aborigines. The leaders of both called at my office with introductions. The first was the Cambridge University Expedition, consisting of Professor A. R. Radcliffe-Brown[1]

---

[1] Now Professor of Social Anthropology at the University of Oxford.

and Mr. E. L. Grant Watson, both of Cambridge. The second was a party of Swedish scientists, led by a Mr. Laurell. This party was bound for Kimberley, and none of its members spoke English, depending mainly upon French as a medium of conversation.

Professor Radcliffe-Brown, on his introductory visit, informed me that he had finances for no longer than six months. Knowing that time to be inadequate for any research of value, I arranged an interview with the late Mr. S. P. Mackay, a well-known and wealthy pastoralist of Munda-bullangana Station, and asked him point-blank for £1,000, to make possible at least two years of field work for the Expedition. He immediately forwarded a cheque for the amount.

It was then suggested that I accompany the Expedition, and the Under-Secretary (Mr. North) obtained the Colonial Secretary's consent. I was appointed a travelling protector, with a Special Commission to conduct inquiries into all native conditions and problems, such as employment on stations, guardianship and care of the indigent, distribution of rations, the half-caste question, the morality of native and half-caste women in towns and mining camps, and many other matters affecting their welfare from an administrative point of view. Sir Gerald Strickland, then Governor of West Australia, showed a deep personal interest in the expedition, and his wife, Lady Edeline, supplemented my equipment with a medicine chest.

Before we left Perth, news came that the civilized and semi-civilized circumcised groups of Lake Darlot had descended in a raid upon a native camp at Lancefield, near Laverton, killing eleven men, women and children. The groups had scattered, and the police had found none of the murderers, much to the consternation of the peaceable natives and white settlers in the district.

We booked our passages on the little coastal steamer *Hobart*, packed our equipment and supplies on board, and were so eager to be off that we embarked a few days early on a southern trip, and after an unpremeditated voyage to Bunbury, had to return to the vessel, and sail north with her to Geraldton, from which we went by rail to Sandstone. The party consisted of Professor Radcliffe-Brown, anthropologist, Mr. Grant Watson, biologist and photographer, myself as government attaché, and Louis Ohlsen, a Swedish cook. A few miles from Sandstone, we pitched our tents among the natives gathered there, our travelling equipment consisting of a large fly for our dining and community room furnished with folding chairs and other luxuries, the men's tent, Louis's portable kitchen, and my quarters. We were surrounded by nearly 100 natives from near by districts, and there was obvious ill-feeling and friction among the groups. I spent the afternoon making new friends, greeting old ones, and, with their assistance, digging out some honey-ants, which I proffered to the Professor for supper. Grant Watson would have none of them.

It took some time to convince the natives that my companions were not policemen, of whom, for their own reasons, they lived in an unholy fear at the time. After some vain endeavours at explanation, I found it easier to introduce them as my two sons! Professor Radcliffe-Brown immediately interested himself in the their string games, similar to cat's cradle, and cross-sticks, and other small primitive handicrafts with which they occasionally pass the time.

After distributing generous rations and discussing family gossip, we were just beginning to make a little headway in questioning them regarding genealogies and customs when, to our surprise, a police raid was made upon the camps at dawn, and six of the natives arrested as the Laverton murderers. Several shots were fired by the police, and some of the fugitives tried to hide in our tents, but no one was hurt.

On the principle that "one nigger is as black as another," the constables had arrested one Meenya, whom I knew did not belong to Darlot, and who had only just arrived from his own country. I saw Meenya in prison, quite naked, as he had been arrested while sleeping. After establishing his identity, I took him back to the camp, where his relatives cried with joy. Gooll-gooil, Jooloor, Dhoolanjarri, Yoolbari, and Dandain, remained in custody.

After the raid, our natives scattered, but returned to tell me that there was another policeman coming with a "big mob." This proved to be Constable Grey, appointed to inspect for symptoms of disease and to gather in half-castes from the camps. The natives were afraid to approach him until I explained that he was a doctor coming to look at us all. When I went myself into the tent, they followed with confidence.

With Professor Radcliffe-Brown's assistance, Grey made his examination, collected a few old men and women, and drove them away in his cart to join the unfortunates waiting in Sandstone. I shall never forget the anguish and despair on those faces. The poor decrepit creatures were leaving their own country for a destination unknown, a fate they could not understand, and their woe was pitiful. The diseased and the young half-castes were housed in different sections of the gaol in Sandstone, and the grief of the aboriginal mothers at this enforced parting with their children was pitiful to see.

So turbulent and so distressed was now the condition of all camps in the vicinity that it was useless for us to remain longer. Professor Radcliffe-Brown, Grant Watson and Louis the cook sailed for Carnarvon. I returned to Perth with my reports and notes. The Laverton murderers were travelling in custody on the same train, and my special commission entitled me to question them in private. For some hours I sat alone with the chained prisoners in the railway carriage, and learned the reason of the raid.

They explained that the Lancefield and Laverton camps had transgressed the bounds of every native law, that they were living in incestuous depravity with sisters and immature children to such an extent that the usual marriage exchanges were not possible. So the Lake Darlot tribes, unable to procure wives, took the law into their own hands, and planned to kill the men and seize the women. They had descended on the camp at dawn, and in the battle of flying spears some women and children were

accidentally killed. I reported the circumstances to head-
quarters, and there was no trial. The natives were detained
only until the departure of the next train. I later sailed
north to rejoin the expedition at Dorré and Bernier Islands.

Dorré and Bernier Islands: there is not, in all my sad
sojourn among the last sad people of the primitive Australian race, a memory one-half so tragic or so harrowing,
or a name that conjures up such a deplorable picture of
misery and horror unalleviated, as these two grim and
barren islands of the West Australian coast that for a
period, mercifully brief, were the tombs of the living dead.

In accordance with its policy of safeguarding the aborigines, the West Australian Government, in 1904, had
authorized Dr. Roth, a Queensland anthropologist, to inquire into native conditions. After intensive study of the
problem, Dr. Roth made the suggestion, among others,
that all diseased natives from the whole of the North-West
should be isolated for treatment. The Government immediately adopted the suggestion, the unhappiest decision
ever arrived at by any humane administration, a ghastly
failure in the attempt to arrest the ravages of disease, and
an infliction of physical and mental torture that it could
not perhaps have been expected to foresee.

At the cost of many thousands of pounds, the authorities
established an isolation hospital on two islands bordering
Shark Bay, some thirty miles from Carnarvon. These islands—Dorré and Bernier—have never been inhabited before or since. A medical officer and staff were installed in
permanent residence, and two or three little cutters plied
backwards and forwards carrying medical and food supplies. Diseased natives were gathered in, by policemen and
other appointed officers, over an area of hundreds of thousands of square miles. Regardless of tribe and custom and
country and relationship, they were herded together—the
women on Dorré and the men on Bernier. Many had
never seen the sea before, and lived and died in terror of
it.

When I arrived at Carnarvon, I found the town inun-
dated by the Gascoyne River in flood, and lost no time
in arranging my passage to the islands. There was no

regular communication, but two cutters, the *Shark* and the *Venus,* were at my disposal, and one of them would sail whenever the skipper, an old sea-dog named Henrietta, felt inclined. In due course, with my baggage and provender, I boarded the *Shark* and crossed to Bernier, where the expedition had already established itself in a cove of the lee shore. I selected a neighbouring cove, and there Louis set up my camp.

Dorré and Bernier, with a smaller island, Koks, shelter Shark Bay from the the Indian Ocean. Barren and forbidding, a horror of flies in summer-time, their western shores are undermined by the sea into steep overhanging cliffs, which sweep down in terraces of sand to the calmer waters of the bay, covered by spare scrub with never a tree worthy of the name. A narrow race of water runs between them with sweeping tides and tremendous tide-rips tumultuous in wild weather.

On Dorré, where the women were segregated, was a well-equipped hospital with doctor's residence, laboratory, nurses' quarters and dispensary. A skilled bacteriologist was in charge. His staff consisted of dispenser, matron and two nurses. In his own cutter the doctor periodically crossed the strait to attend the men on Bernier, but sometimes when he was needed most a storm or heavy swell made it impossible for him to come.

When I landed on Bernier Island in November 1910, there were only fifteen men left alive there, but I counted thirty-eight graves. The doctor's assistant and the orderly staff occupied a wooden building on a rise, the hospital was a tent, and the sick were housed in three-sided huts of canvas, each with a half-roof of corrugated iron. The natives on both islands preferred the open bush to all the hospital care and comfort.

Deaths were frequent—appallingly frequent, sometimes three in a day—for most of these natives were obviously in the last stages of venereal disease and tuberculosis. Nothing could save them, and they had been transported, some of them thousands of miles, to strange and unnatural surroundings and solitude. They were afraid of the hospital, its ceaseless probings and dressings and injections were a daily torture. They were afraid of each other, living and dead. They were afraid of the ever-moaning sea.

The hospital was well kept and the medical work excellently performed, but the natives accepted all the care with a frightful fatalism. They believed that they had been brought there to die—what did it matter if the white man had decided to cut them to pieces first? More, they were undernourished. They were strangers to the island, and the seeds and berries and fish food it could have yielded them. There were plenty of wallabies, but most of the natives were too emaciated and ill to go hunting. Sometimes, when the *Shark* and *Venus* were weeks late, the position became pitiable.

When the bleak winds blew, the movable huts were turned against them, facing each other, regardless of tribal customs, which meant mistrust and fear. Now and again a dead body would be wrapped in a blanket and carried away to burial in the sands, and the unhappy living could not leave the accursed ground of its spirit. Some became demented and rambled away and no one of an alien tribe would go to seek them. One day an old man started to "walk" back over thirty miles of raging waters to the mainland. These shores are infested with sharks and he was never seen again. Another hid in the thick scrub and died there, rather than be operated upon. A third sat on the crest of a little rise all day long, pouring sand and water over his head, wailing and threatening, in his madness.

There were seventy-seven women on Dorré Island, many of them bed-ridden. I dared not count the graves. A frightful sight it was to see grey-headed women, their faces and limbs repulsive in disease, but an even more frightful sight to see the young—and there were children among them. Through unaccustomed frequent hot baths, their withered sensitive skins, which are never cleansed in their natural state save by grease and fresh air, became like tissue-paper and parted horribly from the flesh.

Companionship in misery was impossible to them, for there were so many spiritual and totemic differences. Some of them were alone of their group, and they could not give food or a firestick to a possible enemy or a stranger for fear of evil magic. A woman would be called upon to bath and feed or bury another woman whose spirit she knew was certain to haunt her.

Restlessly they roamed the islands in all weathers, avoiding each other as strangers. Some of them cried all day and all night in a listless and terrible monotony of grief. There were others who stood silently for hours on a headland, straining their hollow, hopeless eyes across the narrow strait for the glimpse of a loved wife or husband or a far lost country, and far too often the smoke signal of death went up from the islands. In death itself they could find no sanctuary, for they believed that their souls, when they left the poor broken bodies, would be orphaned in a strange ground, among enemies more evil and vindictive than those on earth.

The benefits devised by the white people and the endeavours to lighten their pain were only so much the greater aggravation of their exile. Such benefits left no impression because the iron of exile and the frightful condition of rubbing shoulders with possible enemy magicians had filled their souls. All was new and strange to them, but endured often with that fatalism that lets the white people go on in their own way. These haunting terrors they could not communicate to those who were set to guard over them and who, without knowledge of these tribal beliefs, could only reply by kindly efficiency. They wanted nothing in the world but their old sand-beds and shelters and little fires, the smell of their own home area, every secret familiar to them, and the voices of their own kind. There is nothing you can give them but freedom and their own fires—hearth and home.

The horrors of Dorré and Bernier unnerve me yet. There was no ray of brightness, no gleam of hope. In an attempt to escape them I too would roam the islands, finding them grim and dreary. The wail of a curlew crying along the sands would startle me and set me shivering with remembrance of the dying, and the soundless wings of the giant wedge-tailed eagles, as they flew over, cast a sinister shadow on the sunny day.

To question the poor shuddering souls of these doomed

exiles was slow work and saddening, but as I sat with them in the darkness of their *mias* at night, the torture of hospital routine was forgotten, and harking back to thoughts of home, they were, for an hour or so, happy. Of all the tribes there so dismally represented, from Hall's Creek to Broome and Nullagine, from the Fitzroy River to Winning Pool and Marble Bar and Lake Way, I learned much of infinite value in vocabularies and customs and pedigrees and legends. The scientists, I think, made intermittent headway.

"Your two sons—why are they afraid of us?" I was asked more than once. The answer was obvious. Grant Watson was physically ill one day after taking a photograph. However, they helped him to collect shells and insects occasionally, and obligingly sang the songs of *woggura* and *wallardoo*—crow and eaglehawk—into Professor Ratcliffe-Brown's phonograph. He in return regaled them with *Peer Gynt* and *Tannhauser* and *Egmont,* to which they listened politely.

It was a woeful Christmastide at Dorré Island. There were six operations that morning, but a Christmas dinner, with pudding and gifts and sweets was provided for the other sixty women, with some semblance of goodwill and pleasant contact on their part. A few days later the schooner *Anthons* arrived, bringing eighteen natives from Broome. A nurse travelled with them, but some had died on the way down. The *Anthons* was followed almost immediately by the *Venus* from Carnarvon.

Corporal Grey was due to arrive with new consignments of unfortunates collected throughout the vast State, and I went over to Carnarvon to meet him. He was camped four miles away on the outskirts, with about 133 natives, all stricken with disease. Carnarvon citizens justly objected to their entering the town.

Shall I ever forget the surge of emotion that overcame me as they saw me, and lifted their manacled hands in a faint shout of welcome, for many of them recognized me? There was a half-caste assistant with Grey, and all the natives were chained to prevent them from escaping on the way, as it was quite probable that they would have been murdered had they attempted to reach their homes through strange country. In one donkey-wagon were forty-five men, women, and children, unable to walk.

During the week that followed, 122 natives were shipped to the islands in cutters. On one occasion 90 were slung from the high jetty at Carnarvon in baskets, and, the boat being overloaded, many were taken off again and walked back to the camp. I returned to Dorré on an 18-feet cutter with 27 natives in the hold, all suffering from sea-sickness and weakness and fright. Although I had been but a short time absent, I found 14 new graves there. When the natives were discharged as cured, they were generally sent in charge of a nurse by steamer to their nearest port or landed upon the mainland and left to find their own way to their homes, sometimes hundreds of miles eastward, and through the country of stranger tribes. Now and again I arranged a passage for them with a camel team, or under the protection of a travelling station owner.

It was my adopted kinship that made it possible for me to be accepted by the aborigines. At Dorré and Bernier, among the central and north-west groups gathered there, I was again allotted my proper class division, Boorong, which corresponded to the Pooroongooroo of Broome, and the Tondarup of the Bibbulmun. This relationship opened the way to their confidence. For me these travesties of humanity tried to dance their old-time dances, but being among hostile groups, these were invariably war-dances, the *jallooroo, dhoolgarra, djoolgoo,* corroborees of defiance. Those unable to stand upright swayed their bodies to the tune of remembered songs, beating the ground with little bushes. Some groups were represented by one aged man, or two old women, and the voices were so low and feeble that I had to stoop to catch the weak words. Often, in the midst of their posturing, they would crawl whimpering with pain into the darkness of their shelters.

In the course of my official duties I was a constant traveller between the two islands and the mainland, sometimes journeying far inland. On every journey I became postman of a score or so of letter-sticks *(bamburu),* the crudely marked piece of wood that is the aborigines' only attempt at a written language, saying little, and that only by signs, but carrying loving wishes and assurances to wives and husbands and friends. To watch the poor fellows in their fatal lassitude trying to mark the *bamburu* they wanted to send along to their women was a pitiful sight, but to see the joy on their faces when I returned with *bamburu* from the absent loved ones was heart-rending.

Between Dorré and Bernier and all over the central North-West, I delivered these letter-sticks, bringing back the gossip of camps, news of the births, deaths and marriages, of initiations and corroborees and quarrels, to the interest and delight of the dying exiles.

I did what I could among them with little errands of mercy; distributing rations and blankets from my own government stores when boats were delayed; bringing sweets and dainties for young and old, extra blankets in the rain, and where I could a word of love and understanding. To the grey-headed, and the grey-bearded, men and women and children alike, I became *kabbarli,* the Grandmother. I had begun in Broome as *kallauer,* a grandmother, but a spurious and a very young one, purely legendary. Since then I had been *jookan,* sister, among the Bibbulmun; *ngangga,* mother, among the scattered groups of Northampton and the Murchison, but it was at Dorré Island that I became *kabbarli,* Grandmother, to the sick and the dying there, and *kabbarli* I was to remain in all my wanderings, for the name is a generic one, and extends far among the western-central and central tribes.

Our Expedition parted company in March 1911. Professor Radcliffe-Brown continued his researches, taking a northward route through the sheep and cattle stations of the mainland. Grant Watson sailed for Perth. I turned my footsteps to the head of the Ashburton, Gascoyne, Murchison and Fortescue Rivers, once a great highway of aboriginal trafficking.

Upon the ghastly experiment of Dorré and Bernier Islands it is not good for me to dwell. Not very long after our visit, the costly hospital project and the islands of

exile were abandoned. On his return to England, Grant
Watson made them the fantastic setting of a novel *Where
Bonds are Loosed*—a story of illict love with a background
of horror and heartbreak and unutterable woe.

Chapter X

I INHERIT A GOLD MINE

IN DEALING WITH THE AUSTRALIAN ABORIGINES, IT IS
only too easy for the anthropologist to elaborate a fantasy
based on theories and the foreign logics of other native
races, and then proceed to build it up in his field work.
The Australian follows the line of least resistance with
the white man. He will always respond as desired to a
leading question, eager to please, whether he understands
it or not.

The first lessons that I learned were never to intrude
my own intelligence upon him, and to have patience, the
patience that waits for hours and years for the links in
the long chain to be pieced together. A casual soul, he
knows no urgency. Yesterday and to-day and to-morrow
are all the same to him. Naturalness in white company
comes from long familiarity. Only when you are part of
the landscape that he knows and loves will he accord you
the compliment of living his normal life and taking no
notice of you.

His unconscious confidences are by far the most valuable. Most of my data is the gradual compiling of many,
many years. Quite often I have chanced upon the clue to
problems long after I had given them up. Of unfinished
legends begun at Broome and Beagle Bay in the North-
West, I have written the *finale* at Ooldea in the centre.
Some of the straying threads of my ethnological study are
still in midair. I shall perhaps never find the source, nor

know their conclusion. Only in God's good time will you begin to understand the riddle of the native mind. It is the study, not of a year or two of field work, but of a whole lifetime.

Westward and eastward and northward in these northern areas I went, constantly travelling to and fro, and hither and thither by train, or buggy, or horse. I alighted whenever I saw a native and made friends with his little group. I lived their lives, not mine. Whenever I camped with them, they did not trouble about clothing of any kind, innocent and natural as children. Was I not their ancestral grandmother, spirit rather than woman?

Everywhere was evidence of the encroachment of the circumcised groups upon the uncircumcised. I found that the Bibbulmun area had once been far greater, and had gradually narrowed through the centuries, as the first hordes were driven to the coast. From Jurien Bay northward to Ballaballa, along a narrow strip of coastline, were certain isolated uncircumcised groups, each having its own initiation ceremonies, but always adhering to the fundamental totemic and marriage laws. These groups called themselves Ingada, and the Aggardee, or circumcised, tribes bordering them would make contact with the families, and then take the boys away to be circumcised. The Ingada kept their laws, but they gave their boys under compulsion. As civilization went on, their little spaces narrowed, and their marriage laws were no longer possible. I met the derelict members of about forty groups, and each had the same sad story to tell me. The tribes of Geraldton, within twenty years of the white man's coming, had been absorbed, for the second hordes had reached the coast round them, under the protection of the white settlers.

The four-class marriages between Boorong and Banaka, Kaimera and Paljera, as here they were called, had been completely broken down in both the centre and the central west for centuries. The beginning of the breach was probably when certain young men, tired of waiting for their affianced wives to grow up, had seized their father's sisters, who were their potential mothers-in-law, and run away

with them into the vast scarcely-occupied areas south and
south-east of Nullagine, extending down to near the
Nullarbor Plain. There they sat down beside a water-
hole and either established a little group, or merged into
the nomad tribes they met. The children followed the
example of the fathers. Irregularity crept over until there
was not one straight marriage among the thousands I
encountered. Intercourse was not only promiscuous but incestuous. The old men would speak to me about these
things as though I were a native.

Often I came upon a mixture of northern, eastern and
south-western families gathered in one group and living
amicably together, and, in one instance, a group of Bibbulmun in the centre of the Aggardee. I also found traces
of types distinctly Dutch. When Pelsart marooned two
white criminals on the mainland of Australia in 1627,
these Dutchmen had probably been allowed to live with
the natives, and it may be that they and their progeny
journeyed far along the river-highway, for I found these
types as far out as the head-waters of the Gascoyne and
the Murchison. There was no mistaking the flat heavy
Dutch face, curly fair hair, and heavy stocky build.

Baby cannibalism was rife among these central-western
peoples, as it is west of the border in Central Australia. In
one group, east of the Murchison and Gascoyne Rivers,
every woman who had had a baby had killed and eaten
it, dividing it with her sisters, who, in turn, killed their
children at birth and returned the gift of food, so that the
group had not preserved a single living child for some
years. When the frightful hunger for baby meat overcame the mother before or at the birth of the baby, it was
killed and cooked regardless of sex. Division was made
according to the ancestral food-laws. I cannot remember
a case where the mother ate a child she had allowed, at
the beginning, to live.

I obtained a photograph of this group unexpectedly. I
was camped among the Meekatharra tribes, some distance
from the township, devoting myself to the aged and the
ailing, engaged mostly in compiling dialects and map-
making, with the aid of the natives. (The map-making

method was simple. I gathered the men of the different groups about me, and with a sheet of brown paper and a pencil, constructed an early history of their home waters and wanderings. I would start from a given point—Meek-atharra, Peak Hill or Wiluna—plan out the district according to its natural features, mark off the waters, put down the tracks to and from fathers' camps and grandfathers' camps, denoting localities with their native names by means of elementary questions as to where they "sat down." Distances were calculated from "how many sleeps?" allowing so many miles to a day's journey. I have many of these maps in my possession, an intensive geography covering hundreds of square miles, and invaluable in marking the tribes and groups and countries and permanent and other waters of the west of West Australia before it was peopled by whites.)

One evening, an hour or so after dusk, I sensed something moving in the low scrub to northward. Without appearing to take any notice, I perceived a number of native men approaching quietly, all decorated, and carrying their spears and spear-throwers. I looked over to the Meeka-tharra camp, which had become strangely silent. The fires were banked and covered with sand, and there was no stir of life—sure sign of fear of the stranger. I went quietly on making my toast and tea.

The men came slowly closer, still hiding behind the trees. They stopped at some little distance. Without looking up, I called, "Come on, *boggali!* (grandchildren). Come to the fire. You must be cold!" At last eight men came into the clearing, and very sheepishly approached, saying nothing.

"Sit down and have some food," I invited them. "Where are your women?" They gave a short call, as one would call a dog. Several women came out of the bushes. My supper had, of course, to go by the board. Bringing out flour and water, I started them making dampers, and with a casual question or two learned that they had just come from far beyond Peak Hill to see me. Bush telegraph had sent the news of my arrival at Meekatharra, and they had walked over ninety miles, with little food on the way, to see *kabbarli*.

Next morning I took them over to the camp and made the introductions. There was armed neutrality for a while, every man with his spear in readiness, and indeed there were, after I had left them, a few thigh-spearings in revenge for the unlawful appropriation of a woman at one time or the other, but no serious trouble.

In this comparatively desolate country, the totems were entirely different from the brotherhood with nature and the food-totems of the Bibbulmun. Kangaroo, emu, and dingo-totems are common throughout Australia, and here, among them, I met men of the *moolaiongoo,* or wombat snake, and the *goorara,* or prickly acacia. The *goorara* provided the best *bumburu* sticks and also the wood for the best come-back boomerangs.

The age-old feud of the blood and lice totem groups was told to me in the Leonora and Laverton areas. *Kooloo*—lice totem men—sent lice sores to the *ngooba*—blood totem group—and when a blood totem man or woman died, blood magic was sent back to claim a victim among the lice men. As far as I could ascertain, the blood totem groups were tubercular, and, a gruesome and curious fact, this was one of the few totems that might be "passed on" regardless of heredity. When I first visited this group area, Muri and Jinguroo, two lice men, had been arrested for the murder of a blood man and sent to Rottnest Island prison. At that time there were very few of either group living. The blood totem men had been more successful in passing on their magic than the lice men. The area of the groups was in the broken country north-west of Leverton. None of these natives had been in contact with any white people until the end of the nineteenth century. I found one lice woman near Meekatharra far north-west of her home ground. She had escaped the blood magic, but all her fathers and brothers had died of it.

These two groups are typical of the group systems of the circumcised people, which maintains armed neutrality except during the assemblies for initiations and other ceremonies. Tales came to me of one group completely annihilating another with its magic, but I found only one instance of annexation of a group area whose owners had been killed by their more powerful neighbouring group. An area bereft of its owners is "orphaned" land and no neighbouring group would think of annexing it, but when the last Meekatharra man died a Lake Way native, strong in his magic, annexed that group area, while still keeping his hold on his own Lake Way ground.

One evening, as we sat round the camp-fire, this native, Jaal, by a weird aboriginal sleight of hand, apparently from his stomach produced an initiation knife, and with it a piece of dark stone shot through with veins of galena —or was it gold? I did not know. He gave them to me. "This," he said in his own language, "is what the white man likes, but we don't let him come for it. The knife is from Maiamba, and it is my totem, *'jeemarri.'* "

I questioned him further, and found that the *jeemarri* group was the most important in the widest area that I could compass there. *Jeemarri* knives were peculiar to the region, of a hard dark flint. The shrine Maiamba was a secret and sacred place visited only by the older men, who are possessed of the magic of extracting these initiation knives from their stomachs. The surroundings of the shrine possessed a peculiarly Scottish name, Munro, and the area was called Yarnder. The *jeemarri* found there were bartered south and west and north to the confines of the continent. They were so hard and strong, and having come from the stomachs of the old men, their magic was so potent that they could be sold for "spears and spears and spears," making the group a rich one and of outstanding importance.

Jaal told me that he was the last man of his group, and to me he left this shrine Maiamba, from which he and his people had headed off the white man who had come many times looking for gold. I was not to take anyone there until all of the natives who belonged to it were dead and gone, and Maiamba an orphan water. Jaal said he would go with me to Maiamba, but soon after this episode he was taken to Bernier Island. I showed the stone with its rich content to an assayer. He was deeply interested.

"An excellent specimen, Mrs. Bates," he told me. "Seventeen ounces to the ton. Where did it come from?"

"I am not sure of the white name of the place," I evaded. "A native brought it in." Jaal's country and its Maiamba shrine lay east of Meekatharra at Lake Way, now the extensive gold mines of Wiluna, to which by right of bequest, I am the hereditary heiress, for the *jeemarri* area is mine, by deed of gift of my last grandson there.

A long way from Peak Hill, and near a pool called Jilguna, I "sat down" with a large group, among which were many elders, and one old patriarch, Ngargala. Ngargala was nearing his end, and it was he who gave to me the magic *bamburu* which has been my passport among all the central circumcised tribes through the years. I shall never forget the ceremony of the presentation.

The dying man reclined upon a little slope, and I sat beside him, with the group chanting in low tones. From a bundle beside him he brought out a package of emu feathers and human hair, from which he drew a magic *bamburu* of fine light yellow acacia wood, exquisitely curved and etched, with the crude form of a woman its centrepiece.

He pointed to the figure and said, "That is you, *kabbarli, dhoogoor kabbarli* (woman of the dream-time)."

I replied quietly, "I know that, *boggali* (grandson)," and handed it back.

"I am old," said Ngargala. "I give you my magic and you will keep it with your *bamburu*."

As he said these words, he placed his hands upon my breast, and I placed mine on his. Then he placed the *bamburu* between us, with its blunted ends pressed against our bodies, and with his black hands gathered the magic of his heart and stomach, drew it slowly and firmly along the *bamburu,* with one closed hand at the other end to catch it and impregnate it into my breast.

At last I said, "That is all, *boggali*. Now I have your magic and mine. We two are strong for all time. This *bamburu* will never leave me. It will sit down with me daytime and night-time."

I rose from my cramped position, and, emptying my bag of rations, left the group in silence.

I never saw Ngargala again, but those of the groups who were then present would always know me, and many a time have repeated softly by way of greeting and recognition the chant that they sang during the transfer of the old man's magic *bamburu.*

Always, wherever it happened to be, and without referring to the matter, I would go over and take their hands in mine and they knew I was a "mason."

Now the heiress of an undiscovered gold mine and a repository of dream-time magic, there was yet another inheritance that came my way before I left this district. While I was at Cue, one of the natives, a man of the red ochre totem, wished to show me his home-ground, where there was still a motley little group of many families. We obtained a passage to a place called Mindoola, eighty miles away, in a dray carrying provisions to a few old miners. It was a long and arduous journey, for most of the way I tried to make myself comfortable sitting on a sewing machine to be delivered at some outpost station.

On the way we passed a beautiful pool full of pelicans, and then entered the ranges. I had previously learned from the natives of a "stone man lying down," a dark scoriated heap of stone boulders that, from one aspect, appeared to be a gigantic recumbent figure. Should strangers approach the place, according to native belief, the stone man rose in anger, and they died, for the stone sleeper was Barlieri, a legendary father.

As we approached this, I gazed upon it intently. "You see," I said in an undertone to the native at my side, "Barlieri knows me. He knows I am coming. He is glad. He does not rise against me." I felt the native gradually edging closer.

I was wearing, I remember, a cream holland coat and skirt. When we came to Wilgamia, the red ochre deposits, I left the man with the dray, and with my native guide went up the hill and into the hill, cut about in rough excavations. In and out and up and down through hæmatite we went, sometimes seeing the remains of a tiny fire. This hill has been a source of much-valued red ochre for perhaps centuries, for far away in the north I had seen this greasy hæmatite from Wilgamia in the south.

Everywhere the black fellow crawled I followed, until we came to the place they had been digging for the last two or three hundred years. There, with a piece of flint, he cut me a piece, marking his own forehead with it before he gave it to me. 'When I finish, all finish," he said. "Your Wilgamia now."

I came out a Woman in Red. There was not an inch of me that had not been ochred all over, even my face and hands were smeared with the greasy stuff.

Chapter XI

WITH THE DESERT TRIBES

THE END OF THIS PILGRIMAGE IN THE CENTRAL WEST marked the termination of eight years of intensive study and ethnological research for the West Australian Government. I returned to Perth in 1912, and delivered my completed manuscripts to the Registrar-General's Department. Chapter by chapter, these manuscripts had been submitted to Dr. Andrew Lang in England for his revisions and annotations, which I value highly. There was a change of government at about this time, and the manuscripts and photographs were later presented to me with the right to publish them in book form.

By this time I was a confirmed wanderer, a nomad even as the aborigines. So close had I been in contact with them, that it was now impossible for me to relinquish the work. I realized that they were passing from us. I must make their passing easier. Moreover, all that I knew was little in comparison with all there was yet to learn. I made the decision to dedicate the rest of my life to this facinating study.

I admit that it was scarcely a sacrifice. Apart from the joy of the work for its own sake, apart from the enlightenments, the surprises, the clues, and the fresh beginnings that were the stimuli of every day, the paths to never-ending high-roads and byways in a scientific study that was practically virgin country, "the freshness, the freedom, the far-ness," meant much more to me now than the life of cities.

A glorious thing it is to live in a tent in the infinite—to waken in the grey of dawn, a good hour before the sun outlines the low ridges of the horizon, and to come out into the bright cool air, and scent the wind blowing across the *mulga* plains. My first thought would be to probe the ashes of my open fireplace, where hung my primitive cooking-vessels, in the hope that some embers had remained alight. Before I retired at night, I invariably made a good fire and covered the glowing coals with the soft ash of the *jilyeli,* having watched my compatriots so cover their turf fires in Ireland. I would next readjust the stones of the hob to leeward of the morning wind, and set the old Australian billy to boil, while I tidied my tent, and transformed it from bedroom to breakfast-room.

As the sun came up, it changed that plain white room into the most exquisitely-frescoed pergola, with a patterning far surpassing the best of Grinling Gibbon's handiwork. In a constant play of leafy light and shadow, I would eat my tea and toast in absolute content, while outside the blue smoke of the fire changed to grey in the bright sunlight.

The mornings were spent in wandering from camp to camp, attending to the bodily needs of the scattered flock. I knew every bush, every pool, every granite boulder, by its age-old prehistoric name, with its legends and dream-time secrets, and its gradual inevitable change. There was no loneliness. One lived with the trees, the rocks, the hills and the valleys, the verdure and the strange living things within and about them. My meals and meditations in the silence and sunlight, the small joys and tiny events of my solitary walks, have been more to me than the voices of the multitude, and the ever-open book of Nature has taught me more of wisdom than is compassed in the libraries of men.

After a brief pleasant intellectual respite with my own kind in Perth, I pitched my tent again near the Maamba Reserve. There was scarcely the need for it any longer. The indefatigable Ngilgi was still an occasional visitor, and Monnop, noticeably approaching his end, but still hoping vainly to be her suitor. For the rest, a few half-castes and mixtures. Monnop retraced his steps to his own country of New Norcia shortly after, and died there within a year, the last of the dingo-people.

About the same time I made occasional journeys to Rottnest Island native prison, and to New Norcia, a seminary town and an agricultural district of great importance, mother-house of the Benedictines in Australia.

For many years deemed uninhabitable, Rottnest, about 1858, became an aboriginal prison, where native prisoners from the whole State were subsequently herded together in penal servitude. Their offences ranged from the sometimes brutal murder of white colonists to sheep-stealing and cattle-killing, and other breaches of the white man's law of the enormity of which they were, for the most part, ignorant.

Shipped in batches, sometimes 1,000 miles from the tropic north, to their trial and sentence in Perth, chained in gangs on the islands, in the heat and the wet weather and biting cold, they worked in the salt lakes, or at road making, and at tilling a small area for cultivation, the corn being reaped by hand and thrashed by an old-fashioned flail. From the terrible treadmill of a labour quite unnatural to them, they were shepherded at night into the clammy cells of a low-roofed stone gaol, cells filthy and fever-ridden, with walls many inches thick. In these vaults they existed on prison rations. There were no fires. Give a native a fire, and he will survive starvation itself. Feed him and clothe him as much as you like, and deprive him of his fire, and he will die.

These unfortunates died in appalling numbers. At one time there were 800 of them on the island, and twenty-four deaths were recorded in one day. Few returned to their own country when their sentences had expired. Several made the attempt to swim to the mainland, but fourteen miles of tempestuous seas made the island a fortress, and there is no evidence that one of them succeeded. The supply of fresh prisoners, however, continued unabated for years, until northern gaols were established, at Carnarvon, Roebourne and Broome, which alleviated the position in that, at least, it kept the natives in their own climate.

Rottnest Native Prison was only another tragic mistake of the early colonists in dealing with the original inhabitants of a country so new and strange to them. The island is a tourist's paradise nowadays. It was still a native prison when I was there in 1911, but I think it was totally abandoned as such soon after. I camped in my tent there, and, when the weather was squally, occupied one of the administration houses. The low-roofed stone gaol was well in evidence, a house of horror of the past. The conditions of the prisoners had infinitely improved, although they were regrettable even then. Just as there was little understanding by the black man of the white man's law, so there was little by the white man of the black's. Natives were thrown together in a cell, regardless of group antipathies and evil magics. There I met again Jingooroo and Muri, serving their sentence for the murder of the blood man at Meekatharra. Jingooroo was far gone in consumption, Muri was only slightly infected, being a younger and stronger brother. To add to their woes, a blood totem man arrived at Rottnest, Thuradha, recently sentenced for another murder of a lice man at Meeka-tharra. The cells accommodated five or six, and Thuradha was shut in with his hereditary enemies! What to do? The only thing was to have myself locked in with them for some hours at night, and take both magics away, which I did.

The evil accumulated in poor Jingooroo, had, however, taken complete hold. One of my saddest memories is the recollection of my last day at Rottnest. I had been with the dying man throughout the evening, by the light of a lantern which I had given him to hold, by virtue of its warmth. Suddenly he stood up, and laying his hands upon my shoulders, said, *"Kabbarli!* That blood magic; How strong it was to cross the big water and find me!" A heavy hæmorrhage followed, and in a short time Jingooroo's grave was added to the many hundreds on the island.

Now an opportunity came for me to travel to Eucla, the Great Australian Bight, and fresh fields. From Albany, I took passage on the cargo steamer *Eucla.* We called at Esperence, Israelite Bay and Point Malcolm, delivering cargoes and stores at the jetties to be carried to stations inland, and throughout the journey I kept a sharp lookout for natives. The original groups had almost gone, trekking north to the gold-fields. At Cape Arid I reached the point where the circumcised groups had encroached upon the uncircumcised. My old friends Dib and Dab were still alive, the last of the Bibbulmun on this borderland.

Ethnological study now became new and difficult, for there were no class-relationships to guide me, and the totemic divisions seemed to be mostly incestuous. Wild cherry men would take wild cherry women to wife, and their children would be wild cherries. They themselves knew that these marriages were wrong, and called their wives *ngammin-wuk,* unlawful. I found but three living members only of a true cross-cousin marriage group whose area was at Twilight Cove. Other than that the area was purely totemic. There was a continual traffic between all the circumcised natives over immense distances, from Eucla to Balladonia, Fraser Range, and Boundary Dam, but there was also a murderous enmity.

Eucla is nowadays nothing but a name on the map, eight miles west of the South Australian border, a street of ruined houses almost completely engulfed in the sand, just at the point where the majestic cliffs of the Great Australian Bight recede inland for sixty miles, to form the western edge of the vast Nullarbor Plain. In 1877, the telegraph line was constructed round the shores of the Bight, and following the gold discoveries of the 'nineties, Eucla became a large repeating station. Thirty telegraphists

DAISY BATES
Photographed by Douglas Glass, 1948

*At the time of Presentation to the then Duke and
Duchess of York in Perth,* 1901

North-west native, showing mud-curls and scars of the dingo totem

In full Corroboree paint

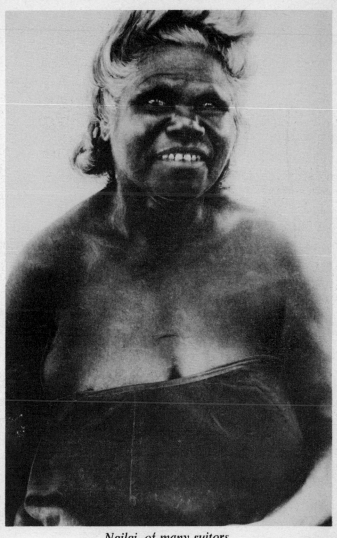

Ngilgi, of many suitors.
One of the last of the Busselton natives, a Bibbulmun
of the South-west

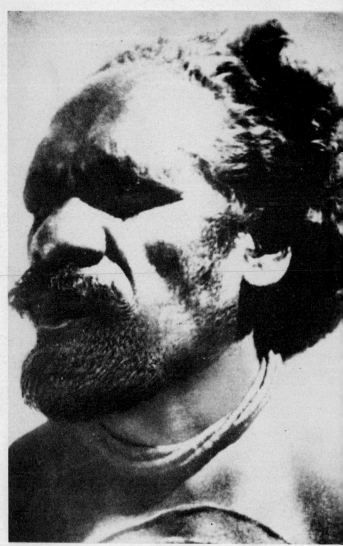

A native of the hardy tribes in the Western Desert of Central Australia

An aboriginal boy of the Murchison district

A shelter (wurley or gunyah) constructed by the Central Australian aborigines on the rare occassions when they remain for more than a few days at the same spot (LAMSHED)

An aboriginal family having a meal of witchetty grubs lightly roasted. In the background is the head of the group, 45 years of age, who had five wives

Aborigines approaching the Adelaide University's
Anthropological Camp at Mt. Liebig.
The two in the centre have bones through the
septum of the nose (LAMSHED)

Central Australian natives decorated for an aboriginal
ceremony. The patterns, which vary according to
the ceremony, are picked out in relief with down
from the breasts of birds, after the designs have
been traced on the skin in blood

*At Ooldea with aborigines who have been in
civilization only a few years and who, in their
native state, are cannibals*

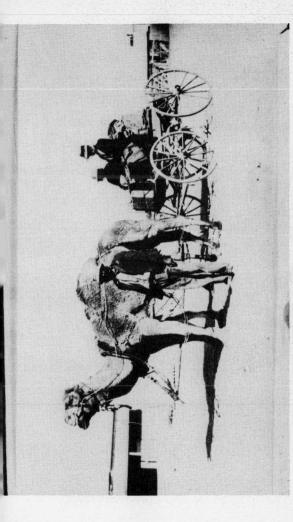

The journey with Gauera and her fourteenth husband across the Great Australian Bight by camel buggy

At my tent

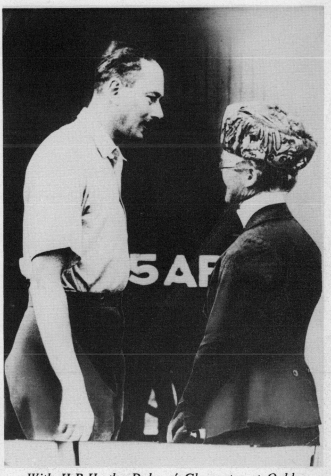

With H.R.H. the Duke of Gloucester at Ooldea

Tending Jinnawillie at Ooldea

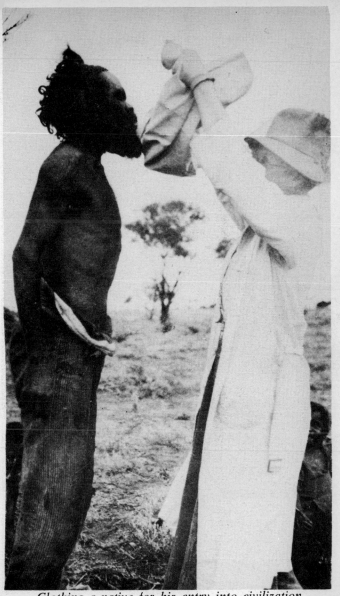

Clothing a native for his entry into civilization

The Author

and their families constituted a permanent population of at least sixty or seventy, and thousands passed through on their way to Coolgardie and Kalgoorlie. The installation of automatic telegraphy and later, the reconstruction of the line in a straight 2,000 miles along the Transcontinental line to avoid coastal atmospheric disturbances, left Eucla the deserted village that overland tourists taking the coast road find in the sand to-day.

The town was in its decline when I was there in 1912. I pitched my tent two miles from the settlement, near the beach. From a hollow in the sandhills, I could look out upon the great sweeping billows of the Southern Ocean rolling in in thunder, sometimes a single wave two miles in length.

About thirty natives were camped in the vicinity, but only one of the Eucla tribe, whose ancestral ground, *jinyila,* had been taken for the telegraph station, was still living. There were a few whose connections had been Eucla people, the last holder of the two true totems,[1] the wild currant *(ngoora),* and *nala* (the edible bark of the root of a species of mallee).

The currant-bushes were about three feet high, covered with small red gluey fruit in their season, and a diverting sight it was to see the wild-currant men sitting round bush after bush until they had cleaned up the berry harvest. The turkey totem belonged to the outlying country adjoining. The turkeys fed on berries, and the natives fed on both, and so became what scientists might call "associated totem groups."

Cannibalism had been rife for centuries in these regions and for a thousand miles north and east of them. When I made inquiries regarding the murder of Baxter (who accompanied Eyre in 1843) by the two Port Lincoln boys who stole the stores and fled back to their own country, I was told that they did not get very far before they themselves were killed and eaten. While these blacks had been under the protection of the whites, they were safe enough,

---

[1] The native word for totem was also the word for home, hearth, fire—*wamoo.*

but the moment they left them, they were descended upon and killed. Some years before my arrival, two white men, Fairey and Woolley, had mysteriously disappeared in this country, but of this comparatively recent affair, the natives would give me no information. I did hear of one instance of cannibalism at the white man's expense, a shepherd whose name is known to me, found dead in the country to westward, with his thigh cut away.

Between Eucla and Eyre a group of six-fingered and six-toed natives existed. They had been seen by Helms as late as the 'sixties, and though they were extinct in my time, I learned both from the natives at Eucla and from Mr. Chichester Beadon, that they had come from the Petermann Ranges, and had intermarried with the five-fingered groups. These six-fingered men were believed to transmit their peculiarity to their off-spring, as were the left-handed groups that I have myself often encountered.

The last manhood ceremony of Eucla was held in 1913, when Gooradoo, a boy of the turkey totem, was initiated at Jeegala Creek, some sixteen miles north. A great crowd of natives straggled in by degrees, remnants from all round the plain's edge, from Fraser Range, Boundary Dam, Israelite Bay, as far east as Penong, and as far north as Ayer's Rock, in the very heart of Australia, 700 miles and more of foot-travelling. There were numbers of women among them, as in all these gatherings an exchange of women is an important part of the ceremony. For the ceremony there must have been more than 200 assembled.

In physique these border natives were fine sturdy fellows. In their own country they were cannibals to a man. "We are Koogurda," they told me, and frankly admitted the hunting and sharing of kangaroo and human meat as frequently as that of kangaroo and emu. The Baduwonga of Boundary Dam drank the blood of those they had killed. The Kaalurwonga, east of the Badu, were a fierce arrogant tribe who pursued fat men, women and girls, and cooked the dead by making a deep hole in the sand, trussing the body and there roasting it, and tossing it about until it cooled sufficient for them to divide it. Another group would cut off hand and foot, and partake of these first, to prevent the ghost from following and spearing them spiritually.

Although they camped about me for many days, I was sufficiently acquainted with their disposition and their customs to know that my own position was secure. All knew of *kabbarli* and her grandmotherly magic, and I look upon this exciting period at Eucla as one of the most illuminating contacts with this primitive race that I have ever made.

At about this time, I sold my pastoral properties in the Ophthalmia Ranges, and so could provide liberal flour, sugar and tea for the forthcoming celebrations.

A few days before the celebrations a curious ceremony took place on the arrival of a contingent from the east. No fires of welcome had been lighted. Because there were so many factions tension grew and grew until one day I found a raging crowd, with spears and spear-throwers and clubs, ready to fall upon each other. I had gone over to choose those who would see to the damper-making for the day, and penetrated right to the centre of the angry mob— a delicate moment!

I looked round. "All you *boggali* (grandsons) bring your spears to me," I said quietly. "I will sit down and take care of them, and then you can go little way and have a good fight, and come back for food."

To my astonishment, old Ngarralea and Dhalja and other totemists of the loudest voices and most belligerent attitudes put down their spears beside me. The others followed. I carefully arranged every spear in order of tribal eldership in its right totem-group. Then I said, "Now go and have plenty talk and little clubbing. I will wait." They went a little way only, and I could hear the shouted grievances and antipathies in a wild medley of argument and accusation. Then without rancour, they came back, ready for a meal.

The strangers came down in a line, and stood on the slope near my fire. The men from the other camps gathered in an orderly throng five deep, and approached the new arrivals at a trot, their women like camp followers behind. As they advanced, they now and then stopped, formed into a dense round mass, and gave a deep throaty shout. All were fully armed.

When they were within twenty paces, they suddenly turned towards their own camp, and ran round in a great circle to behind the strangers. This was repeated again and again—a greeting of armed neutrality, a temporary truce. The men then approached the camps of the new-comers, where bartering took place.

From them I discovered an avenue of inquiry of considerable scientific interest, for the new arrivals, I learned, were the men of the Wanji-wanji travel dance.

A great aboriginal trade route circles the continent. As already I had found evidence of a stone-age barter, pearl shell of the north treasured as magic in the deserts of the south, red ochre and flint knives traded across many hundreds of miles, I now learned that this barter includes all exchangeable articles, and is continent wide. Notwithstanding the hostility of groups and tribes, barter went on all the year round along this great highway, which abutted directly on the north and south coasts, and branched off to the eastern and western coasts so that no groups were isolated. All along the main road were by-roads and branch-roads. Every group in Australia, except those of the coast, had four roads of exit and entry, east, west, south and north, where they could send their local products and obtain desired goods. Spears made of certain hard and durable woods, spearheads of varied stone for various uses, fur-string belts and forehead bands, curiously shaped meteorites, little white tail-tips of the tail of the rabbit bandicoot, clubs made from strong roots, Murchison ornamented shields—all found their way for immense distances along this great recognized continental route, prized for their good or evil magic, or their usefulness, and increasing in antiquity and value as they travelled farther and farther.[1]

_____

[1] Bull-roarers, the most sacred Central Australian objects, were brought by the Bibbulmun, whose children whirled them in play. An imitation of the Malay *kris*, made on the north coast, was bartered as far south as Cooper's Creek. A ground (Neolithic) axe from East Kimberley reached the Perth Tribes.

The great continental trade-route probably originated with the second horde that arrived in Australia. Century by century, generation after generation, they penetrated farther south and east and west, buying and selling, bartering their women and girls for boys, whom they adopted and reared and initiated. Saleable goods and human possessions were not the only traffic.

Two great dramatic performances travelled with them, the Wanji-wanji, and the Molong-go. The Wanji-wanji came down along the river-heads, and the Molong-go travelled south from a point east or south-east of Darwin. These dances took one or two generations to traverse the continent. The Wanji-wanji was an ancient dream dance, a dramatic rendering of the arrival of the second horde into Australia. It had reached the Bibbulmun long before white settlement in the South-West, and was known there as the wanna-wa. There were only a few old Bibbulmun who had been able to tell me about it, and according to them it came from the man-eating groups on their north-eastern border.

The Wanji-wanji I saw at Eucla coincided with the initiation ceremonies. It had come by its old traditional inland road from the north, along the Fortescue, Gascoyne, Ashburton and Murchison Rivers, east of the goldfields, then south. It lasted about a fortnight, and there were three performances daily, at 4 a.m., 2 p.m. and at about 8 p.m. Day after day, the same songs and motions were demonstrated and practised until the participants became perfect. I attended every performance, right to the close, when the sacred and secret parts of the dance, forbidden to women and girls, were enacted at a spot five miles from my camp. Neither those who brought the dance, nor those who watched it, could interpret the words or the actions, but they had a fine quick ear, and reproduced them perfectly. The Wanji-wanji finished its last grand tour at Eucla, for although the mixed groups gathered there took it on to Tarcoola and Kalgoorlie, these great traditional dances demand a large number of performers and audience, and for lack of them, petered out.

Old Tharnduriri, who was over 70 years old, remembered parts of the dance, which he had seen at Ayer's Rock in his boyhood.

A few still remain who remember the Wanji-wanji, and I had but to sing the opening stanza—

> Warri wan-gan-ye,
> Koogunarri wanji-wanji,
> Warri wan-gan-ye,

and they would remember, and join in exact time and tune and words.

When the ceremonies of initiation were about to begin, an interesting incident occurred. The boy initiate, Gooradoo, was taken out on a fishing excursion by the white telegraphists one day in a dinghy. A north wind blew up suddenly at Eucla, and Gooradoo's father entertained grave fears for his boy's safety. His panic was such that he cursed and stormed impartially at the whole assembled camp until Gooradoo returned. Reassured and full of contrition, the father immediately set out to walk fifteen or twenty miles to bring a turkey to the group totem people, an edible totem being the customary peace offering after injustice or rage.

The initiation corroborees began at Jeegala Creek. Night after night the orgies continued in excitement so intense that one man, having danced himself into a frenzy of heat and passion, lay on the damp ground, was seized with paralysis, and died. He was of the edible bark (*nala* tree) totem. My camp was beside a *nala* tree, and when I came back from his grave, and was about to set my fire for tea, I looked up and perceived what I thought was rain falling from out of the branches. Rain-water being infinitely precious, I ran for my bucket, to see that the sky was clear. Yet water, beyond all doubt, was falling from the leaves of the *nala* tree!

I called Dhalja, one of the old men of the totem.

"Dhalja, you look! What for the water come from those tree leaves?"

Dhalja looked closely for some moments at both me

and the tree. Then he pointed to the ground. *"Nala* man dead," he said.

I have never been able to find a logical explanation of this singular occurrence of leaves dripping water from one branch only. When the period of mourning was over, and they were allowed once more to eat of the totem, Dhalja brought me a wooden scoop filled with this edible bark, telling me that as the tree had shown it, I belonged to his totem. The bark was sweet and not unpalatable, and I returned the compliment in sugar, which he found sweeter still.

When the initiation and the Wanji-wanji were over, the times came for the grand finale of these ceremonies, the introduction of new members into the totems, and the addition of new boards to the sacred store. It was then that I myself was initiated into the freedom of all the totems, in a purely religious ceremony intensely impressive.

All natives who could claim connection with the remnants of the Eucla totem group had gradually assembled in the vicinity of my camp—mallee-hen, curlew, native cat, wild currant, kangaroo and emu and dingo, edible bark, turkey and many others. The elders of the various groups brought me portions of their traditional totem foods, all cooked except the water-roots, and presented on a bark scoop. Very early one morning I was awakened by the insistent clicking of boomerangs outside my tent. I went out to find a long file of more than fifty men forming a half-circle. All carried spears, and all were naked except for the decorations—crazy stripes of red ochre and white pipe-clay, crests of cockatoo feathers, hair-belts and tassels reddened with blood, and waist-belts with a tuft of emu-feather behind. The camp was silent, for the women and children had been sent some miles away.

In my sober Edwardian coat and skirt, a sailor hat with fly-veil, and neat high-heeled shoes, I took up my position in the centre. We must have made a quaint assembly indeed. We took a track beside the receding cliffs for some miles as the totem shrine was a spot called Beera, some five miles or so west of the Telegraph Station. Two natives of Willilambi (Twilight Cove), Wirrgain and Karnduing, of the eaglehawk and sacred spear totems, ran on either side of us, sometimes covering their mouths with their hands and emitting long blood-curdling tremolo "eagle-hawk" screams that echoed eerily along the cliffs. Every now and again, we came to places along our road where fires had been lighted, tended by other men who beat upon the fires with fresh green branches, and solemnly steeped us, one and all, in the dense smoke that arose.

At length we reached a wide totem road, with cleared spaces some fifty yards in diameter at either end. A great fire was lighted in the centre of this. At a given signal, we each gathered a mallee branch to hold in the right hand, and spread out in a wide-flung half-moon, of which I still held the centre, all sitting in a semicircle and facing the road.

On a shrill, high note, with the branches beating the ground, began the song of the totems, native cat, curlew, eaglehawk, kangaroo, wallaby, emu, mallee-hen, and so on through the whole gamut of those assembled.

"*Yudu!*" came a shout from one of the elders. ("Shut your eyes!") With bowed heads, in a tense silence and with closed eyes, the great crowd of squatting natives bent to the ground. I ventured to watch.

At the other end of the road, in the cleared ground that was, at it were, the altar, or sanctuary, appeared an ancient tribal father, an extremely tall and imposing figure with a long black beard, Wardunda. He was holding before him a totem board at least fifteen feet high, a *koon-dain*, the father of all totem boards, deeply-grooved and painted in red ochre and white pipe-clay with the sacred markings of Maalu, the kangaroo. Arriving at the centre of the cleared ground, he turned to face the prostrate circle, and lifted the *koondain* in the same manner and to the same hushed reverence as the elevation of the Host in the Roman Catholic Church, or as Moses lifting the serpent in the wilderness.

At a whispered word the natives raised their eyes. Immediately a frenzied chanting arose, the song of the kangaroo, ringing and echoing from men's throats in that lonely place to the rhythm of beating branches, while man and board remained absolutely motionless. The board was then slowly lowered, and as it lay flat on the ground, Wardunda prostrated himself upon it, then rose and reverently carried it out as the singing died away. A smaller kangaroo board, about four feet long, was silently placed in my lap from behind.

Again *"Yudu!"* was the cry, and a second long totem was exhibited. Again a smaller board, with its special markings, was given to me in the same way, until I held twenty or thirty boards of groups living and dead, identical with the large ones, long seasoned with age and weather, bearing the concentric circles, diamonds, squares, and transverse markings and crude drawings signifying birds and animals. These totems have their sacred significance back in the dreamtime, and hold the mystery of life. No native knows more than that.

We now rose to our feet. The natives, still in single file, twice made their circuit of the ground, then all stood with their spears in fighting position while Jilburnda came towards me. Taking the boards, which I held in my arms, he touched me with every one of them, upon breast, back, shoulders and knees, finally laying them at my feet.

The young men who were witnessing this ceremony for the first time stood at either end of the semicircle, and these were now motioned to come forward to the fire. This they did, trembling. The songs of their totems were sung, and they also were touched, with their own sacred boards, on back, breast, shoulders and knees. Jilburnda signalled me to rise and approach the fire, where I was touched again with the boards, which were then laid at my feet.

Once more *"Yudu!"* was called, and there followed a second exposition of Maalu the Kangaroo, and the singing of its song.

I was then asked by Jilburnda and Ngailgulla to carry the boards to the storehouse. I walked in the centre of the totem road, accompanied by the men, who formed a file at each side. I was told that the little storehouse of mallee branches, cunningly hidden, was but a temporary shelter, the cave that had been their resting-place through generations having once been entered by white men, who carried off as souvenirs and museum pieces the sacred objects they found therein. I placed the boards on a bed of fresh mallee-leaves, the opening was carefully covered, and we turned southward without retreading the sacred ground.

With smoke signals to tell the camp of our return, we hastened back in the growing darkness.

As keeper of the totems, I had now free access to the place, and it was my duty to grease and freshen these boards occasionally, and to hide the place of their storage from white men.

Chapter XII

ACROSS THE BIGHT BY CAMEL BUGGY

I REMAINED AT MY EUCLA CAMP TILL 1914, WHEN AN invitation came to attend the Science Congress to be held in Adelaide, Melbourne and Sydney. To get to that heaven of contact with my own kind, I hired from the local storekeeper a substantial camel buggy and a pair of camels. I left my tent and its contents in care of my native friends, instructing the storekeeper to supply them with my usual rations. The initiation parties had dispersed, and only a few families remained. As we should pass many little groups on the 240-mile journey, it was a problem to load sufficient to provide hospitality along the Great Australian Bight, and also to select my travelling companions, everyone being eager to come. At last I chose Gauera and her latest, and fourteenth husband, who had bought her a few weeks before from his brother Ngallilea for two shillings and a well-seasoned pipe.

We started one fine morning along the sheep road that had been the old track of the Bight Head and Nullarbor natives for generations. The track up to the cliffs was called Yeergilia, from which the name Eucla had been distorted by the white men. It was a steep and dangerous road for vehicles, and the camels concentrated all their viciousness into the pulling. Soon we were on the crest of the cliffs, the southern edge of the Great Nullarbor Plain, that stretches for 450 miles east and west, and about 250 north and south at its widest. We paused for a moment to send a smoke signal of farewell, receiving an answering smoke wishing us good luck, and to look back upon the little telegraph station on the sandy rim of the great blue Southern Ocean.

Nullarbor was named by the surveyor Delisser from the Latin, *nullus arbor,* for the great plain is utterly tree-less, covered with salt-bush and blue-bush and other low and inconspicuous herbage. The natives believed it to be the abode of a mighty magic snake called Ganba or Jee-darra which ate any human that entered his territory. None of them ever ventured far out. They might chase kangaroo or emu some twenty miles from the edge, but invariably returned to their camps at eventide. The Nullar-bor is a series of subterranean shelves, with many caves, underground lakes, and possibly rivers. Scattered over the surface are numerous blow-holes through which the ocean winds sweep violently and hot gusts of summer are sucked down with a loud roaring. According to the natives, the blow-holes are the gates through which Ganba passes to his sea home.

The Plain has yet to be surveyed. From the shelving nature of this old sea-bed, it will not be surprising to find that the sea runs for many miles under the lowest shelf, and perhaps the course of the two lost rivers east and west of it may also be located, and their waters tapped for pastoral purposes. The cliffs are precipitous and there are but five possible landing places in some 200 miles.

Balgundra, who belonged to the Balladonia opossum group, was paying his first visit to the Bight, but Gauera had been backward and forward with various husbands. Our daily journeys were lengthened and shortened as we came to good patches of camel-feed, and at night my travelling tent was quickly slung between the buggy and a mallee-bush, and while Gauera put on a breakwind, Balgundra went exploring for possible food. One evening he returned with a tawny frog-mouth, which he called *munnarn*. While he told me the *munnarn* legend he had heard from his father, Gauera cooked the bird for his tea. Our camping places were often ten miles and more from the cliffs, and yet as I lay on the ground I could hear the monotonous beat of the sea as if beneath me.

Our first welcome from the eastward was a smoke from Koombana, forty-five miles from Eucla. Here, in a small group, we met Ngallilea, Gauera's former husband. He invited himself to join our party. Here I had occasion to mark the nice sense of honour that exists among these people. Ngallilea had sold, not lent Gauera, and though she built his breakwind, he lit his own fire and took his food alone.

For about sixty miles the coast is fringed with gnarled and twisted trees in which road and track are easily lost. Here and there we found little mounds of the edible ant, its totem mate, *kailga* the lizard, and the land-snails mentioned by the explorer, Eyre.

All four in the buggy, we wiled away the hours singing the songs of the Wanji-wanji, about thirty all told, the words of which I had written in my notebook for reference, and discussed native matters that could be spoken in the presence of Gauera. At the men's camp at night we whispered the secrets a woman must not know.

A few miles from Koombana, we came upon Goonalda Cave, with its big underground lake, and descended with the aid of a rope for water, and then to our first vermin fence near White Wall Sheep station, set like a toy house on the treeless flat surrounded by towering sandhills moving in every wind. Here I was able to replenish my stores. At Ilgamba, the head of the Bight, I found but one representative of the dingo group left, a fine wiry old fellow named Koolbari, who was glad to meet Kabbarli and tell her another legend of Munnarn, a pillar of rock on the crest of the sandhill, a dreamtime man who had once stolen two boys and drowned them in the sea near by, and also Bai-ongu-mama, father of all porcupines, who was now changed into porcupine grass. Three of the five landing-places along the cliffs are dangerous climbing, but Koolbari and his people had scaled them frequently, to catch seal, penguin and other sea-creatures. The old man told me that the sulky magic snake of the Plain had pushed up the land with his shoulders so that he could swim along under the cliffs.

In the first months of telegraph settlement, when Eucla's mails depended on the irregular visits of the little steamer *Grace Darling* from the west, Koolbari's services had been enlisted as postman from Fowler's Bay, 480 miles on foot to and fro, and he never failed to deliver the bag intact at either end. On one occasion, however, meeting a large group of his friends and relations coming in for their ceremonies, he cunningly hid the mail-bag until the visitors had departed, arriving three weeks late. He and Beenbong his woman were the last of their respective groups, and were well provided for in their old age by Government and white settlers.

Ilgamba is an Arabian desert in little, its sands of hourglass fineness, continually encroaching and changing the landscape, sometimes completely obliterating the old telegraph lines and posts. From there we travelled eastward through country thickly timbered with mallee and other eucalypts. Birds and animals were plentiful, but Koolbari called the area "orphan country" because its own native gooseberry and kangaroo groups were extinct. Ilgamba was also orphaned ground.

In these undulating hills, my camels travelled easily. I sometimes walked beside them for exercise, as did the native men, seeking lizards and grubs and edible gum, while Gauera sat aloft in the buggy cursing the camels and feeling very important. We now resumed our smoke-signalling, to tell the tribes of our coming, choosing always a tree with a pile of dead leaves beneath it. With every group, or rather the remnants of every group, landless and listless, I camped and asked questions. One of the old civilized men, surprised at my sudden appearance, hastily buttoned himself into a pair of ancient trousers, wrong side before, in his eager haste to greet Kabbarli.

Rabbits and sparrows were then making their way across the Plain into Western Australia, and the fox had reached this timbered country. I saw sparrows at White Well Station. They had taken ten years to reach there from Fowler's Bay, where they had been seen in 1905, but it took them only three years to go from White Well to Eucla, a good season or two helping them along. The rabbits easily acclimatize themselves to any conditions. In the worst droughts they devoured the bark of sandalwood and other trees, and dug up the roots of the smaller bush plants. I myself saw them climbing the mulga to nibble off the young shoots.

Both fox and rabbit gave good meat food to the natives, but none were so sweet as their own natural fare, lizards, snakes, grubs, and the sweet white manna from certain eucalypts. Their methods of cooking kangaroo, emu, wombat, wallaby and other large game are to me unequalled in bringing out the flavour. They cooked me a delicious meal, a wallaby tail, with the skin left on, thrown into the ashes, and a long fat carpet snake called *goonia* rolled into lengths and roasted. Several wombat snakes called *moolai-ongoo,* and wombat itself, were also eaten. Balgundra's excitement when he handled the first wombat he had seen was amusing. His sharp eyes took in every detail of the strange beast; then he turned it over, pressed its hind foot into the ground, and shouted with delight, "Look, Kabbarli! the track of a baby!" The wombat was four hours in the hot ashes before it became edible—tender and tasty as roast pork.

At Fowler's Bay, at the kindly invitation of Mr. and Mrs. George Murray of Yalata Station, I remained for a few weeks. Yalata was a shining example of the old-time out-back hospitality. Everyone was sure of a greeting, and every derelict native of the eastern and northern edge of the Plain found sanctuary there. Men of the district came back to it to live and die, and new groups were constantly arriving from the central areas. Old and young sat behind the wool-shed or round the wood-heap off and on for years, mostly gossiping and loafing, always sure of a sympathetic understanding with plenty of good food and kind treatment from Boonari, as the Big White Boss was called, notwithstanding the fact that the native dogs played havoc with the sheep.

There I left Balgundra and Gauera to return to Eucla with the buggy, while I journeyed down the West Coast of South Australia by boat. How vividly I can still remember the vision of green beauty of those Adelaide hills as we entered the river in the early morning, lovely as a series of Constable pictures to eyes weary with the glare of the sandhills.

Members of the Congress—the Association for the Advancement of Science—leading men of their day from the leading universities of the world, were due to arrive, and I was busy with the compilation of my notes and deep in the joys of anticipation when one day, as I walked along King William Street, my attention was struck by the newspapers announcing the declaration of war—England and Germany, Russia, France and Belgium, the whole world, in turmoil. My own thought had been so remote from international concerns for so long that I stood aghast.

For a little while the daily routine was undisturbed. The scientists arrived. There were German and English Professors of great attainment among them, and in perfect amity the congress was opened in the Town Hall, Adelaide. Among the visiting anthropologists were men of the standing of Professors Bateson, W. H. R. Rivers, Haddon, Malinowski, Sir Everard im Thurn, Graebner, Hartland and many others, leaders of thought in their own countries, seekers after knowledge in Australia. I accompanied the congress to Melbourne and Sydney, a happy and exhilarating association from beginning to end, and then returned to Adelaide, where I was asked to deliver lectures. This aroused the interests of the women's organizations in my work, and a deputation was made to Sir Richard Butler, then Minister in control of the Aborigines' Department, that my services be retained for

South Australia in the same capacity as they had been in the West. Pending his decision, I returned to Yalata, and made the return journey by camel buggy for my camp equipment at Eucla.

Chapter XIII

WIRILYA'S PLEASANT VALE

I RIGGED MY FIRST LITTLE TENT HOME IN SOUTH AUStralia on the hills West of Fowler's Bay in 1914. Koolbari and Beenbong built my breakwind and settled down beside it with remnants of many groups of the eastern, western and northern edge of the Plain. Among them were three who were blind and helpless, Dowie of the Boundary Dam mallee-hen; Jinjabulla, last of the emu men of Ooldea; and Binilya. a *wirongu*—rain or cloud woman of Tarcoola.

Binilya, though totally blind, had the reputation, like Canute, of being able to control the elements. To see her haranguing the lightning and brandishing her digging-stick at the scowling skies in a thunderstorm was a sight to be remembered. When the thunder died away, an expression of the utmost self-satisfaction overspread her eager, listening face, and she would go back to her camp-fire happily singing the rain-songs of Wirongu.

These sightless ones had been deserted by their own last of kin, and suffered many disabilities and small persecutions until one day I delighted them by striking camp and taking them with me to a little haven of their own, a place called Wirilya, twenty-six miles from Yalata. I put up my tent in a grove of acacia trees, and, because they had such great need of me, "sat down" with them there for two or three years.

Wirilya had never been a group camp, as there was no

permanent water, but after rain, when the rock-holes were filled, the passing tribes would stay for a little while demolishing everything edible. From my camp in a little grove of *kardia* I was encircled by a ring of soft green vales which, again, were bounded on their farther side by the blue mallee hills of the coast and the purple-brown *kardia* of the inland slopes.

It was all limestone area, offering little resistance to weathering and levelling agents. Nearer the coast the valleys were formed from more recent sea inlets, and in digging down into these depressions stratum upon stratum of small shells, sometimes one inch, often three or four inches in depth, was disclosed, each species of small shell, clean and whole, forming its own stratum; and on the limestone slabs that have formed, and that now lie exposed in some of these depressions near the coast, are numbers of footprints, called by the natives *"nyeerina jinna,"* of humans, animals and birds which walked over the soft mud of long ago to get the oysters, mussels and other shell-fish whose fossils line the shallow banks girding them. A granite boulder, a white flint, a waterworn stone, some odd geological feature which even the natives knew was foreign to the district, formed with the footprints the basis of many a native legend accounting for their presence in such strange surroundings. Farther inland the valleys were covered with grasses, samphire, saltbush and other metamorphosed sea-growths, and creeping slowly over many of them the *kardia* was gradually covering their surface, so that in many places one looked across dark-green forests of *kardia* to the deeper greens and browns of the slopes beyond.

At all times it was beautiful, whether in the quivering heat of summer which sent waves of soft colours dancing over still trees and brown surface, or in the cool and misty winter mornings, when just to look upon its beauty was an ecstasy; the tall golden grasses nid-nodding with every breeze, the growing greens of tree and bush mingling in utmost harmony with the greyer or browner older leaves, the tree-tops of the edging slopes beyond the vale silhouetted against a brilliant sky, or rising out of a white lake of morning mist; and all round and about, winter and summer, the wild life of the bush adding its voice and movement to the general harmony.

There were well-defined gullies on some of the deeper slopes that told of a heavier rainfall in days gone by, and in the good winter and spring kangaroo, emu, and turkey came in plenty to feed on the luscious grasses and herbage of the verdant slopes. Edible roots and fruits, native currants, peaches and the like, were also plentiful in good seasons, so that in the winter and spring the South Coast men,[1] in whose tribal run Wirilya was included, were able to perform ceremonies if they did not last too long, for beyond a few shallow clay-pans and rock-holes, filled only in good seasons, there was no permanent water at Wirilya. Groups of males often came to catch that great native delicacy, the emu, and to feast on its blood. Women were not allowed to come to these feasts for emu was forbidden meat to them, and they could not drink the blood of emu nor even see their menkind drink it.

Several roads, which were expansions of old native tracks, ran from Wirilya to Yuria Water in the north, to Bookabi and other rock-holes in the east and south-east, and to Binjumba and Kooluna in the west and north-west, but there were no deep native tracks such as were to be found round permanent watering places, and until the white man's sheep came to Wirilya it was mainly left to the birds, animals and reptiles and insects that flourished on the plains and slopes, the swamp and low scrub round and about Wirilya knoll.

Wirilya abounded in bird life, its soft and musical name deriving from the little "wirily," a species of ground lark that lives on the plains and the grassy slopes.

When the first aborigines arrived at this point, they had apparently formed their own exogamous[2] laws, and they noticed that the wirily[3] chased the young male birds out of the family to go and make their own group elsewhere. Then probably arose the legend that wirily were at one

[1] *Yulbari nunga.*
[2] *Thar-burda* and *narrumba.*
[3] "Ily" as in *fauteuil.*

time men, and when they changed into birds they kept
their laws, and married without breaking the moral law
of consanguinity, and so the home of these law-abiding
birds was called Wirilya.

There is something extraordinarily human about the
wild life of the bush, and the lonely camp-dweller and
lover of the wild can easily understand the translation of
bird and animal into the legends and traditions of the
aborigines. Like the natives themselves, birds are far
keener observers of the white man than he is of them, and
have a much greater intelligence than the most observing
of us credits them with.

Whenever I pitch my camp I become at once an object
of scrutiny to the bird life surrounding the spot I have
chosen. Each bird has its own method of observation,
some peer stealthily, watching my movements from hidden
spots, others are openly curious and perch anywhere round
where they can get a good view of the intruder, others
come mocking or uttering unfriendly warning, or even
contemptuous notes. Every species of bird has its own
personality, so to speak, and in the native bird legends
their personality is always taken into account. Again, too,
as with the natives, themselves, some birds are friendly
towards some of their kind, adopt an armed neutrality
towards others, and are at open and constant enmity with
yet other groups; and where bird or animal becomes the
totem of a human group, the same distinction appears to be
observed by the aborigines as prevails amongst the bird
groups. A native of the eagle totem will be friendly with
a kangaroo totem man, but will wage war with a crow
man, a wombat totem man will be the enemy of a wild
dog man, and so on. Totem is the general American term
applied by the scientist to the peculiar connection existing
between the aborigines and certain birds, animals, reptiles,
etc., their belief that the bird or animal is "the same as"
the man whose totem it is, for every aborigine fully be-
lieves that in the dhoogoor or dream (ancestral) times
his own ancestors were birds like that which is now his
totem, and which he calls his brother or son, sister or

daughter according as the bird is old or young, male or female.

A man may kill and eat his own totem in some districts, but unless very hungry, he will not kill and eat its young ones, for they are his *gijjara* (children), and their shadow or spirit (called *ngwan* in the Eucla area) is always inside his own body, but he will kill and eat, and give to his friends to eat his "totem brother," the deliberate giving of which alway cements their friendship. All bird and animal totemic ceremonies that I have seen are simply legends dramatized, for bird legend and totem are inseparable in the native mind.

One must love solitude for its own sake to taste in its fullness the perfect happiness that these beautiful open spaces give.

> Wind and sunlight and wide clear spaces—
> Dawn and evening and bright clear stars.
>   . . . and desert places.

Often in the evening dream echoes of native voices come, borne on the winds, singing weird cadences that seem to take one's soul into a barbaric past in which it had once lived and moved. The croonings and keenings of the natives of to-day are the same as those sung by their far-off ancestors. The meaning of song or recitation is never expressed in the few words crooned or sung, for inside the singer there may be a wealth of meaning, a dirge for the long dead but still remembered friend, a long story of ancestral travelling, a hunting exploit, a kill, a song of prowess, a dramatic episode, or just emotional phases passing through the singer's mind; any one of these giving rise to song. Many of their keenings are strangely like those of the Celt and Oriental, and between these three races—Celt, Oriental and Aboriginal—there is also the link of fatalism. It is impossible to describe these songs adequately even when one is familiar with the trend of thought, daily life and speech and the cadences natural to the expression of aboriginal emotion. If you are a Celt you can sense what the singer is unable to express, and feel the varied emotions passing through him. Subjects that have lent themselves to epics in other lands can only be rendered by the aborigine in a crude sentence. His totem songs—a few words at most—are sung with a wild abandon, the emotions they stir within him becoming stronger with every repetition, until finally, from excess of feeling, the singer will often fall unconscious, to be roughly massaged into life again.

Sunsets blaze and fade, and blaze again in these great empty wilds, and dawn sets her diadem over them. The light loitering winds carry delicate perfumes hither and thither, but all these places that once echoed with song or war-cry are now left to the birds and animals whose forebears witnessed the arrival of the humans, and who themselves are now witnessing their passing.

Night comes to us with its shadows and misty veilings. Our bird friends are sleeping contentedly in the trees round about us. What night life there is moves noiselessly, and this is the time for legend or tradition or narrative of exploits of young days. The natives' voices attune themselves unconsciously to the hushed immensity round us, and lower and lower the words are uttered until the story ends between words and silence. Then perhaps someone will start a sort of crooning lullaby, the soft melody rising and falling like an aboriginal Gregorian Chant, a song of the dream times, an echo, "*wongai arga argarn*," that has come from the past.

At Wirilya my blind natives and I lived in contentment. I daily hunted rabbits and lizards for their food, cut wood for their fires, guarded them from setting alight to themselves or wandering into danger, cooked their meals and cared for them, lighted their pipes, and sometimes led them, by means of a long pole, for pleasant walks in their beloved bush, talking of old times. Always I respected their own laws. For instance, Jinjabulla and Dowie must never touch each other, as Jinjabulla had once given blood to Dowie at an initiation ceremony. Both being wanderers and both blind, many a time I called a warning that only we three could understand. Dowie's life history was a

THE PASSING OF THE ABORIGINES

terrible one, given me partly by his contemporaries, by Binilya and Jinjabulla and Eucla and Bight Head derelicts.

Dowie was a Baadu of Warrdarrgana, the son of Karil-danu, a Baadu and mallee-hen totem man, and Bildana, his wife, a Ngallia and of the emu totem from the North-East. When he was a little boy he was given four baby sisters to eat and he was rubbed over with their fat. This made him grow so quickly and so big and strong that he was initiated at the same time as boys much older than he, but not so big and broad and fat. He was hairy and tall and big-mouthed, and from the moment when he first tasted the flesh of his baby sisters, he developed a taste for human food that grew and strengthened with his years. He was taken north to the spinifex country for his initiation, and while living with the North-men he heard in the evening tales told by the elder men of spirits (white-men) that had been killed and eaten by those tale-tellers, but that did not taste as good as their own human food. He was told of his great ancestor's travels north, and the travels of Ming-ari (Mo-lock Horridus). He heard too of the huge snake, "like a hill walking about," who went and sat down by Milbarli's iguana water at Wandunya and would not let Milbarli women come near the water. Milbarli, Meeda (small iguana) and Yoong-ga fought Ganba, who tried to hide in the sand that covers Wandunya Water, but Milbarli pulled him and Meeda hit him and Yoong-ga pushed him, and all the women helped their husbands. And at last they killed Ganba and he turned into stone, and he is there now by Wandunya Water. And Milbarli and Yoong-ga made a dance and many songs of the great battle and all the Waddi now dance the "beeja-beeja-ma" to show how their dreamtime brothers and sisters killed the huge Ganba. Dowie saw the dance, but he did not like it, because wo-men had too large a part in it and he despised women.

He hated his mother, Bildana, and his other mothers and his sisters, and all his brothers. He would have eaten them all as he had eaten the others, but they were older than he was and so could not be given to him to eat. He never played with girls without fighting and beating them, and he beat his mothers with sticks and stones, and threw sand in their eyes. He was the constant cause of camp battle, so that when his initiation came, all those in charge of him had some grudge against him, and at the *Wa-warning* (throwing the boy in the air) they let him fall again and again, but he was so fat and strong they could not break his bones, or cripple him. Then, at the beating, he was thumped hard on the chest and heart, but no blood came. At the blood-drinking he drank greedily of the blood that filled the scoop and wished the ceremony lasted longer than a day. All Baadu are blood-drinkers, but Dowie liked blood to drink more than water. The voice of the bull-roarer soothed him while the severer ordeals of his initiation were gone through. Every detail of the ceremony sank into his being and as he had been dealt with, so also and more hardly did he deal with the boys whom he initiated later. He made his own scars, for there was neither brother nor friend who wished to scar him in amity, and though the four men who held him had to make their sisters his potential mothers-in-law ("forbidden") the sisters were only too glad because he was now *oomari,* and, therefore, could not touch or beat or look at them any more, but they hoped no girl babies would come to them, because one of his *oomari* had lost an eye through his wicked sand-throwing.

His initiation finished, he was free to join the others in their exchange and barter journeys, but there was never a journey in which he took part that did not end in bloodshed and a feast of human flesh.

Dowie had passed his initiation and was claiming one of the wives that had been promised him when the shock of Giles's expedition passing through Boundary Dam[1] sent the tribe into such a panic of fear that several died afterwards from the magic of its passing. Among them were Dowie's brother and two sisters. White men and horses had been previously described to Dowie, who saw them for himself, and he feared and hated them, yet dared not lift spear or boomerang to hurl at them.

Cruel, blood-thirsty and quarrelsome in his manhood,

---

[1] Warrdarrgana.

he demanded and obtained his first wife, hurrying up the
ceremonies connected with her entry into womanhood. He
flung the human and animal meat payment to the girl's
family in more and more contempt as the days passed and
her initiation was delayed. His huge mouth twisted and
moved with every ugly emotion of his mind; he was the
scandal-monger of every group and his eyes and ears were
constantly on the alert to see and hear things that, when
repeated, led to killing and eating. And when he stood in
the row of young men into whose mouths Kommuru
(mother's brother) threw pieces of liver,[1] however large
the piece, Dowie caught and swallowed it and only showed
his satisfaction when the portion was unusually large.
Neither the hands nor the teeth of the young men must
touch the liver, and if their stomachs reject it they will
die, or if they attempt to masticate it they will die. Kommuru cut larger and larger pieces for Dowie hoping that
he would fail to swallow them, but Dowie never missed,
though other and better young men of the group missed
and died and became themselves human food.

Dowie brought home many human bodies for he would
stalk human game in murderer's slippers,[2] and he loved
the flesh of man, woman and child. When he brought his
own "kill" into camp, he claimed those portions that im-
part the strength of the dead man to the eater. And so he
waxed in strength and cruelty. He beat his first wife Yoo-
bana immediately after she was handed over to him,
because she cried from fear of him, and he continued to
beat her until, tired of her tears, he knocked her on the
head and shared in the distribution of her body afterwards.
Then Diongu was made ready and was passed over to him,
and she was also killed and eaten, and so were Nyiranunga
and Wanbiana. Now, wanton women in any camp may
lawfully be killed and eaten, but these women were not
wanton, yet none dared to remonstrate.

His four wives finished, he looked for others, and took
Narrilyana from a Wong-gai-i Waddi, which was wrong

---

[1] Kammarndi.
[2] Muldharra.

or the Waddi and the Baadu could not intermarry. Then
ne took a Munjinji woman and a Ngallia, and Mardu-
wonga, but these all died quickly. All those who opposed
nim he fought and killed and helped to eat. Yangaij was
nis next capture but her own man stole her back again,
and about this time there came a diversion, for news was
brought to the Baadu that white men had come to Yooldil
(Ooldea) Gabbi, and, as the Baadu and Yooldil men had
often exchanged boys for initiation, a party set out from
Boundary Dam. Some of the older Baadu had already
mixed with and worked for and bartered their women to
he white kangaroo-hunters, and others on the plains and
lsewhere, and when this new way of living presented
tself to Dowie's own eyes, he picked up Koondhaing, who
nad drifted down as a young girl, and had attached her-
elf to a white man. With some of the emu men from
Ooldea and the Wirongi from Winbera (Wynbring) he
assed down to the West Coast through Ooldilbina and
Turia Waters into Bookabi. An endeavour to chop wood
t the command of Koondhaing's white husband lost
Dowie his eye, a splinter flying into it and destroying it.
o he ceased to chop wood and lived on the food his
oman brought from the white man's camp, beating her
hen she did not bring him enough.

The chief native courtesy between tribes, and the great-
st guarantee of friendship, is the interchange of boys for
nitiation, so when the Jinyila Minning (Eucla men) heard
nat a mob of Baadu (with whom they had already ex-
hanged boys) and Yooldil men and Wirongu had come
own to the coast, they invited them all to an initiation
eremony, although full of fear of the Northern men, for
ney were slippered men, and had caught and eaten many
Minning. However, the invitation was given and accepted,
nd members of the three groups went to Jinyila, amongst
nem being Dowie and Koondhaing.

Each visiting group hunts and finds its *dhoogoor*
(dreamtime) totem food while visiting but only to give it
o the owners of the country while they receive in ex-
nange the *dhoogoor* food of the country visited. Dowie
unted for mallee fowl, and although it was strange coun-

try to him, he always came home well laden, for then h
got the best of the meat foods of his hosts. While he wa
away on what proved to be his last hunt, a violent hail
storm, with thunder, lightning and great wind, came u
suddenly and quenched every fire in the camps.

Dowie had been tracking a fowl, already full of fear c
the magic of which strange country is always full and wit
a hundred other fears that beset the native when on terr
tory other than his own; and when lightning, thunder an
hail played about him and the hailstones beat upon hin
and he could see no reassuring smoke from the camp
and when he remembered the evil magic that was in a
the elements that were now having their way with hin
Dowie's brain snapped, and he became demented and a
the while the storm raged he rushed through the bus
screaming and crying, breaking down the obstacles tha
came in his way, but with no purpose or direction in h
wild rush. Hither and thither he ran, stumbling and fal
ing, but never ceasing his mad cries. Meantime the cam
was one confused mass of terror-stricken occupants, son
of the older men, the sorcerers of the group standing ov
in the open with spear or digging-stick, pointing to th
direction the storm should take, for "they had done n
wrong," others, lying face downwards, trying to cove
their bodies with sand, and women and children and me
huddling in groups, all crying or scolding at the top o
their voices. One of the Jinyila men, as soon as the storn
showed signs of abating, started off with a friend to whei
they had seen a shea-oak burning some days before, an
from this tree they brought back firesticks, which restore
the camp to comparative quiet.

Dowie's loud cries now began to be heard fitfully, b
neither his own people nor his hosts attached any undt
meaning to them other than the terror that a great stor
always inspires in the native. But night came on but st
the cries were heard. There was no friend there to bra
the awful darkness, and all through the night the ma
shouts sounded, until in the early dawn one of the old me
of his group said, "Dowie is mad." Then someone went
fetch him, but Dowie presented such a fearful spectacle-

covered with blood, and with his one eye fixed and glaring, his club held high, while he smashed at every obstacle —that he feared to approach him, and returned to the camp without him. They knew that the thunder magic had at last caught him, and no one in all the camps was sorry that the full power of the thunder had gone into him and left them untouched.

With the quiet hours that followed the storm the violence of his attack lessened, and eventually he was brought back by a relative subdued, but mad, for all to see. The ceremonies were hurried to a close, and the departure of the visitors speeded. There would certainly have been a fight, and perhaps killing, had not Dowie been so universally disliked, even by those who had met him for the first time. His own people did not sorrow for him, but they began to be in greater fear of him now, for his madness was homicidal, and, having got possession of a tomahawk, he made frequent wild rushes at Koondhaing and others, which, however, by degrees became less and less dangerous, for his dementia hastened the destruction of his remaining eye, and in his killing fits, all were now able to get out of his way. Koondhaing, the only one whom he could have compelled to serve him, now fled from him in his blindness.

Dowie never went back to Warrdarrgana. The groups separated after the initiation ceremonies were over, the Wirongu returning to Winbera and the Yooldil men to Ooldea by easy stages. The Baadu became disintegrated, small family groups stopping here and there, some going north where they had an orgy of human flesh after that long abstinence at Jinyila; others going eastward, where a fat baby was killed and eaten. Dowie shred in the latter, but his helping was a small one, for his impotence was manifest to all. He began to wander from the camp, and sometimes he was brought back, but more often he was left to wander in the hope that "finishing magic" would catch him. He roared with rage at times, lifting the sand in handfuls and throwing it about him, hoping that it might blind those who were near. Day after day he sat

alone in the cold and darkness, with only his malady fo
company. He was cunning enough to keep near white set
tlement and so received scraps of food now and then, b
his night wandering frightened the white folk, and thos
of his group who were near were compelled to take him t
their camps and to watch if he wandered. They soon tire
of this state of things, for there is no room in any cam
for useless adults, as all have to contribute their share t
the day's larder; and Dowie blind and demented coul
bring nothing in. Wherefore feed him? A sister dragge
him along at the end of a spear, when the camp shiftec
or when he had to be brought back from his wandering
Then his sister was given to a man and so his last pro
was taken.

In one of his insane plunges into the open he trample
and broke through the shelter and newly made grave o
a newly dead woman belonging to the Jinyila group, whei
the evil had first caught him; and the spirit of the dea
woman that still sat in the shelter became sulky and saic
"You must die in a strange country, too, for you hav
broken my shelter while my soul still sat there." And th
ghost of the dead woman followed Dowie to his shelte
and called him and coaxed him, crying and moaning s
that his daughter and blood-brother covered their heac
and ears that they might not hear the crying; and Dowi
followed the ghost which went round and round the shelte
in ever-widening circles, and he cried out, *"Maami
maamu!"*[1] as he went, stumbling and falling but ever ri
ing to the call of the ghost, which bade him follow to th
place where he was to die.

He periodically ran away, happily when the moon wa
full, so that I could generally manage to track him. H
was always glad to hear my voice, and full of romance a
to where he had been and what he had seen. Sometimes h
became entangled in the ropes and poles of my tent i
the darkness, and wakened me with his shrieks of terro
believing that devils were grappling with him. Then
would gently lead him back, wrap him in his blanke

---

[1] Ghost! Ghost!

stoke up his fire, and then warm his spirits with a drink of tea and a pipe of tobacco and talk him to sleep.

One day he wandered farther than ever, and even scrambled through a sheep-fence. I was five hours searching before I found him naked and exhausted in a clump of bushes. It was bright moonlight, but we were far from the camp. He could not again manage the fence, and Yalata and help were twenty-six miles away. With great difficulty I hoisted the poor old fellow on to my back, and, leaning for support upon my digging-stick, slowly carried him back, half-pushed, half-pulled him through the fence, and was trudging on when the recollection came to me that I was still an absent member of Perth's most exclusive women's club. My very chuckle at the thought made the load lighter, although it was late night when we reached camp, to find Jinjabulla anxiously groping his way to look for us. The close embrace of the two blood-brothers showed me that the long, long tabu was lifted, and that the end must be near. A few days later Dowie died.

With my scoop and digging-stick, I dug a grave seven feet by four, and five feet deep, and with two hanks of the tent-rope drew the body to the brink and lowered it in. Although I had spoken no word of the death to either Jinjabulla or Binilya, I could hear them wailing a mile away as I was filling in the grave.

While I was busy at my sad task, the grey shrike thrush suddenly came out of the unknown, and sitting on the edible gum-tree which shaded the grave, he poured forth his beautiful swelling notes into the air, where the Spirit of Dowie might be hovering; and there he sat and sang while I worked at the grave-digging—the only other mourner at the burial.

There crept into the camp one day another helpless derelict in desperate straits, Jeerabuldara, a woman of about 40 years of age, but a repulsive sight, dying of disease. I had known and tended her at Eucla, and she had walked 200 miles in her terrible condition to find me again. A kindly white dingo-trapper had given the poor creature a lift in his buggy over the last forty miles. She told me that she had been turned away from her own camp, and from all the others, because they could not bear her continuous screaming in pain. So she had come to Kabbarli. Nothing could be done in those last agonies, save to make her passing easier. Day and night for eight weeks, with all the little remedies at my disposal, I tended her, and for the most part she lay on the soft sand, with the warmth of fires about her, contented now save in the dreadful torment of her spasms of pain.

There came a night when she was sinking fast. I sat beside her, holding her hand in the the last hours. Suddenly she sat up in the firelight, searching my face with troubled eyes.

"Yaal yanning?" (Where am I going?) she cried, in fear.

I answered her question with another, very quietly. *"Kabbarli balya?"* (Is Kabbarli good?)

"Kabbarli balya," she answered.

"My Father is sitting down where you are going, Jeera," I told her, "and as soon as I let go your hand, my Father will catch hold of it. He will take care of you until I come."

"Your Father, Kabbarli? Then I shall be safe," she said, and settled down to sleep. I did not know she was dead until her hand grew cold in mine.

That is all the religion that I have ever spoke to them. They had my example, my love and devotion through the years. They trusted me, they were sure of me, and through me they believed and understood a little, I hope, of the All-Loving. My veneration for my own religion is too great for me to reduce it to pidgin English, and I have found it impossible to translate into any one of the 115 aboriginal languages with which I am acquainted. There are no words, no possible association of ideas, in which to convey our own beautiful prayers full of imagery and the passion of supplication. Many, many times have I tried to render the Lord's Prayer in many tongues, and failed utterly in all.

"Our Father" that is simply *"Mama ngalia!"*

"Which art in Heaven"—"Sky sit down"—*"Kalb nyinnin."*

"Hallowed be Thy Name"—"Big Name"—"*Inni bool-ga.*" So far so good. "Thy Kingdom Come"; any country that they did not know and belong to was the country of enemies and black magic. That would not do. "Thy will be done, on earth as it is in Heaven." Again I was baffled. "Give us this day our daily bread." That, of course, was easy. How many times have I heard it at my own tent-flap in the past thirty-five years—a quiet, lagging footstep, the soft insistent hail of *"Mai yua, Kabbarli?"* But "Forgive us our trespasses as we forgive them"—there is no forgiving, the trespasser is punished there and then, with all the revenge and hatred of which the avenger is capable, and the offence wiped out of memory, and very often the offender with it. "Lead us not into temptation" was equally impossible, and "deliverance from evil," with evil lurking in every shadow, and every misfortune, and death itself just magic.

I could have taught them the prayers easily enough, but I did not want parrot repetition, in which they excel. I tried to give them the only Christianity I knew they understood, which was nothing but loving-kindness, and an unfailing trust, and example, example always.

The one great fault in our attempts to Christianize the Australian aborigines lies in our violent snapping of their own traditional beliefs in our endeavours to replace these by teaching them the rudiments of that special creed to which we ourselves belong, or rather to the beliefs which we have reached in our present state of culture. We forget the many, many stages through which these beliefs have passed before they became the supposedly perfected creeds of the present day. We have not taken the lessons of the early Christians to heart. These good men, with characteristic prudence, merged as many of these pagan beliefs into the Christianity of those days as could be safely welded in accordance with the tenets of their religion. Like St. Paul, they were all things to all men, and by this practice made their way among the pagans they had gone forth to Christianize. So the magic of the heathen became the miracle of the early Christian, the sacred stones, mounds and caves of the primitive all over the world the holy shrines of to-day.

The animism and totemism of the aborigine are his religion, the initiation ceremonies his baptism of blood, and are there not sacred pagan places in our own Catholic Ireland? The waved lines, concentric circles, zigzag patterns, dotted rings found in Australian rock-drawings have their counterpart in the rock-drawings discovered in England, Scotland, Ireland, Brittany and elsewhere, and hold similar meanings. Snake and sun worship, totemic food laws, the return of the spirits of the dead to the places they knew in life—all of these show the similarity—between the religious beliefs of savage and civilized peoples, and the isolation of our Australian aborigines from the rest of mankind has but preserved intact the customs and beliefs which were common to the whole human race in its infancy. They cannot catch up with us in one generation.

The morning after Jeera's death, I carried her body—a pathetically light burden—into the shade and buried it, and went back to the others. But now my health began to go, and my strength with it for the time being. Those trying months of constant vigilance, the manual labour of digging rabbits out of the blazing sands, sometimes labouring for hours and then losing my quarry, the hardships and deprivations of a life for months at a time out of touch not only with the amenities, but devoid of the barest necessities, and now these two pitiful burials, had left me a wreck. My eyes were in a serious condition. I suffered from headaches and hopelessness, and could not sleep. I sent a message to Yalata, immediately followed by the arrival of a camel-buggy—one of the thousand kindnesses of my dear friends, the Murrays, during my voluntary exile—and into it I packed Jinjabulla and Binilya and my camp and theirs, and made back to Fowler's Bay.

But not for long. No sooner were my health and spirits normal than I was off again, this time to Yuria Water, some fifty miles north.

Chapter XIV

BY YURIA WATER

ɪɴ MANY OF THE MORE ARID PARTS OF AUSTRALIA THERE
ʀe permanent water-holes round which groups gathered
ɪɴ seasons of drought or for the performance of ceremonies
ᴡhich necessitate the presence of greater numbers than the
ᴜsual family groups, but there was no permanency in these
ɢatherings, and no other bond of unity than that of thirst
ᴀnd hunger or ceremonial observance, and when the
ᴅrought broke up, and ceremonies ended, what might have
ʙeen a community relapsed into its family groups, each
ɢroup wending its way by its appointed roads to its own
ᴡaters.

Yuria Water was one of these gathering places. It is a
ʟarge granite outcrop, situated some fifty or more miles
ɴorth of Fowler's Bay, South Australia, and is the only
ᴡatering-place in the district that may truly be called
ᴘermanent. Its waters never run dry.

All permanent native waters have legends attached to
ᴛhem, legends of the dream times, which go back to the
ᴅays when birds and animals possessed human attributes,
ᴏr were human beings, or were human groups of which the
ʙird or animal was the representative, or were magic
ᴀnimals and birds possessing the power of human speech.
ᴛhe natives cannot say that the "founders" of the various
ᴘermanent waters were altogether human, altogether birds
ᴏr beasts, or half-bird half-human, but the bird or animal
ɴame only is always given in the legend, never a human
ɴame.

135

In the legend of Yuria Gabbi (water), the *walja* (eag
hawk) was the water-bringer.[1]

All roads led to Yuria, which might be called "T
White Rock of the Star," for the red roads radiated fro
the gleaming white boulder like the points of the star. /
round the granite grew mallee and myall and sandalwoo
which provided the materials for weapons, the sandalwo
yielding the gum with which the flints were fastened in t
throwing-sticks. Many luscious roots and fruits were to
gathered at Yuria in their season, and there were certe
sure haunts of the silver-grey and white kangaroo and em
and the mallee hen, which made hunting easy. During cer
monial gatherings in Boogoomarl's time he sometimes ga
permission to good hunters among the visitors to go a
hunt the big game, or his own people hunted and fed t
visitors. The wombat went away with Boogoomarl, a
now there are no more at Yuria.

Each visiting group came along its own road, a
camped beside it during the ceremonies, and thus t
visiting groups kept apart from each other, each in l
own prescribed position. The groups from the north co
only camp on the *allinjerra warri* (north road), those fro
the east on the *koggararra warri,* those from the west
weelurarra warri. The south[2] men were the nearest re
tives of Boogoomarl, and he was not afraid of them,
they camped close by his own *ngoora.*

Many a grave and many a human oven were dug
Yuria Gabbi in those far-off days. When a fight end
fatally, the victim was cooked and shared, unless he w
an important or very old member of a group, then
would be carried back for burial to his own ground. T
bones of the cooked person were taken back to his o
waters, for each must be buried in his own country, or
spirit would find itself in a strange place and be ve
unhappy. When their little growing boys showed signs

[1] In a book that is not yet published I deal at greater len
with the strange legends of the aborigines. As an interest
example, however, I have included this legend as an Appendix
this book.

[2] *Yool'bareri.*

decline or weakness, a baby brother or sister was killed
and cooked, laid on its face upon the hot cinders, and the
fat of the baby was rubbed all over the weakling boy, and
he ate of its flesh in the morning and the evening until it
was all finished, and he had become strong again, and grew
fat and big. Boogoomarl's grave lay in a hollow some distance from Yuria Water, and on top of the grave his
eenma (Churinga, of Spencer and Gillen) which held the
spirit as well (for it showed the markings of the dreamtime
eaglehawk), was laid flat upon the grave. With the long,
long years during which it had lain there untouched and
ungreased it was but a shred of wood when I came upon
it in my wanderings over Yuria ground, but the markings
were still faintly discernible, though the grave had long
ago fallen below the level of the surrounding earth.
Dhoogoor times begin at the great-grandfather period.
Beyond "grandfather's time" is *dhoogoor,* or dreamtime.

The *walja*—eaglehawk—have now entire possession of
Yuria Gabbi, for its owners and their relations have long
since gone to the "spirit of Yuria Gabbi." Near the granite
is an old dead tree, shaped like a rough cross, and upon its
branches a *walja* is always to be seen sitting in the early
morning. Sometimes his wife sits beside him, but the dead
sandalwood has always one occupant upon its branches.
The rabbit has come to Yuria, and dug burrows close by
the water, and three of these burrows are near the dead
sandalwood, so *walja* waxes fat and lazy since food is now
to be got without hunting. And only the cutting flints[1] are
there to tell of the old-time residents or those who passed.

Little special spots were shown to me. Here Yoorbilya

---

[1] These, by their colour and nature, tell the direction from
which they were brought. There are black, grey, brown, red, yellow, white and many other coloured flints amongst them, but all
are roughly chipped palæoliths, the weapon of early man. The
upper millstones were rounded, water-worn stones, of which a
small part was chipped off to give better hold. A wooden scoop
(Thaggulu), a digging-stick *(Wanna)*, and bits of broken spear or
boomerang lie rotting here and there, and will soon be dust, like
their dead owners. It is only by finding palæoliths in quantities that
one discovers the old camp sites. All the flints were brought by the
visitors, for there is not flint formation in Yuria district.

hid herself when she ran away from her initiation, covering
her tracks so cleverly that her pursuing brothers failed to
see them; and it was not until she almost perished from
hunger and thirst that she gave herself up to dreadful punishment and death. There Ngain-miri had beaten his woman so badly that she lay for many days (?) unconscious
and none would go near her, fearing Ngain-miri's anger
until he himself went and beat her back to life again.

The many musical names of conspicuous spots, valleys
hills and plains round Yuria have long since ceased to be
applied to these places. Moonaba, Joorrba (the Yuria people had many of the beautiful Irish rolling "r's" in their
speech), Wajjina, Walbinya, Beerana, Yoolilbinning, all
these are little rock-holes or temporary camping places.
A rock-hole holding a few gallons after rain had been
named after Yanguna, the wife of the errant Koongara. It
is some five miles south of Yuria, and Yanguna had flown
thus far when she followed her husband. The coast hills
were visible from the granite, with a deep, wide, wooded
valley between, such a vale as that in which the Sons of
God might have buried Moses, a beautiful evergreen valley
of waving tree-tops, the swish of whose leaves in a light
soft wind is like the sound of the sea running up and down
a pebbly beach.

There are not many old trees round Yuria, there being
too many destructive agencies at work—white ants and
grubs in the roots, geckos, spiders, beetles and other wood
insects between the bark and the wood, as well as fire and
lightning.[1]

So long is it since the Yuria natives inhabited the district
that the paths and roads, hardened as they were by the
passing of many, many feet throughout the ages, have

---

[1] These old trees that have escaped destruction by fire or lightning are the chosen homes of colonies of the larger winged ants, the
butts near the ground becoming distorted and swollen to an enor-
mous size, and hollowed with cells. Trees and shrubs were valued
for what they produced. A species of sturdy thorn bush bears a
small white, five-leafed, fan-shaped flower of the rarest fragrance,
the flower turning into an edible fruit called *moon-yooin*, but there
is no name for the glorious perfume.

become runnels and miniature creeks in wet weather, emptying themselves upon little open spaces that fill with "button grass" after good rains. And always the blue hills are visible, and always the colours change on hill and valley; yet in the native dialect there is not one expression that would tend to show the native's admiration of his beautiful surroundings. With him tree and bush and plant were valued only for their uses, and were specially named, otherwise trees were *"jeelya,"*[1] shrubs *"warda-dhaddi,"* and flowers *"ngam-boom-barra."* His named colours were *maaru* (charcoal), *durdur* (soft red ochre), *mur-darba* (hard red ochre), *wina* (white pipeclay), *karrgu* (yellow pipeclay). He "bought" these colours from the visiting tribes, and paid in return the meeros, spears, clubs and other weapons, the wood of which was plentiful at Yuria.

In the days to come Yuria will have many farms, and the plough and the spade will cover the palæoliths that still dot the country round, and the spear-mark and the fire-place and the marks of Walja's knees on top of the granite will be broken and cut up for building, so that there will be no native history at all at Yuria, beyond its dialect, its few primitive implements and its soft-sounding place-names. There are no monuments to destroy, no evidences of an older civilization to be uprooted for the new. Nature's obstacles of tree and shrub are the only obstacles to be overcome. Given water, or planted with a corn needing little water, and Yuria in the years to come can be transformed into one of the loveliest districts in Australia. One cannot but regret the passing of its aboriginal inhabitants, and yet, given another thousand years' possession of the country, it would still be *"walja gabbi"* only.

In 1918, a bad breakdown in health brought me to Adelaide for medical attention. When the beautiful Mount Lofty Hills had restored my vigour, I was asked by the authorities to take charge of the Returned Soldiers Home at Myrtle Bank, which needed reorganizing. I readily consented, and the ensuing few months, spent in mothering

---

[1] *"Jeelya,"* corruption of "tree."

the returned wounded there, were, I think, happy ones. Although I knew comparatively little of matronship, as such, I did know a great deal of mothering, and for "wingies and stumpies" as they called themselves, the blind and the maimed who had given so much, all the service and devotion of which I was capable was only too little. These brave boys, crushed in those first years by the weight of their affliction, facing a changed world, were my first white patients.

Chapter XV

FIRST DAYS AT OOLDEA

THE CONSTRUCTION OF THE GREAT AUSTRALIAN TRANS-continental railway line was the end of the native groups north, east and west for many hundreds of miles.

For some years, stray natives had been coming in to civilization, following the tracks of the explorers, Warburton, Giles, Forrest and Maurice. They had looked upon the white men with awe—bearded ghosts with a fire magic that could send little stones into their vitals. "Windinjirri! Run! Run! Run!" they shouted when they beheld those fearsome spirit monsters, the camels, and scattered to the four winds, dropping infants and food in their desperate fright. Windinjirri was the camel's name among them ever after. One woman gave birth to a baby while fleeing from the camels, and no harm resulting, the baby was given the camel as its totem.

At first they lived in abject fear of the *"waijela"* as they learned to call the white man, but after they had talked with him, touched him, and even eaten his food, the fear changed to anger. This *waijela* was killing their meat leaving the bodies of the kangaroos to rot and taking only the skins. He was monopolizing the precious water-hole

for the hated camel, forbidding the rightful owners to approach. Then, little by little, or rapidly, according to local
circumstance, he assumed another, and though they did
not know it, more terrifying aspect. He became a source
of revenue to them, and he had come to stay. They were
always familiar with the traffic in women. That the *waijela*
knew the trade simplified matters.

So with the survey of the east-west railway began the
extermination of the central native groups, not by the
deliberate cruelty of the white man, but by the impossibility of amalgamating two such extreme races, Palæolithic
and 20th Century, and through the natives' ready, and even
eager, adoption of the white man's vices.

As the construction proceeded, with a great influx of
railway workers of all classes and nationalities, along 1,000
miles of previously uninhabited country, they straggled in
to the line in increasing numbers, drawn by the abundance
of food-stuffs and the new fire-drink[1] that made them
"head no good."[2] Each group through whose territory the
line was passing saw its waters used up, the trees and
bushes destroyed for firewood and fence-posts, and the
whole country turned to strange uses. In their eagerness
to "make the most of what they yet may spend," they did
not know that they were bringing about their own annihi-
lation. They thought that the train and its people would
go away, and leave them the things to play with.

Bush rumours travelled far and rumours magnify. From
over a thousand miles north and north-east and north-
west the groups came, amalgamating with the tribes they
met, or killing, on the way; smokes on the horizon telling
of their coming as they skirted the Plain, still afraid to
cross it for fear of the serpent devil. Eastward to Wynbring
and Tarcoola, westward to Karonie and Kalgoorlie, they
journeyed, but more frequently to the traditional camping-
ground on the north-north-eastern rim of Nullarbor, known
to the white man as the Ooldea Soak.

This is the legend of Ooldea Water.

---

[1] *Kala-gabbi.*
[2] *Kooramba.*

A long, long time ago in *dhoogoor* times, Karrbiji, a little marsupial, came from the west carrying a skin-bag of water on his back, and as he travelled east and east there was no water anywhere, and Karrbiji said, "I will put water in the ground so that the men can have good water always." He came to a shallow place like a dried lake. He went into the middle of it, and was just going to empty his water-bag when he heard someone whistling, and presently he saw Ngabbula, the spike-backed lizard, coming threateningly towards him, whistling. As he watched Ngabbula coming along, Karrbiji was very frightened, and he said, "I can only leave a little water here. I shall call this place 'Yooldil-Beena'—the swamp where I stood to pour out the water," and he tried to hide the water from Ngabbula by covering it with sand, but Ngabbula came along quickly and Karrbiji took up his skin-bag and ran and ran because Ngabbula would take all his water from him.

By and by he had run quite away from Ngabbula, and soon he came to a deep sandy hollow among high hills, and he said, "This is a good place, I can hide all the water here, and Ngabbula won't be able to find it. He can't smell water."

Karrbiji went down into the hollow and emptied all the water out of his bag into the sand. He covered up the water so that it could not be seen, and he said, "This is Yooldil Gabbi and I shall sit beside this water and watch my friends finding it and drinking it." Karrbiji was feeling very glad that he had put the water in such a safe place. All at once he again heard loud whistling and he looked and saw Ngabbula coming along towards him. Karrbiji was very frightened of Ngabbula, and he quickly picked up his empty skin-bag and ran away; but fast as he ran Ngabbula ran faster.

Now, Giniga, the native cat, and Kallaia, the emu, were great friends of Karrbiji, and they had watched him putting the water under the sand where they could easily scratch for it and drink cool nice water always, and they said, "We must not let Ngabbula kill our friend," and when Ngabbula chased Karrbiji, Kallaia and Giniga chased Ngabbula, and Ngabbula threw his spears at Giniga and made white spots all over Giniga where the spears had hit him. Giniga hit Ngabbula on the head with his club and now all Ngabbula's heads are flat, because of the great hit that Giniga had given Ngabbula.

Then they ran on again and Ngabbula began to get frightened and he stopped chasing Karrbiji, but Kallaia and Giniga said, "We must kill Ngabbula, and so stop him from killing Karrbiji," and a long, long way north they came up to Ngabbula, and Kallaia, the emu, speared him, and he died.

Then they went to Karrbiji's place, and Kallaia, Giniga and Karrbiji made a corroboree, and Beera, the moon, played with them, and by and by he took them up into the sky where they are now *kattang-ga* ("heads" stars). Karrbiji sat down beside his northern water, and when men came to drink of his water Karrbiji made them his friends and they said, "Karrbiji is our dreamtime totem," and all the men who lived beside that water were Karrbiji totem men. They made a stone emblem of Karrbiji and they put it in hiding near the water, and no woman has ever walked near the place where the stone emblem "sits down."[1]

The Kallaia men of Yooldil Gabbi (Ooldea Water) are now all dead and the last emu man died far, far away

---

[1] Kallaia, the emu, "sat down" beside Yooldil Water, and when the first men came there they saw Kallaia scraping the sand for the water, and they said "Kallaia shall be our totem. This is his water, but he has shown us how to get it." Giniga, the native cat, went between the two great waters, Karrbiji's Water and Kallaia's Water, and was always the friend of both. Ngabbula was killed north of Yooldil Gabbi, but he also had his water, and men came there and made him their totem, but Kallaia totem men always fought with Ngabbula totem men and ate them.

Karrbiji, after his work was done, went north, and "sat down" among the Mardudharra Wong-ga (*wonga-ga*—speech, talk), not far from the Arrunda, beside his friends Giniga, the native cat, and Kallaia, the emu. And he made plenty of water come to the Mardudharra men, and by and by the men said, "Karrbiji has brought his good water to us all. We will be brothers of Karrbiji." In a sacred spot near the water where Karrbiji sat down, there is a stone Karrbiji (phallic emblem) and here all the Karrbiji totem men gathered at certain times, and performed sacred and secret ceremonies to Karrbiji, the water-bringer.

from his water. Jinjabulla was his name, and he was very old and blind when he died.

Ngoora-bil-nga and his brothers, the last Karrbiji totem men, left their ancestral waters and reached Ooldea Water in 1928. They knew Yooldil Gabbi from the Karrbiji legend only. They left the Karrbiji emblem in its old place; but they must never again dance the Karrbiji corroboree, or "fire would come inside them, and burn their hearts out."

Nothing more than one of the many depressions in the never-ending sandhills that run waveringly from the Bight for nearly a thousand miles, Ooldea Water is one of Nature's miracles in barren Central Australia. No white man coming to this place would ever guess that that dreary hollow with the sand blowing across it was an unfailing fountain, yet a mere scratch and the magic waters welled in sight. Even in the cruellest droughts, it had never failed. Here the tribes gathered in their hundreds for initiation and other ceremonies. When all the waters had dried for countless miles, strangers came from afar, offering their flints and their food and their women for the right to share it and live. The emu men of Ooldea had lived and thrived on the renown of their water, watching daily for the light smokes that prepared them for the visit of friends or the heavy smokes that signalled the approach of an initiation party. On the steep hills about the soak, the visiting mobs camped, each in the direction of his own ground. Exchange of totem foods made for friendship—mallee-hen, emu and native cat—and there was always plenty of vegetable and meat food and edible grubs and sweet grasses. Today, in a flintless country cut flints in millions are to be found on the surrounding sandhills and about the site of the native wells, and human bones and skulls are evidence of these great gatherings of long ago.

In the building of the trans-continental line, the water of Ooldea passed out of its own people's hand for ever. Pipelines and pumping plants reduced it at the rate of 10,000 gallons a day for locomotives. The natives were forbidden the soak, and permitted to obtain their water only from taps at the siding. In a few years the engineering plant apparently perforated the blue clay bed, twenty feet below surface. Ooldea, already an orphan water, was a thing of the past. Old blind Jinjabulla, the last of its emu men, whom I had tended at my Winilya camp 100 miles south, was burned to death shortly after I left, in his shelter at Fowler's Bay.

When I came to Ooldea Siding in September, 1919, I found conditions difficult. Some hundreds of derelict natives had established their camps at the sidings, and travelled up and down the line, begging from the train at every stopping-place, a responsibility and a menace in that many of them were already ravaged by disease. There was no control of them. The few filthy rags they wore had been thrown to them in charity and decency. A policeman stationed at Tarcoola and another at Kalgoorlie dispensed rations, but Tarcoola and Kalgoorlie are nearly a thousand miles apart.

The newly formed railway settlements had not yet settled down after the chaos of the very recent construction. Aftermath of war was still in the air, and the unrest among the white communities was almost as distressing as the obvious degeneration of the black. I pitched my tent first on the south side of the line, where there was a small auxiliary railway for carting wood and a pipe-line, and a half-caste teamster camped with a motley crowd of natives. Such a diversity of creatures they were that, among remnants of all the south and central areas, and the east and west, I found an Arunta of the MacDonnell Ranges, a Dieri of Cooper's Creek, and even a Bibbulmun woman from Ravensthorpe in South-West Australia, the wife of this German half-caste, an unhappy creature, who had drifted with him through all the groups between.

Numbers of white derelicts and camp followers were still on the line, strike-agitators, foreigners, pilgrims of one kind and another, "jumping the rattler" between the capitals, or recklessly walking the whole thousand miles, throwing themselves on the hospitality of each succeeding camp of fettlers. Some of them cut the telegraph wires in the throes of thirst, or held up the passing trains in starvation, and most of them stirred up trouble wherever they went.

Prostitution of native women was rife, sought by the blacks and encouraged by the lowest whites, and many unfortunates had already reaped the wages of sin. When the first half-caste babies appeared, the wild mothers believed that they were the results of eating the white man's food, and rubbed them frantically with charcoal to restore their black health and colour, till often they died. Even when they had eaten the fruit of the White Man's Tree of Knowledge, they were not pleased, for they had seen piebald horses, and shared the primitive fear and distaste of the unusual.

News travels quickly by smoke signal, and soon my old Bight and Eucla and Fowler's Bay natives were arriving to sit down with me again. An epidemic of influenza broke out, and in tending and feeding the sick, making the acquaintance of strangers of the desert, clothing them for their first entry to civilization and smoothing out many a social problem, I was labouring every hour of the day when there came the disturbing news of an engine-drivers' strike. The six weekly expresses—three from the east and three from the west—were no longer to be expected, nor the weekly supply train. Moreover, there were rumours that the service would be discontinued for twelve months.

I had few stores in my modest larder for such an emergency, and no facility for obtaining them. Telegrams were useless. The strike was declared on October 30. The fettlers were paid off, and Port Augusta volunteers drove a train to take their women and children into Kalgoorlie. From these departing fettlers, I bought all the flour, tea and sugar available for my natives, and soon found myself the only white woman left on the line, alone at Ooldea save for the two pumpers at the Soak, three and a half miles north, the half-caste teamster and the various camps. Then I learned that a large gathering of natives had come in for an initiation ceremony at Tarcoola, and might be expected at any moment, but I had nothing to give them.

The next eight weeks were indeed difficult. I existed principally on porridge, and sometimes I would give that to my patients, and eke out the next day upon a meagre damper or a potato. Once I made a meal of an iguana that two friends, Nyirdain and Thangarri, caught and cooked for me. Worse than all, our water was limited. As it was no longer needed for the fettlers and the locomotives, the pumpers had ceased to work, and the daily supply had to be rationed scrupulously. I admit that I was on the verge of desperation, with no relief in sight, when there came the glad news that the strike was over. On December 3, by the first train through, I was able to purchase one loaf and a pound of butter. Never did I enjoy such a simple meal so heartily.

Following this harrowing experience, we were blessed for a time with the passing of six trains weekly, in an attempt to reduce the congestion in the railway sheds. The fettlers and their wives returned to their little homes so rudely deserted, and I was able to provide my natives with a Christmas dinner worthy of the name.

My own fare, day after day throughout the years, has always been so simple that to myself I am a miracle. I have consoled myself with the reflection that the simpler our needs, the nearer we are to the gods. A potato in the ashes, now and again a spoonful of rice that nine times out of ten was burned in my absence or absent-mindedness, occasionally the treat of a boiled egg, and always tea—my panacea for all ills—were the full extent of my culinary craft. Even so, after so many hardships, I determined that this Christmas should be a memorable one for us all, and passed the glad tidings of peace and goodwill and plenty *mai* along to the natives.

A big mob gathered about me in expectancy. Fires were quickly lighted and flour was given out for damper making.

"Who can make plum-pudding?"

"Injarradu pudding roongani." So Injarradu was given mutton fat and sugar, raisins and dates and prunes and figs, eggs and flour and carbonate of soda, and baking-powder, holus-bolus in a bath-tub, and duly produced a glutinous seething mass wrapped in one of Kabbarli's old night-dresses and boiled in a zinc bucket. After ten hours of cooking, the centre of the pudding was half-liquid, and its external appearance that of a diseased pancake, but it disappeared rapidly enough, with all the other good things. Each little family sat in such a position that it could not be overlooked by its neighbours while eating. It is an offence for a native to watch another eat, as evil magic might be conveyed to the food—which reminds one again of the old Irish saying, "I'd rather have six atin' wud me than wan lookin' at me." When the dinner had disappeared, they rubbed their stomachs and flicked their thumbs downward in satisfaction.

"*Jooni-bulga, Kabbarli*" (Full up, Grandmother!). They grinned and wended their way over the hill to the siding to beg for baccy on the Christmas trains.

My knowledge of the circumcised troups of Broome, the central west, the south-central west, the Plain and the Plain's edge was now to be concentrated on Ooldea, and the first years there were years of never-ceasing work. The endeavour to reconcile the old conditions with the new was pathetic. My first task, as the groups stepped over the threshold of civilization, was to set them at ease and clothe them, learn their names and their waters, explain the white man's laws and tell them of the resources and the dangers of this new age they had stumbled into. Most of the young people were orphans, their parents having been killed and eaten on the long journey down.

One morning, there arrived at my camp, naked and innocent, a contingent of twenty-six men, women and children from the Mann Ranges, nearly 1,000 miles northwest. They stood trembling and shrinking at their first sight of a white woman, but when I took the hand of the old man, and told him in his dialect that he could sit down without fear, the tension relaxed, and it became a question of clothing my new family.

Just as I was buttoning the men into their first trousers, a thunder came from the Plain. All rose in terror to watch, wild-eyed, the monster of Nullarbor, the *ganba* (snake) coming to devour them. I needed all my tact and wisdom to prevent their flight. Two of the women were heavily pregnant. One of these, in spite of the abundant food bestowed on her, later gave birth to a girl baby in a hidden spot in the bush, and killed and ate the little creature. The other woman reared her child for a year or so, and then, giving birth to a half-caste at some siding, took both along the line and disposed of them either by neglect or design. One of the men survived civilization for a brief period of seven months. He had been taken by the "magic snake" train to Kalgoorlie, where he contracted venereal disease, and returned to Ooldea only to die. On the day following his return we buried him near my tent, with Inyiga, a woman who, after killing her diseased half-caste child, succumbed to pneumonia.

I had eight pneumonia patients at one time, cared for them all, and cured most of them. Trudging many miles, day and night, across the sandhills between camps, my methods were my own, grandmotherly cough mixtures, massaging with oil, nourishing foods and much cheeriness, but most of all the Kabbarli magic that they believed I possessed.

The aborigines have little power of resistance. They may recover from accidents and illnesses that invariably prove fatal to the white man, but a neglected cold frequently becomes consumption, and measles and influenza and other inconsiderable ailments often take a terrible toll. Massaging magic, suction magic, kicking magic and other spells are brought into play by the sorcerers, but I found loving-kindness, simple remedies and common sense the most satisfactory treatment. When the end was inevitable, the patient just turned round on his earthen bed and quietly closed his eyes. Death comes as gently and easily to the aborigine as it does to all other creatures of the wild.

The Death and Burial of Jajjala

Jajjala died at his camp near Ooldea. He was aged scarcely 25 years, a quiet, gentle, naturally well-mannered boy, clever at weapon-making and carving, a good hunter and a generous giver.

He had taken kindly to the mission teaching, and sang and listened with pleasure to the mission songs sung and played by the teachers, but two days before his death, as I sat beside him, he signed to his brother to show "Kabbarli" the *ma-mu-a-bu* (evil magic stone), which he believed had been sent into him and was now causing his death. The object was a tiny piece of some hard substance, thin as the lead in a pencil, and only an inch long, and was said by his brother to have come out of Jajjala's breast, having been pointed at him by a Western[1] emu totem man.

Jajjala died in two beliefs: that the small object had poisoned him, and that he would meet Kabbarli's Great Father, who was waiting for him in the *dhoogoor* Linjiri—the cold west country where all the dingo totem men "sat down." And so he died quietly and peacefully.

Through the last hours of his illness one or other of his brothers sat beside him laying a hand upon his heart to feel the heart-beats as they became more and more feeble; the hand was not removed until the end.

His little group of relatives had sat in darkness, wailing loudly and continually: but when they heard the brother's sudden cry, all ran to his breakwind, and a great keen went up from every member of the group for their newly dead. The men threw themselves flat on the ground, the women flinging themselves on top. Out of the struggling mass of mourners a man or woman would rise, only to fall back again on the living heap or on the bare ground in wild abandon. Men rising would clasp one another, and embrace, crying and screaming. *"Juniyuril"* (bowels moving) is their sole expression of sorrow. Women would rise and lay their foot upon the head, back or shoulder of a father or brother of the dead youth, or would clasp one another and press their stomachs together to feel each other's sorrow. All the relations were naked. The deep voices of the men mingled with the clear, long-sustained note of the women, and wailing and movement, movement and wailing, went on until the violence of the first great grief was spent.

Moondoorr, who was the eldest brother of the dead man, and the oldest dingo totemist in the group, was already busily lighting fires east, west and south of the breakwind where the body lay. Four boomerang-shaped lines, the ends curving upwards, were painted in pipe-clay across Moon-

---

[1] *Weelurarra.*

doorr's chest. He was the only decorated man in the group, and, by virtue of his age, the leader and director of the burial ceremonies.

The body lay in darkness, though surrounded by the great fires, only myself sitting beside it. The younger brothers and two women, one of whom was Moondoorr's woman, who were to dig the grave detached themselves from the other mourners, and each taking a light fire-stick from one of the three fires, they came over in single file to the dead man's camp. They stood a moment while Moondoorr walked inside Jajjala's breakwind and took his stand by the ashes of his dead brother's fire, holding a torch in his right hand and some green branches in his left. Then the grave diggers ran around outside the breakwind three times, crying, "Pah! Pah! Pah!" at intervals, and waving their torches up and down with each cry.

Moondoorr waved torch and branches, and also joined in the cry. After the third circuit had been made, the brother next to Moondoorr led the file towards the spot on the northern slope of the hill where the grave was to be dug. As they ran, the men now and then gave the three short, sharp shouts of the dingo totem group, the two women crying, "Pah! Pah! Pah!" Fires were lighted at intervals along the track to the hill.

The grave was dug with wooden scoops to a depth of nearly seven feet in the sand, and a length and width of five and four feet respectively. Three fires were lighted east, west and north of the grave. From the sand that was flung out a semi-circular mound was made at the head of the grave, and branches and logs were gathered by the women and placed near by.

The grave-diggers then returned to camp and repeated their previous performance, giving the dingo totem shouts and filing around the breakwind, but this time they cried, "Gah! Gah! Gah!" as they circled round. Then they all went back to the place where the mourners sat, and the loud wailing was renewed. Presently one of the brothers came over and silently handed some string to me. I tied Jajjala's legs and thighs together and fastened his left arm to the upper arm, the hand resting against his chin. The right arm was left free and lay across the dead man's breast.

The body was then lifted and carried on the shoulders of the four brothers. Four girl children, little sisters of the dead man, stood nearest the breakwind, with torches in their hands, and behind these the women stood, all crying, "Gah! Gah! Gah!" without stopping. The fathers and mothers of the dead man, with other mourners, remained in the spot where the wailing took place, and did not attend the burial.

As soon as the men had started with their burden, the little girls followed first, with the men and women marching beside or behind them. All except the bearers had lighted torches.

When the grave was reached, Moondoorr and his woman, Nyanngauera, went into it, and covered the bottom thickly with green soft branches of the acacia. The body was then lowered and laid on its left side, the head to the west, the eyes looking towards the north, the free arm laid across the breast. All round and on top of the body green branches were pressed down by Moondoorr and his woman, and then the brother next in age and his woman took Moondoorr's place, and filled every space round and about the body with branches, as no earth must touch the body of a newly dead dingo man. Two more young brothers put the final branches on until the green covering was level with the surface. Then Moondoorr and his brother took the logs that had been placed in readiness, and laid them lengthwise on top of the grave, close together, and well stamped down. On top of the logs more branches were put, and the space round the grave was made clean and level, and the semi-circular mound at the head battened and smoothed into shape with wooden scoops. No one spoke above a whisper, as dingo men don't address the spirits of their dead.

The neat green grave, the mound of white sand at its head, and the clear swept patch around, stood out in the now lessening firelight. There was no moon, but a brilliant twinkling starlight. When all was finished the mourners returned in the same order, the men leading, and giving the three shouts of their totem, and as soon as the camp was reached all gave way to their sorrow. Again and again Ganbia, the mother of the dead man, would rise from the struggling, crying heap of men and women, and lifting her hands and face to the stars would utter a long, loud, heart-breaking cry and then throw herself flat on the ground, beating it with her hands. Both Ganbia and Nyeegala, her sister, are now bereft of every one of their young sons, hence their despairing grief. The burial ceremonies lasted about three or four hours. When grief had temporarily ex-hausted itself, the group gathered its few belongings and left the now "haunted" camp, coming over to the hill near my tent; and all through the dark hours men and women abandoned themselves to their grief. The men sat in little groups crying steadily, but Ganbia and Nyeegala and other mothers and elder sisters of the dead man ran keening and wailing along the valley, throwing themselves down on the stony ground in the excess of their sorrow. One long-sustained cry would go ringing and echoing into the distance, the cool, clear and dewy night sending it far amongst the sandhills.

When the sun rose they all went to the shea-oak hill southeast of the siding, and pitched camp there, the crying and wailing being resumed every night. All the relatives, men, women and children, cut off hair and beard, which was buried here and there near their camps. Jajjala's hair was not cut off after death.

The ceremony of laying or allaying the spirit[1] of the dead man took place a month later. The spirit of the newly dead always "walks about" during this interval between the actual burial ceremony and the final ceremony of bury-ing any evil magic the spirit might have left in the air or on the ground. In this interval, any personal friend or brother of the dead man who wishes to avenge his death performs certain rites. He goes alone to the newly made grave, carrying a spear and a *miro,* the latter grooved and carved with his own and his brother's totem marks on its concave side only. Lighting a fire beside the grave without smoke,

---

[1] *Ko-irdi.*

he places the *miro,* concave side up, close to the fire.
While the fire is burning he thrusts the spear into the
ground on either side of the fire, thereby announcing to his
dead brother that he wishes to avenge him. As the spear
is drawn out of the ground the spirit of the dead man
comes out of the body and sits on the spear-thrower. The
friend or brother now takes the *miro* in both hands and
presses it against his breast and stomach, holding it there
for a moment. When he takes it away the spirit enters
him, and he is not only able to find the murderer, but
the spirit helps him either to spear his enemy fatally or to
use the poison bone with equally fatal results.

The performance of this rite requires great bravery on
the part of the young man, for the fear of spirits is in-
eradicable in the aboriginal mind. If it happened that in
thrusting the spear into the ground it broke through meeting with some obstruction, the young man dropped it in
fear and terror, and, believing that the spirit was "sulky"
with him, rushed frantically and blindly away from the
grave until he dropped from fear and exhaustion. He
would never return to his camp, but would remain on the
ground where he had fallen and pine away and die. His
relatives would shift camp when the time for his return
had come and passed, their fear of the spirit compelling
them to leave him to his fate.

In the early afternoon of the final ceremony Jajjala's
brothers came with several other relatives who had that
morning arrived from the east, many young children being
amongst them. The near relatives of the dead man were
naked. Men and women held green branches of the water-
bearing mallee tree, but the men carried also a short club
covered with blood, with both ends shaved about one or
two inches from the point, the shaving and club ends being
left white and clean. Moondoorr led the large party to the
dead man's camp, all crying, "Gah! Gah! Gah!" the men
now and then giving the three shouts of the dead man's
totem group. When they reached the breakwind, Moondoorr and two brothers went inside the breakwind, and
stood by the ashes of the dead man's fire, while all the
others ran round in single file, waving their branches, and

crying, "Gah! Gah! Gah!" Moondoorr and his brothers cried, "Pah! Pah! Pah!" swished their branches and waved their bloodstained clubs as the groups filed out three times round the breakwind. Then all moved along the track to the graveside, crying, "Gah! Gah! Gah!" all the way.

They stood close round the grave, the men waving branches and clubs downwards towards the grave. Then all the children, boys and girls, were laid in turn across the grave on top of the logs and their bodies and faces were rubbed with sand from the ground or mound beside the grave, their mothers, fathers and elder brothers performing this rite. When all the children had gone through, or been passed through, this ceremony, the young initiated brothers of the dead man lay across the grave and their elder brothers rubbed their faces, legs and arms with sand. When this was done, all the branches were thrown on top of the grave, and Moondoorr and his brother, going to the grave's head, pulled the logs from the foot of the grave and set them upright at the head, the end of the logs resting beside or on Jajjala's head. The branches fell down into the hollow thus made, and then the decorated clubs were thrown in. With a scoop and hands the grave was partly filled in with sand, but the mound at the end was not touched. The clubs and the branches thrown upon the body took with them any evil that might be about camp or grave. The blood, the shavings and bared ends of the clubs all had reference to Jajjala's initiation into manhood, and the part his "blood brothers" had taken in it.

Jajjala was now *barndi mannainyi* (good smelling) and the children and young men who had lain across the body and were rubbed with sand would grow up strong and clean.

While the grave was being filled with sand the women and children sat crying near by. The men worked in silence, but when they joined the women and children all broke out into fresh wailing.

Chapter XVI

A REVOLUTION AND A ROYAL VISIT

IN FEBRUARY, 1920, I WAS APPOINTED A JUSTICE OF THE Peace for South Australia, being the only woman at that time to hold such a commission in two Australian States at the same time. A few weeks later I was asked by the authorities to arrange a display of aborigines at Ooldea, in honour of His Royal Highness the Prince of Wales, who was to pass on the east-west railway on his tour of Australia.

There was excitement in the tiny outposts whose residents did their utmost to provide a worthy welcome at every stopping-place of the royal train in its passage of the desert. But the exhilaration of anticipation, the constant discussion of plans and the high enthusiasm found its reaction among certain strife-makers in the camps. I have said that the unrest of war-time was still in the air. Many of these men were unemployed, and found mischief and a certain type of humour in an attempt to stir up a rebellious spirit among whites and blacks. Soap-box oratory appealed to the scamps among the civilized natives. They listened with interest and mimicked it well.

It had been a trying summer, with temperatures for days at a time touching 120 degrees, and unending dust-storms and disappointments. The meat-supply of dingo and rabbit had failed. Little food remained in my store, and that was reserved for the delicate children, the ailing women and the old. A new mob was expected for an initiation ceremony, and the camps were hungry and disgruntled. As I went quietly about my work for the sick, I could hear the banging of boomerangs and clubs and loud chatter of voices in the men's camps, those of Nabbari,

Dhanggool and Winnima, three of the most civilized, raised above the others. My only fear was for the safety of the new-comers. I never dreamed of anything so intense or so intelligent as an organized revolution among the world's best communists, but I waited patiently for enlightenment.

In the afternoon of April 26, I was enjoying a cup of tea when one of the women, Comajee, sitting outside my breakwind, called a word of warning and, to my surprise, ran and hid among the trees. Down through the sandhills came an angry mob of about eighty men, not walking in single file, native fashion, but in a body, not a woman or child among them. I could see that something was seriously amiss. For the first and the only time, I opened the break-wind and brought them in to sit round the fire before I would hear a word.

Ranging themselves according to their totems— kangaroo, dingo, eagle-hawk and mallee-hen—they took four fire-sticks from my fire, sign of blood-relationship. I then addressed myself to Nyimbana, one of the ring-leaders.

"Naa?"

"Black-fella king belong to this country!" shouted Nyimbana in English. "We don't want waijela[1] here! This *gabbi* our *gabbi!* Chasem waijela long way!"

I spoke quietly. *"Yaal wonga?"* (Who has said this?).

"I *wonga!"* said Nyimbana threateningly. "We don't want waijela king. We want our king."

When Nyimbana had finished, Waw-wuri spoke, in his own language.

"White-fellows have frightened all our game away and taken our waters. The Kooga will come back when the white men goes. This is our country. White-fellows took it away, and brought their sheep, bullocky and pony to hunt our totem meat away. You send paper to Gubmint and tell them we don't want white-fellow king. We want our own king and our own country!"

I remained silent for some minutes—silence in a tense moment terrifies the natives. Then:

---

[1] Corruption of "White-fellow."

"Who will you have for your king?" I asked.

"Nabbari our king."

Nabbari, a dingo man, was the most cunning in camp, an excellent beggar, one who ate his meat in secret and always had money to spend. It was his brother, Dhanggool, who had spoken. Nabbari was conspicuous in his absence.

"Sit down, *boggali*," I said. They sat down. "Kabbarli understands you now. This country belongs to blackfellow, and you want your own king. You all like Nabbari to be king?"

Cries of "No!", "Yes! Yes!", "I don't want him", "Nabbari king!"

"Which of you owns the water of Yuldil?" I demanded.

"Yuldil orphan water. People dead."

I turned to the kangaroo men. "Will the men of the grey kangaroo sit down under a dingo at this water?" I demanded. There was no answer.

Then Draijanu, one of the oldest and normally one of the gentlest, stood up and faced me angrily. "This country black-fellow," he shouted, in exact reproduction of the soap-box manner. "Waijela gubmint take dousand, dousand, dousand pound—close up five pounds! Wheat-amanning (taking wheat), potato-amanning, weijela stealem our country. We take back. Yuldil we take, Tarcoola we take, Port Augusta we take, plenty flour blackfellow all time. We kill waijela!" There were grunts and shouts of approval. The temper of the crowd was ugly. I knew that there were but fifteen white settlers, men and women, and no policeman nearer than Tarcoola, 170 miles away.

In their eyes was the fanaticism of initiation time, and nothing short of fire-arms and a posse of police would remove them from the district. It needed little encouragement to provoke serious trouble—a raid on the settlers' cottages for the food there, with burning and violence; for all that the hungry black-fellow can think of is food, and these men, I knew, were hungry.

"Nyimbana, fill the big billy," I said irrelevantly, and Nyimbana willingly went to do it, while a faint stir of

ulterior interest ran through the mob. All were watching
my face intently.

"Draijanu, Nyimbana, Dhanggool, Winnima there, hiding behind the bush, all *boggali*, you hear Kabbarli now,"
I said. "This young white king come this country, my
king, your king, too, father, grandfather, right back
dhoogoor. Big flour-giver. He tells all his white men to be
good to *waddi*. He tells me give you food." (They knew
that I had denied myself to give to them.) "When this
young king comes, he will give you plenty flour, sugar,
blankets, tobacco. But you don't want that. You want to
kill white-fella. When all the flour and tobacco that you
take from the white men are gone, who will give you more?
Who will plant wheat, who will build fences for nani and
bullocky? Suppose you make Nabbari king, all right.
Maadu queen. Our king's wife we call queen, so Maadu
your queen now."

They all knew Maadu. A shrill termagant, greedy and
bad-tempered and ultra-civilized with a great command of
black-fellow and white-fellow Billingsgate and no mercy,
Maadu was not popular. Their expressions changed. No
aborigine will recognize the authority of woman. I knew
that I had struck the right note, and went ahead in honeyed
accents, selecting from the little crowd the ones that hated
her most.

"When Maadu queen, Thanyarrie must build her breakwind. Dhanggool will bring her firewood. Maradhani will
hunt for rabbits and snakes and mallee-hen's eggs and
bring them to Maadu, and Nyimbana will carry her *gabbi*.
Everybody look out every day, plenty work, dig up
ground, put up fences, grow wheat, make flour, and all
will 'eat behind,' when Nabbari and Maadu have had
enough. Everything Maadu say, you do. That good for
Maadu when Nabbari king."

There was a general scowl, and I heard mutterings and
protests. The idea of raising the native woman to such a
status appalled them.

"No Maadu!" shouted Draijanu.

"Very well. King must have wife. You give Nabbari
one of your own women, whichever one he wants." There

was a loud outburst. I turned aside to hide a smile, then
"Nabbari king?" I asked again pleasantly. This time there
was silence. They were thinking it out.

"Boggali," I said lightly, "I think those white men make
mock of you. They not good white men. You see policemen take them away. Suppose black-fellow talk like that,
he take black-fellow away. You know Nabbari can be old
man only at Loondadhana—*gabbi,* his own water. Our
king *koojiba, koojiba, koojiba*—different—big king all
country, far over the sea. He 'lookout' after 'dark one
waddi,' 'white one Koonga,' just as Kabbarli 'looks out'
for you—"

Here the billy boiled. I brought out my tea-caddy, and
used up the supplies of the month, making it very strong
and very sweet. Everything edible in my little tent was
needed to go round.

"Ngooranga—go to camp now!" I said, "and don't let
the white-fellow make mock of my *boggali."*

They trailed out over the sand-hills and that night the
camps were quiet. Next morning I was sharing my porridge with Angalmurda at the pipe-line when Nyimban
passed by.

"Going to find some grubs for Queen Maadu?" I asked
mischievously.

"I don't find grubs for any woman," he grunted.

When the Prince of Wales passed by there was nobody
in all Australia to give him a more exciting or more heart-
felt welcome than the cannibal rebels of Ooldea.

The display was to take place on July 10 at Coo-
eighty-six miles West of Ooldea Siding, and I started o-
to collect the natives at the various sidings within a radi-
of two or three hundred miles. They numbered about 1:
in all, and I travelled the line with them in the goat-va-
of a goods train, the two distinct odours definitely co-
flicting. We brought supplies of wood and kangaroo-f-
and other materials to be used in a demonstration of nati-
arts—spear-making and spear-throwing, the manufactu-
of boomerangs, hair-spinning, flint-cutting, seed-sifting a-
other primitive aboriginal handicrafts. A bag painted w-
the crude effigy of a human body was the target for t-

spears, and the Yuala, a dance of magic, was selected as the most spectacular.

The natives now understood that the coming of the *King-King-Kadha* (the King's son) meant new blankets and pipes and unlimited food and tobacco, and they were all excited and eager to do their best. There were innumerable deputations to Kabbarli for advice and encouragement, and I knew not a moment's peace.

Cook Siding, in the very heart of Nullarbor, is bleak and cold in July, but boughs and branches had been freighted in by the trains for over 100 miles across the treeless plain to provide shelters and camp-fires. A temporary platform of railway sleepers was the royal dais. My presence was necessary throughout, there were so many mixtures, uncivilized, semi-civilized and fully civilized, the last named by far the worst to deal with. As there was nobody to feed and care for Janjinja, Jungura and Angalmurda, three of my oldest and most helpless charges at Ooldea, I decided to bring them with me. Two newly circumcised boys, who must on no account come in contact with the women, travelled with me in the goat-van. With the extreme courtesy and delicacy of feeling that I have always encountered when dealing with native men, they were good travelling companions, and always turned their backs to look out of the window while I was dressing.

I superintended the preparations with much anxiety. I was afraid that a sudden outburst of hostility, personal or tribal, at any moment would result in chaos. Carefully choosing my words, I explained the position to the natives in that, as they sent their sons to their people, so our great and good white King had sent his son to us all as we are his people. Some of them may have had the idea that the Prince of Wales was on his way to our initiation ceremony. Loyalty and enthusiasm ran high, and by keeping them busy, and stressing the importance of their best and brightest, I looked forward to success.

Cook Siding in 1920 was a long string of two-roomed houses, a bare little village of the Plain, with the two steel lines of the railway running east and west to infinity. I camped in my railway-van and busied myself with the arrangements of the fantastic decorations, and with rehearsals, a railway employee representing His Royal Highness on the dais, and I joining the dance and the singing by the way of exhortation. There were many small squabbles that might have become serious, but somehow trouble was avoided for the time being, and I spent the eve of the royal visit cleaning my goat-van, which was in a woeful condition. There was no broom available, but I managed to achieve some effect with newspapers and an old totem board with the sacred woman markings, and boiled a little water for my bath at an outside fire.

At last the great day dawned. Stripped to waist, decked in corroboree paint and feathers, the mobs quietly awaited the arrival of the royal train. Among the gifts they had made was a boomerang with a welcome inscribed in Central Australian dialect—*"Gan'ma nyinnin nyoora nongu; wan'yu ngalli-anning"* (Glad you here to see—come again).

At 3.45 the train stopped half a mile from the siding, and the Prince and suite alighted. H.R.H. first inspected a corps of returned soldiers under Captain Lindsay, and then took his place on the dais. The corroboree began with a native shout of welcome and the singing of the women, and in a few minutes the Yuala was in full swing.

Lord Claud Hamilton had been requested to present me to His Royal Highness, and when I made my curtsy, the Prince asked me to join him on the dais, where I explained both dance and dancers, both being cinematographed and cabled round the world. The Prince, deeply interested, then came down from the platform for a closer view of their native crafts, and tried his skill at flint-chipping and spear-throwing, to the delight of both natives and white residents.

Marburnong was the flint-chipper. Without any self-consciousness, he guided the Prince's hands in the art. *"Balya! balya!"* he grunted at last, giving praise, but not until it was due. Inyadura ground the seed splendidly, and blind Janjinja wove the string on her thigh like a seeing woman. Men, women and girls brought their gifts to the platform. "Thank you very much!" said His Royal Highness to each and every one, with a smile of appreciation

"*Dango berra-anujy,*" they gravely replied, while the women and children lowered their heads and hid their eyes. The two young initiates were brought forward, with their elaborate decorations and head-dresses, emu chignons, cockatoo feathers and paint. And the greetings ended with the booming of the big bull-roarer, the welcoming voice of the wilderness and its savage people. His Royal Highness remained some two and a half hours at Cook, intensely interested throughout, and as the royal train pulled out across the Plain, the Prince driving the engine, the natives gleefully turned to the feast of roast sheep and flour and tobacco that their King's son had given them.

Joonguru died that night. We buried her about a mile from the siding in the hard limestone of the Plain, her head towards the East. I returned to my goat-van, but not to sleep. So intense had been the anxiety of preparation and the excitements of the day that I could not rest. I remember that I sat up all night, trying to read *Our Mutual Friend* by the glimmer of a solitary candle I had bought from a fettler's wife.

Chapter XVII

INTRODUCTION TO CIVILIZATION

OOLDEA SIDING, IN FULL VIEW OF THE TRAINS, WITH many passers-by, was scarcely the place to accomplish good work for the natives, and it was not long before I transferred my camp to a sandy gully a mile north, on the track that led to the Soak, with a convenient tap in the pipe-line for water supply. There I built an enclosing breakwind of mulga bushes, and set up the little household that was to be my domain for 16 years.

There was an 8 × 10 tent for my living and sleeping;
an upturned tank which my natives and I rolled many
miles across the plains where it had lain stranded for
years, and which I utilized as library, storing there my
manuscripts and my books; a bough shed "storehouse"
that held everything from my daily provender and supplies
for the natives to their most sacred totem boards and
initiation properties, and a smaller bough shed on the
crest of the hill, with a ladder leading to its leafy roof, that
was my observatory. Here in the bright, still evenings, I
studied the skies, astronomy being an old love of mine,
and compiled my aboriginal mythologies, many of them
as poetic and beautiful as are the starry mythologies of the
Greeks. A prickle-bush—"dead finish," as old white prospectors call it—was my barred gateway at night-time, a
barrier for privacy passed by few in all my years of residence. Outside, the natives would come to await my attention, old friends sitting patiently beside the pipe-line, and
naked new-comers shyly flitting about among the trees
sometimes two days before they summoned courage to
approach this Kabbarli of whom they had heard so far
away. Innocent as children, they would make their fires on
the sand-hills and camp contentedly while I made or obtained from my store the clothing they needed before they
approached the siding, too soon to learn the art of
scavenging and selling all that was saleable.

They came to me from the Mann, the Gosse, the
Everard, the Petermann and the Musgrave Ranges, occasionally from as far away as Tanami, from Kalgoorlie
and Laverton in the West and Streaky Bay in the East,
and from far across the north-western borders of the
State. Sometimes two years on the journey, zigzagging in
the desert for food and water, they followed the tracks
of those who had come in before them, disintegrating, re-
uniting, mourning and rejoicing, and every moon fleeing
farther from their hereditary waters. At last the remnant
arrived on the rim of civilization outside my breakwind.
As each little group appeared, I was made aware of its
arrival by the wailing and shouting and spear-rattling of
the groups already there. Every native who steps over his

own boundary is in strange country and hostile. There are no groups in the lower centre now, only little mobs continually changing. The amalgamation of the totems is their frantic effort to coalesce. Each mob was more reckless and difficult to control than the preceding ones.

My duty, after the first friendly overtures of tea and damper, was to set them at ease, clothe them, and simply to explain the white man's ways and the white man's laws.

Sometimes a group of forty and more would arrive, families and vagrants following each other, finding their way across the desert, drinking water from the tree-roots, and setting fire to the bush as they came, hunting kangaroos and emus. They had fought and killed on the way south, and their only safety from each other now lay in their proximity to the white man. His novelties were also exciting. The first few weeks of their arrival were usually spent in ejaculating "Irr! Irr! Irr!" at the trains, the houses, the white women and babies, paper, pannikins, tea, sugar and all the mystifying belongings of the "waijela." Biscuits and cake and fruit were thrown to them from the train windows, while boomerangs and native weapons, and their importance in the landscape as subjects for photography, brought many a shilling and sixpence for them to spend, which they promptly did, without any knowledge of its value, and sometimes were wickedly imposed upon. The train was their undoing. Amongst the hundreds that "sat down" with me at Ooldea, there was not one that ever returned to his own waters and the natural bush life.

There was never a camp, through my thirty-five years of service, where my small mercies were not constantly in demand, but here they were called upon to the utmost. There were sometimes as many as 150 natives in the vicinity of Ooldea. Among them I found sufferers from venereal disease, debility, senility, ophthalmia, bone-magics; broken wrists, burns and spear-wounds, with the occasional outbreak of an epidemic of ring-worm, measles, sandy blight and pneumonia, which meant unending ministrations.

No more half-caste children were born in Ooldea from 1920 onward until the temporary cessation of my work there in 1934, nor was any half-caste ever begotten in any of my camps. I had my own way of dealing with the problem. Like Agag, I walked delicately, by quiet persuasion preventing the black girls from haunting the white men's huts, and by equally quiet persuasion, from a different angle, deterring the white men from association with them, an appeal from a woman of their own race and colour to play the game that never failed. Three half-castes had been begotten at Ooldea in the year before my arrival. One was taken to the German mission on the west coast of South Australia. The other two were destroyed in infancy, one of them thrown into a rabbit-burrow, and the other scalded to death by a billy-can of hot tea thrown over both mother and child by the black husband.

Never at any time in any Ooldea camp did I receive government rations for distribution or public charity of any kind. By this time the proceeds from my north-west station properties were wholly exhausted. I still possessed a freehold in Perth, a small residential estate overlooking the banks of the Swan River, upon which it was my intention to build a home for my declining years. So many times had I beguiled away the loneliness and hardship with architectural plans of that little home, envisioned its simple comforts, and worked and idled in its gardens— a dream that was not to be, for here I found a need far greater than my own. I ordered the sale of my freehold in my first year at Ooldea, with most of the personal possessions that remained to me, including my side-saddle and bridle—last relic of a happy past. When this money, too, was engulfed in the usual routine order of flour, tea, sugar, onions, medical supplies, dress material, shirts, trousers, and a little tobacco for comfort, I depended wholly upon the earnings of my pen, contributing to Australian and Home newspapers my scientific gleanings of general interest, the legends that had occupied years in the collection, and the human stories of the curious people to whom I have devoted my life.

When visitors and friends from interstate and oversea showed interest in my work, and wished to send donations, my expressed wishes were always for flour and tea and sugar and porridge. It sounded greedy, but it meant so much to see the little ones *jooni-bulga* (tummy-full).

Young and old, they were all my children, children always hungry, and my love for them was interpreted always in the litany of flour, tea and sugar. No sooner did I obtain supplies than they wanted to sit down and eat up the whole lot "quick-fella." It was of no avail rationing them weekly, for they would promptly devour the lot. My own living never cost me more than 10*s*. a week and sometimes considerably less. My own food-bill from December to March totalled £4.

The weekly stores obtained from the supply train consisted of two loaves of bread, toasted to the last stale fragment, one tin of powdered milk, a pound of rice or sago and a pound of butter when I could get it. A tin of jam lasted six weeks, and a pound of tea over two months. An occasional cabbage or lettuce was eaten leaf by leaf, day by day, and 12 lb. of dried potatoes lasted nearly four months. When friends sent me delicacies such as preserved fruits or tinned goods, gladly I exchanged them with the fettlers' wives for flour and tea and sugar. When times were lean, and the natives had only a small damper, they could be sure that I had an even smaller piece of toast. One day Gindigi misunderstood me, thought I was hungry, and brought me a billy-can of broken bread he had begged from train-passengers.

I discouraged this begging to the best of my ability, but it was of no avail. Occasionally trouble came of it. One day a mean-spirited tourist, after some twenty minutes' haggling over the customary "tchillin" for a boomerang, kept possession of the curio till the moment of the train's departure when, with a wink at his fellow-passengers, he climbed on board and threw the puzzled native a penny. The enraged boy hurled a stone that broke the carriage window, and the natives were warned from the line for a period, but they were flies about a honey-pot and it was impossible to keep them away. It was old Kattigiri, climbing a moving van eager to be first for the sheep's head and other butcher's offal, who fell beneath the train and was cut to pieces. On another occasion, old blind Janjinga, something of a wit and always lucky, struck a group of particularly generous travellers, who loaded her with good things. As there were still more gifts and givers coming, Janjinga ripped off the travesty of a frock that was her only garment, spread it on the ground, and stood with arms outstretched, wearing nothing but her smiles of gratitude. She could never understand why all her bene-factors suddenly disappeared, fleeing for the carriages to hide their blushes, while the siding rang with shouts of ribald laughter.

It was no unusual sight to see anything up to 100 of these cannibals, men, women and children, several of them but a week in civilization, climb aboard an empty truck and go off to an initiation ceremony farther up the line. I use the word cannibal advisedly. Every one of these central natives was a cannibal. Cannibalism had its local name from Kimberley to Eucla, and through all the unoccupied country east of it, and there were many grisly rites attached thereto. Human meat had always been their favorite food, and there were killing vendettas from time immemorial. In order that the killing should be safe, mur-derers' slippers or pads were made, emu-feathers twisted and twined together, bound to the foot with human hair, on which the natives walk and run as easily as a white man in running shoes, their feet leaving no track. Dusk and dawn were the customary hours for raiding a camp. Victims were shared according to the law. The older men ate the soft and virile parts, and the brain; swift runners were given the thighs; hands, arms or shoulders went to the best spear-throwers, and so on. Those who received skull, shoulder or arm kept the bones, which they pol-ished and rounded, strung on hair, and kept on their per-son, either as pointing-bones or magic pendants.

Every one of the natives whom I encountered on the east-west line had partaken of human meat, with the exception of Nyerdain, who told me it made him sick. They freely admitted their sharing of these repasts and enumerated those killed and eaten by naming the waters, and drawing a line with the big toe on the sand as they told over in gruesome memory the names they dared not mention.

My first words to them were always "No more man-meat." From the weekly supply train, I would procure part of a bullock or sheep and show them the game food areas, mallee-hen's eggs, rabbits and so on, that must be their meats now, with as many dampers as I could provide, and a drink of sweetened tea.

One morning very early, the news came that Nyan-ngauera had left the camp, taking a fire-stick and accompanied by her little girl. No one would follow her or help to track her. For twelve miles I followed the track unsuccessfully, but Nyan-ngauera doubled many times and gave birth to a child a mile west of my camp, where she killed and ate the baby, sharing the food with the little daughter. Later, with the help of her sons and grandsons, the spot was found, nothing to be seen there save the ashes of a fire. "The bones are under the fire," the boys told me, and digging with the digging-stick we came upon the broken skull, and one or two charred bones, which I later sent to the Adelaide Museum. A grown man will never avenge the death of his own child, nor will he, under any circumstances, share the meal.

The late Frank Hann, on a survey exploration, conferred the name of Mount Daisy Bates upon a height a little south of Mount Gosse. I discovered that it was the area of one of the worst groups of cannibals in the Centre.

Such were the men and women who came to my camp at Ooldea during the whole of my residence of sixteen years. Derelicts of the desert, these people knew no marriage laws nor traditional relationships, for their groups were scattered and mixed. All were potential enemies living in an armed truce, with fires lighted about their shelters to shield them from each other's magic, and spears standing ready. As each little group arrived, I was advised of the fact by wailing and shouting and rattling of spears. There were many family wrongs to be avenged. Thigh-spearing and duelling were frequent, but I knew the dangerous sounds and I casually asked them to tell me when they wanted to fight. They laughed, and said, "We will tell you, Kabbarli, if a spear is thrown to hit."

Certain duels, among brothers, I allowed, always standing by the duellists. When a slight wound was inflicted as punishment, a brother would invariably share food with the wounded, and the quarrel was forgotten. On one occasion, a boy ran away from his initiation and placed himself under the protection of the white settlement. He later aggravated the offence by taking a wife. He was caught by one of his initiated brothers, and a duel with clubs ensued. The kindly but mistaken intervention of the offender's white friends resulted in his being taken to a hospital, and that quarrel is neither avenged nor forgotten to this day.

Chapter XVIII

MY FRIENDS THE BIRDS

EVEN IN THE WILDERNESS OF OOLDEA, I COULD YET GATHer wealth to my mind, find solace in the solitude. Those who have passed the siding in the west-bound express know all there is to know—four little boxes of fettlers' huts in an arid monotony of sand-hills and low scrub on the rim of the desolate Plain, yet not so desolate, for I found my recompense.

I might be solitary, but I was never lonely.. The breakwind that enclosed my garden of sand was a veritable sanctuary of wild life. The birds and the quaint little burrowing creatures of earth were all my friends. They, too, came to Kabbarli.

I invariably rose at sunrise, when the days are at their most glorious, and the whole world is full of beauty and music and dreaming, waking from its slumbers under the mists. I made my toilet to a chorus of impatient twittering. It was a fastidious toilet, for throughout my life I have adhered to the simple but exact dictates of fashion as I left it, when Victoria was queen—a neat white blouse, stiff collar and ribbon tie, a dark skirt and coat, stout and serviceable, trim shoes and neat black stockings, a sailor hat and a fly-veil, and, for my excursions to the camps, always a dust-coat and a sunshade. Not until I was in meticulous order would I emerge from my tent, dressed for the day. My first greeting was for the birds.

In myriads they came to the water-vessels ranged about the camp, ready for the showers that never came and daily replenished from my water-cart. All through the fourteen hours of stark daylight there were visitors to my crumb-ground, for which I saved every morsel. To my 120 native dialects, I now added the language of the birds. I welcomed them in their own sweet accents, and knew them always by the aboriginal names that in many instances are a triumph in onomatopœia, infinitely more delightful than the stilted English or the sonorous Latin of the ornithologists.

With a flash of bright wings and an excited chattering they were all about me. Melga I loved above all. These little spotted and chestnut-backed ground-thrushes became tame chickens, and would walk sedately through my tent as I sat reading and writing, and preen themselves in the sunny doorway until Jaggal, the bicycle lizard, came along. Miril-yiril-yiri, the blue-backed, black-backed and white-backed wren, and Minning-minning his wife, were other cherished friends. These three separate wren families lived with me in perfect harmony, and allowed me to feed their babies with white ants and other writhing morsels. Nyiri-nyiri, the finches, came in hundreds drinking four kerosene-tins full on a hot day, and taking shelter beneath my stretcher. Burn-burn-boolala, the Central Australian bell-bird, was a gifted ventriloquist. He could stand on the top rung of my ladder observatory, and pretend to be miles away. Juin-juin, the babbler, was insulting. "Yaa! see! Yaa! see!" he would call in derision, then fall into a recital of cheap slander. Koora, the magpie with its liquid throaty warble of extraordinary beauty, was a rare and welcome visitor; Beelarl, the pied bell-magpie, with his wild double note and his quaint impatience with his greedy lazy son; and Koolardi, the butcher-bird, ringing the mellow changes, set me a task in musical exercises— while Gilgilga, the love-birds, and Baadl-baadl, many coloured parrots, all the smaller varieties of parrots furled their gay wings on the *"boggada"* mulga above me and made cave-shelters from the heat in the shaded sands. Geergin and other hawks I discouraged—they were a menace to the little birds; and I was not too friendly to Kogga-longo, the white cockatoo. Kalli-jirr-jirr, the blackbreasted plover, lays four speckled eggs in a small shallow place on the Plain with no cover—the speckles are its protection in that mottled limestone—but the fussiness of Kalli-jirr-jirr drew the attention of hawk and butcher-bird, and she would appear at my tent-flap wih a shriek, "Come and save my eggs!"

Weeloo, the curlew, had more than one group totem all to himself throughout Central Australia, but, saddened by his weight of legend, he was ever mournful, and there was that about the hard cold eye of Rool, the sacred kingfisher, that is fatal to the natives. A lone pilgrim, he wanders where he will, and is the Bird of Death.

My reptilian friends were many, and they, too, gave me joyful hours.

Among the fauna peculiar to the Australian region there are two species to which early observers applied the condemnatory term devil—the Tasmanian devil and the York or mountain devil. The Tasmanian devil well deserves the name bestowed upon him, but the little creature known as the mountain devil[1] is sadly misnamed, for it is

---

[1] It is known to the aborigines of the inland areas by three native names: *"Minjin,"* from the Murchison and Gascoyne rivers to the goldfields of Western Australia; *"Nai'ari"* on the borders of South Australia and Western Australia and Northern Australia's southern and south-western borders; and *"Ming-ari"* in the south central area and all around the edges of the Great Australian Bight. As *ming-ari* is the most widely known term amongst the central aborigines, I suggest its general adoption, especially as the name signifies its principal and only food, the little black ant. The word is derived from *minga*, small black ant; *ari*, many, belonging to, full of.

one of the most harmless as well as one of the most useful creatures in Australia.

Mountain devils occupy a unique position in aboriginal stellar mythology, for they have a part of the sky belonging to them into which no man may enter. In the dreamtimes of long ago, mountain devils were women who never mated with men; they travelled to and fro over their own territory, always accompanied by big and savage dogs which guarded their camps from all men.

Mountain devils travelled all about, and wherever they rested they left babies behind them, telling their children that they must never speak or whistle, or the men would hear them and come and take them away. At Kallaing, Jalgunba and Bilgin waters they sat down and left many babies in the spirit stones within or beside these waters, which are called *ming-ari* waters today.

By and by, when the mountain devils were changed into the little creatures we mortals know, they were still voiceless, because their mothers in the dreamtimes had never allowed them to speak or whistle; and no one has ever heard a sound coming from them. But they were given very keen eyes and their bodies were covered with thorns, so that they might keep their enemies away.[1]

Mountain devils are very tenacious of life, and will live a long time without food. Their chameleon-like quality of changing colour with their surroundings is interesting to watch. In times of great heat they dig themselves a little

---

[1] Little is known of the habits of the mountain devils. They have but one food—the pestiferous little black ant—and they will place themselves beside an ant "road" and eat and sleep and wake and eat throughout the day. The females are superior in intelligence to the males, and the adult female will scratch the surface of an ant bed if the supply ceases. They need special intelligence to cope with the intelligent black ant, and pit their wonderful eyesight against the ant's wonderful hearing. When a number of ants make an attempt to hunt them away from their nest, they raise themselves on all fours and swell their bodies roundly, thereby putting into business trim every thorn on their many-thorned hide. The ants crawl all over them, but only very rarely get a "nip" at the only vulnerable part—the inner lower lip. When this happens the mountain devil raises its head like a racehorse and shakes it viciously, but after a while settles down again to passive resistance.

tunnel four or five inches long, where they remain during
the heat-wave, but if exposed to the sun on a very hot day
they quickly turn a bright yellow, with a few red-brown
patches, and die. Excessive cold or cold rain will also kill
them. They loved to lie on my warm palm on a cool day.

By their aid I keep my tent from the pestiferous little
ant. They may consume anything up to a thousand ants
a day. I have sat beside them for an hour and counted
over a hundred ants caught and eaten by each one.

Jaggal, the bicycle lizard, was so self-confident that he
would sit upon me and catch flies as I lay dozing in the
excessive heat. These little creatures that live on insects
were a valuable asset. I have given Jaggal a live red-
backed spider, which he enjoyed, first tossing it about until he had subdued its fighting power.

The combat of these diminutive reptiles was an epic.
The males fought incessantly in mating-time. I often re-
flected that if the combatants could be enlarged to saurian
size, the battle would make the most interesting prehistoric
reptile film in the world. The manœuvring and circling for
the final rush, each aimed for the head and mouth of the
other, the false clash and parting and manœuvring again,
the beautiful war-colourings—red, yellow and blue of
bodies, black expanded throat, erected spikes along head
and neck, quick angry movements of their orange-and-
black banded tails, made these duels of the summer-time
a spectacle to behold. Once a Jaggal had its wide mouth
split and broken. I immersed it in warm Condy and fed
him with flies and applecrumbs and beetles until it healed.

These masterful little creatures were jealous of my
birds, and would take the centre of the stage to frighten
them away. Neither Jaggal nor Mingari has a voice, but
their intimidating appearance, their fearsome attitudes and
their angry darting were sufficient. Both go into deep
sandy tunnels in the cold season.

Moordin is a little night lizard, snake-like in its sin-
uosity, with a brown skin patterned in swastikas. Both he
and she would emerge from under deed-box and tucker-
box, and go hunting by candlelight. Moordin males fought
like Kilkenny cats, each with a firm grip on the other's

tail, which they ate if it broke off or they could bite it off, but they fed their young and acknowledged them, which Jaggal and Mingari never did. Beeburr, the grey gecko, was another camp-follower, clinging with his feet along the ridge-pole, wagging his cone-shaped tail and catching flies and eating tiny portions of apple, or a beetle which I would hold up to him, but perhaps the quaintest little friend of all was Wiru-Wiru, the dancing caterpillar, a small green species that in certain seasons miraculously appeared in myriads on the mulga. It was old Draijanu who showed me that, if you bob a little stick up and down in front of him, wiru-wiru dances to it, holding firmly to the branch and nodding his long horny head for as long as you care to stay. An army of these dancing on the low mulga was a quaintly funny sight.

I taught my natives to consider my breakwind a haven for all bush creatures. "Don't kill Jaggal," they would say, "that is Kabbarli's dog." If a *mingari* were found with a little piece of red wool hitched to his hind leg, they promptly removed the wool and sold him to me as a new one. I bought one of my *mingaris* six times over, and at the sixth time I looked hard at the little chap. "Here you are again, Mingari," I said. "Yalli-yalla always tells me you are somebody else, but Kabbarli knows." The wise cock of the bright black eye greatly embarrassed Yalli-yalla.

In all my walks through the bush, my tracks were followed by the natives. On one occasion I went twenty miles, to Bimbalong and back, the highest hill in the Ooldea Ranges, and that less than 100 feet. Dingoes howled on the sand-hills all night through, and sometimes came in to the siding and killed the fettlers' goats and fowls: the natives told me that before the days of the white man, they had been known to slink in to the breakwind shelters at Uldilgabbi and attack the babies. When blood-curdling howls made night hideous, a shot from my revolver restored the silence and peace of the starlight.

Children, white and black, have always been a passionate love of mine, and to the little ones of every camp I

was an ever-loving Kabbarli. Some were orphans whose
parents had been killed and eaten, and until they learned
to catch reptiles and rabbits to make propitiatory offer-
ings to the men of the groups, these led a life of semi-
starvation up and down the line, and became my particular care. Merrily we all played at "Here we go round
the mulberry bush," which I translated into their language,
which just fitted the lilting tune:

> Ngannana boggada yangula nyinninyi,
> Boggada boggada yangula nyinninyi,
> Ngannana boggada yangula nyinninyi,
> Ungundha nyeenga aaru.

Their aboriginal games were much the same as children's the world over, cat's cradle, hide-and-seek and
marbles being the most common. In cat's cradle games
with hair-string, they delighted to make turkey's feet and
kangaroo paws. Often have I joined in "Katta-gor-gor"—
"I spy" for the fun of watching the little things turn themselves into a log of wood, lying or standing, and looking
so exactly like the bark of a tree that only their own playmates would have a hope of finding them. Marbles were
played with the round kernel of the native peach and
other fruits.

I obtained many an ethnological item of value by watching the children playing. Taken to all the ceremonial
corroborees, and believed to be sleeping, they were unconsciously schooled into their place in the tribe. Almost
as soon as consciousness comes into the baby's life, he
begins his mastery of women, and most of the terms of
disrespect or reproach are couched in the feminine, extending to mother and grandmother. Yet the mother's
duty and love to her child, provided she has allowed it
to live, never cease. There is nothing greater in aboriginal
life than mother-love, a love of never-ending service.

A sad fatality occurred one day after a game between
two little girls. I had watched their play. Gooburdi lay
down under a bush to sleep, having first made sure that
there were no tracks. Presently from behind the mulga

came Boonggala, club in hand, watching lest she should
tread upon a stick, and so warn the sleeper. Raising the
club she struck Gooburdi just below the temple. Gooburdi
quivered and lay still, while Boonggala made believe to
light a fire, carefully dispersing the smoke. The game was
then repeated with Boonggala as victim. Gooburdi's blow
was stronger than she knew. Boonggala's ear and lower
temple were affected, and she sickened and died. Gooburdi sat by herself. My little gifts of sweet and biscuit
dropped out of her hands, and, mourning for her dead
mate, she herself lived only a few weeks after Boonggala's
death. Gooburdi's mother, Gowadhugu, a gentle, loving
creature, went away to Tarcoola, where the curse of
disease fell upon her, and she returned to die in my arms.
Her husband, Munra-ambula, showed more of real sadness and feeling at her death than I have ever encountered in an aborigine. We buried her near my camp, with
the wailing of the group. Because I had loved the gentle
soul so much, I gathered bush flowers and put them on
the grave. To my surprise, when Munra-ambula returned,
he too brought flowering branches and placed them on
the mound—a unique action, showing his love for his
little wife. Another of his women succumbed to civilization a few weeks later.

So the years passed, and tragedy stalked with them. By
the end of the great drought there were nine graves in
the sand-hills about my tent, Marradhanu and Inyiga we
had buried there in the first year, 1920. There was Joon-
dabil, an old man, who had for his wives successively
mother, daughter and granddaughter. And Gowadhugu
and Draijanu, who died from trying to mix the white
men's medicines, for he sent his daughter Weejala to all
the fettlers' camps to beg from them, and drank everything hot, from cough mixture to embrocations.

Chapter XIX

IN THE GRIP OF THE DROUGHT

As the years passed, I was more and more convinced that it was impossible to leave these people, to be deaf to their appeal for human kindliness, and of the hopelessness of any movement except one of help and comfort to the individual, and personal example. So savage and so simple, so much astray and so utterly helpless were they, that somehow they became my responsibility. All along the thousand miles of railway, there was no other sanctuary, no half-way house, as it were, between the white man's traffic and the native intelligence, five thousand years behind.

I did my utmost to arrest the contamination of civilization. Many times I sought facilities to pitch my camp at Boonja Water, sixty miles north, or at Wandunya Water, 140 miles north-west, where I might have retained many of the natives about me, to lead their own natural lives without clothing and without cunning. At Ooldea, not wishing to interfere in their associations with the white people, who were always kind to them, I could do no more than think for them with my "black-fellow's mind," dispensing my Kabbarli wisdom for what it was worth from the knowledge gained through half a lifetime, and my Kabbarli comfort to the very limit of my means and my physical endurance. I could not keep them long enough with me to hope for the humblest results, for even when I had plenty of food for weeks, they would still go on, up and down the line, wandering for any reason or no reason. *"Koorda kombinyi!"* (Heart getting hot!) they told me, and, clambering on the trains, would be off, in their nomad eagerness, to Tarcoola, to Kalgoorlie, to anywhere between.

Apart from the effects of malnutrition and epidemics and disease, death-magics and bone-pointing had always to be combated. When they believed that the bone of a dead man had been levelled at them by an enemy, they would lie down in their little beehive bough-shelters and refuse all food unless I took the magic out of their bodies. I was generally successful in my treatment of these purely psychological but often fatal illnesses, and would solemnly remove and burn and bury the offending magic, gaining a great reputation as *dhoogoor maamu ngangarli* (doctor of old-time witchcrafts).

Death quickly claimed the weakest of the new-comers. It is sad reading in my diary of the deaths of young people in those days at Ooldea. Some had been but a few months in touch with civilization when they turned aside from their groups to die, and those who had drifted away came back always with their numbers lessened.

There were a few who assimilated easily and survived amazingly. Nyan-ngauera, who came down with the first group in 1920, is still on the line, a case-hardened beggar. With another group from the border was one little girl, Nandari, about nine years old, of marked intelligence and spirit. After a few days she set off by herself on a goods train to Cook, where she changed for Kalgoorlie, and was so delighted with the adventure that she spent most of the next three years travelling up and down on every train that would give her a footing.

My work, as always, was confined to attendance upon the sick and feeble, the very old, and the very young. For the full-grown healthy male natives I had neither rations nor blankets. I encouraged their hunting-crafts and the subsistence upon their own foods, which were to the natives plentiful in good seasons, nourishing and suitable.

In that grey and apparently barren bush, where a white man would starve to death if left to his own resources, the healthy native could find food in plenty, mulga apples, acrid but sustaining, quandongs white and red, *kalgula* and *koolyoo,* a potato-bulb creeper trailing

over the jam-wood trees, fruits and roots and berries innumerable, edible grasses and beans. Kangaroo and emu
had become rare, but the white man's rabbit had taken
their places in myriads. There were mallee-hens in the
valleys and frogs in the swamps. A harrowing thing it is
to see them squeeze the water from these frogs and throw
them on the coals. Everything is eaten half raw, save the
rabbit, which is well cooked, and every bird and beast and
creeping thing provided a meal, including the banded ant-
eater and the barking lizard. Many of the interesting botanical and reptilian specimens that I have forwarded to
Australian and British Museums were rescued from anni-
hilation in the natives' evening fire. The only living thing
they conscientiously objected to devouring was the marsupial mole, that quaint little creature of the Nullarbor
Plain so seldom unearthed that the natives believe that it
never brought forth a baby. The *mawgu,* or witchetty, a
delicate white grub found in the roots and bark of mallee
and mulga and other trees, with its creamy almond flavour,
was the favourite dessert, but, though highly popular
throughout Central Australia, it was eaten sparingly by
the wise, who found it rich to biliousness.

As each group came and went, it left me the legacy of
its derelicts. Veiled from the flies—and the flies of the
Ooldea mallee in the summer season are a monotony of
torture—I threaded the camps in some miles of difficult
sand-walking, with the day's provisions slung over my
shoulder in calico bags. The frocks I distributed to the
new arrivals were frequently burned in a night from igno-
rance or carelessness at the sleeping fires. The food would
be shared with all who laid claim to it. There was a terrible instance of this in Ngannana, a woman who came
in with six or seven men, all naked and very primitive.
showed her how to make a damper and gave her a ba;
of flour. Next day I found her savagely mutilated, an
learned that the men who could lawfully do so had take:
all the food from her. When her great hulking son ha
come in to find none spared for him, his fiendish reveng
was the act of a wild animal.

When Mooja-Moojana's mob came in, some semi-civ

lized relatives showed the man a tomahawk. It was such a vast improvement upon his old flint *yabu* that Mooja felt its edge in wonderment, kept it near him as a treasure, and when his woman returned from the day's reptile hunting, almost cleft her buttock in two as an experiment. I confiscated the tomahawk, spent the morning refining the subtle differences between "waijela" and "waddi" in this regard, and threatened to call in waijela policeman *(baleejeman)* should he offend again.

In November, 1920, an epidemic of sandy blight broke out among the natives young and old, and in attending them I developed the complaint myself, a very painful granulation that resulted for a time in almost total blindness. The nearest doctor was at Port Augusta, 427 miles away. I dared not venture beyond the confines of my breakwind, but I could thread the well-known tracks within it without injury, and grope my way to the pipeline for water. By covering all the things I used most with white tops, I could manage to attend to my own needs, and to feed the natives, who daily brought me firewood. They were amazed at my affliction and looked upon me with "Physician, heal thyself!" written very legibly upon their faces, for was I not *ngangarli,* doctor of all magic healings? The recurrent attacks of this malady that I endured alone in the ensuing years were the most difficult periods I have known in all my life. Not once but several times, bending over my open fire-place to make my cup of tea, a smell of burning has been my only warning that my clothing was on fire. So grave and so prolonged was this first attack that I believed I was threatened with permanent blindness, and early in 1922 made the thousand-mile journey to Perth to consult an oculist. That was to be the last holiday—if holiday it can be called—for twelve years of so much increasing difficulty and disheartenment that, had it not been for the guiding light of my ideals of service, and my deep love and sympathy for the natives, I could never have lived them through.

Twenty-five, and sometimes forty at a time, would come to me for food and clothing. I loved to hear them chattering outside the breakwind, and if I had recently received a cheque for an article, there was plenty for all. There was an eclipse of the sun on September 21, 1922, and the natives ran to me in fear. They told me that the hand of *maamu-waddi,* the spirit man, was covering the earth while the sun and moon were *guri-arra*—husband and wife together. They believed that it presaged disaster, and clung to my clothing as I sat with my smoked glasses, quietly observing the phenomenon.

"You see," I said, "Kabbarli gathers the *maamu* to her, so that it cannot hurt you," and they were quietened.

Nevertheless, disaster was on our track.

In 1922, two bores put down at the Ooldea Soak resulted in an outgush of—salt water. It was the beginning of the end of this magical Yuldil-gabbi that had not failed its people in hundreds, perhaps thousands, of generations. In the few brief years since the white man's coming, 52 wells had been sunk, providing 70,000 gallons a week for the railway. The late H. Y. L. Brown, one of Australia's greatest pioneer geologists, had advised that no boring should be undertaken, but in continual experiment the blue clay-bed that formed a natural reservoir had apparently been pierced. The waters became brackish, injurious to the engines, unpleasant to the taste, and gradually seeped away. In October, 1926, Ooldea Soak closed down. The two towering tanks at the siding, from which supplies had been freighted up and down the line, were now useless. A number of 400-gallon tanks were installed at each siding and the fettlers' weekly supplies were brought from Kingoonya over 100 miles eastward, and Kalgoorlie, 600 miles west. The natives were forbidden access to these tanks and forced to procure their water direct from the Soak three and a half miles away, where one well even yet yields a limited supply. The valuable pumping machinery was guarded against them, and they had to beg for their water.

My only recourse was to carry my supplies a little over a mile across the steep sand-hills in two four-gallon kerosene tin buckets twice and sometimes three times a day. The unaccustomed strain on my arms led me to try all sorts of ruses. I first adopted the old English dairy-yoke method, but my digging-stick was unsteady and galled my shoulders. I tried a series of billy-cans and more frequent journeys, very wearying in the hot sun. I even emulated the natives by balancing a kerosene-bucket on my head with a *monguri*—a circular head-pad stuffed with hair and fur-string—but stumbling and stubbing my toes often sent the bucket flying, deluging me with my supply. I could never accomplish more than eight gallons in one journey, and when a thirsty native came out of the wilds and pointed to his lips, I would give him a gallon in one gulp. Restrictions were rigid. I was in honour bound to give my water only to the weak, and had to watch till they finished it, otherwise it would be wolfed by the others, or poured on their heads for coolness.

Water-carrying became more and more strenuous, and as I approached the allotted span I sent a request to the railway workshops at Port Augusta, asking that a little go-cart to carry two tins might be made. The cart duly arrived, in the nineteen-thirties, and the makers refused payment, a kindly gesture that I appreciated. The weight of water over the rough track twice broke the wheels in the heavy sand, and eventually iron wheels three inches wide had to be fitted. The empty cart was heavier than the full cart, a matter I have never been able to explain. To the very last week of my camp life I trundled this heavy load over the sand-hills, in the summer making three and sometimes four two-mile journeys in the day.

The failure of the water-supply coincided with the commencement of an eight-year's drought, perhaps the worst in South Australian history. Year after year, little or no rain fell upon the parched earth. The mighty Plain was but a shadow of the pale empty skies. Native foods dwindled and vanished, fruit and root and berry. All the rain-songs were in vain. Now and again *gabbi-jean* (the rain clouds) mercifully covered the sun for an hour or more, but before their promise could be fulfilled a barbed spear of wind would send them flying across the scattered hills of Wilba-thali, kicked up helter-skelter in the dreamtime by Wilba the Wallaby to confound and confuse his enemy. Raging winds scoured the plain, coming together with a clash in the visible combat of the whirlwinds, at which the women, in fear, threw handfuls of sand lest it should give them a baby. When they saw me whirled round and about in these opposing forces, with no evil results, "What big magic belongs to Kabbarli!" they said in wonderment.

Summer temperatures soared to 114 and 120 degrees for weeks, even months, at a time, culminating occasionally in a shade record of 126 degrees. At ordinary times the average rain in a year was less than four inches. I have often watched heavy curtains of rain falling from a cloud high up, to evaporate somewhere in the hot dry dome above the plain, and many a heavy oncoming storm mill away in the wind like the steam of a railway engine.

Sand-storms raged for hours at a time, and the world was darkened. When the heaviest gusts threatened to rob me of house and home, I clung frantically to the ridge-pole of my tent, pitting my slender weight against the strength of the elements, and when they abated crept in exhausted to find my stretcher, my table and everything else within covered in nearly a foot of sand. I built my breakwind up to twelve feet high in order to protect my tent in these ruinous winds and sweeping sands, but it was of little avail.

To write the newspaper articles that meant the sustenance of so many under such conditions was at times impossible. My first typewriter became a ruin. The second baffled me in that my hands were so painfully burnt and blistered with the heat and dryness, the wear and tear of constant water-carting, and my years of attendance on the sick that at one time I essayed the art of typewriting in seven finger-stalls and failed dismally.

Only once, when tying up poor Jajjala's arms and legs for burial at about 2 a.m., having had to hurry to their call, did I forget my gloves. A needle had run into a finger-nail that day, and into this tiny crevice poison entered. For about six months I kept up a counter-irritant by putting my finger into *boiling* water, healing and again blistering, and so saved finger and nail, so that to-day only the tiny needle-point route can be seen.

Many people, both in private and in the Press, have expressed amazement in that, in the heart of the Australian desert, I have always adhered rigidly to the incongruity of gloves. The explanation is simple. From the time of my first ministrations to the diseased—often repulsively diseased—natives of the north-west and the south-west of Australia, gloves have been my safety from contagion. I have kept dozens and dozens of the cheapest always ready, and immediately on my return from the anointment of sores, the bathing of eyes, and septic wounds, and other dangers of infection, both gloves and hands have been steeped in boiling water. It was a drastic safeguard but a very necessary one.

In 1925 Ardana brought in his contingent, all young men and all orphans, their fathers having been killed and eaten before their initiations. Mirnaambula came with the men, women and children in his group, and others from east and west with boys for the manhood ceremonies. The transcontinental and its traffic clashed noticeably with these age-old rites. The old men and brothers-in-law sometimes arrived by train, wearing felt hats and calling themselves *"dokkatur,"* with the initiation knife, whittled from a glass bottle, a pointing-bone, some hair-string and various magics carried in a "doctor's bag," an old suitcase they had picked up along the line. Their fees, in the matter of food, were high, and for the most part provided by me. Occasionally a boy, if closely associated with the white people, was completely overlooked, and I have seen an uninitiated boy daring to take a woman— a matter of instant death under the old law—actually daring to throw his spear into the camp, demanding that she should come to him, regardless of marriage restrictions, which no longer existed.

In the midst of Juginji's blood-drinking period, when he was isolated from his group between my camp and the Soak, some excitement carried those responsible for the boy's sustenance away to some other siding, all save his brother, Waueri. I accompanied Waueri to where the boy was hidden, and swung the big bull-roarer over the two, while Waueri tied a ligature about his arm, dripped the blood thereof into a wooden scoop, and gave it to the boy to drink. I then produced a big damper and a billy-can of tea and gave them to the famishing initiate. It was against the ceremonial law that the boy should have any other sustenance than human blood at this time, but there were none who dared to question Kabbarli.

I kept religiously to their prejudices and tabus, and was as mindful of their tribal restrictions as they were themselves. By attending their totemic and initiatory ceremonies I tried to keep alive in them the will to live.

The totem ceremonies had also degenerated. One early morning I was called out by the usual native signal—a sort of insect buzz. On the hill-top three natives were sitting beside the huge effigy of a snake and its eggs, the snake fastened to a straight pole, about ten or more feet between its curves. It was made with grass and covered with dirty rag in lieu of the human hair which is its proper decoration, with ochre, pipe-clay and birds' down; its eggs, two concentric circles, ochred and outlined with white down. The men scooped out a long narrow hole in the sand and we all stood round as two of them reverently lifted the snake and set it standing on the hill-top. Behind us the deserts of emptiness, and a mile south civilization and the railway. The female of the *jeedarra* was then produced, the woman emblem an ancient motor tyre, also on a pole, ochred, with its circles covered with down. I was asked to take charge of these sacred totems, and keep them from the women and children.

My funds were low indeed through these years of drought, and there is many a famine noted in my diaries, and few are the records of our feasts.

My success throughout all my camps in tending them in sickness was that I never attempted to alter their natural habits and environment. White medicines are not in harmony with the native constitution, and the white man's hospital only aggravates their sickness. Whenever a native feels ache or pain in any part of his body, he lights a tiny fire and keeps the affected part close to it. This course I followed, keeping them in their own little bush shelters under the branches they loved, with their own people about them. For diarrhœa I gave them the edible gum from the jamwood tree, and for constipation a cooked iguana liver and as much of the reptile as they cared to eat, and a few barbaric grubs, with other homely remedies for various complaints, and no patent medicines. Their own methods were crude. A tightened head-band allegedly alleviates headache, and a magic string would be expected to cure most other complaints. To amputate a limb they made a small bright fire and, placing the broken and probably gangrening wound on top, they burned off the leg or the arm, cauterizing the ragged bones still attaching to the upper limbs.

I had subsisted for a month on porridge . . . warm in the morning and made into a damper-cake for my supper—when two unexpected cheques endowed me with sudden wealth. One was for the amount of £7 10s. from an American university for a detailed survey of the "Sex Life of the Australian Aborigine." The other, from the University of Adelaide for a series of anthropological notes compiled, was a generous grant of £60. I immediately allotted £40 of this to the replenishing of native food supplies, and devoted the other £20 to recuperating my own health with a series of nourishing, well-cooked meals purchased with the consent of the Commonwealth Minister of Railways from the dining-saloon of the passenger expresses passing four days weekly. I enjoyed those luncheons and dinners with the appetite of a healthy child. I had not realized how hungry I was! The water-carrying was no longer a bugbear, nor the drought a dragging nightmare. For the first time in years Kabbarli herself was *jooni boolga*. The old joy of life and delight in service came back to me. I could wake to face the day with a sense of well-being and a full heart.

· The drought dragged on and on, until in 1929 the dry earth was tinder in the heat. Food was always scarce. The fruits and berries had shrivelled, the succulent *mawgu* grubs were no longer to be found in the withered mulga and mallee; mallee-hens and their nests had disappeared from the valleys, and the white man's rabbits were rarely to be seen on the sand-hills they had infested in their millions.

The natives travelled miles upon miles in their hunger hunting for lizards. It was Dhalberdiggin, the son of old Jinnawillie, one of the skeletons of the desert whom I was at the time endeavoring to restore to some human semblance with all the nourishing foods at my disposal, who brought upon us the menace of the bush fire—evil genius of the Australian drought. He had chased a long-tailed iguana into a low clump of bushes at Inmarna Siding, twenty-one miles east of Ooldea, and had begged or stolen a box of little fire-sticks from a fettler, ran the fire-stick (match) along its "magic board" and set fire to the bushes. Dhalberdiggin got his iguana, all ready cooked, sat down to eat it, and lazily watched the flames spreading and running all round the compass with the playboy winds.

The temperature was 110 degrees at Ooldea, and it was a few days before Christmas. We saw a great bank of smoke on the horizon, too low for the deceptive rain-clouds that always so dishearteningly passed us by. Next day came the sound of section cars moving rapidly up and down the line. Panic was afoot.

On Christmas Eve the fire was raging round us, a fury of smoke and flame on the nine hills and valleys of withered mulga that lay between the Soak and my Camp. The ganger came to warn me of its steady approach along the line, realizing that my little tent was in danger.

For myself I knew no trepidation, and my personal possessions were few. It was for my precious manuscripts that I feared, the thousand notes and note-books that represented a lifetime's ethnological work, accumulated through 35 years and thousands of miles of wandering.

On Christmas morning the camp was surrounded by a dense haze of smoke in heat so intense that I thought it was already too late. One spark meant ruin. It seemed that in a few hours my life's work would be nothing but a little heap of ash.

Yalli-yalla, Mooja-moojana, Mooloor and others who were watching the onrush came to my assistance. The sand was our salvation. In a frantic effort to save the manuscripts, we dug a pit six or seven feet deep and buried the boxes, covering them well. Then all hands set to work clearing every bush and tree on the sand-hills near until we had a fire-break of 50 yards and more. Luckily my years of gathering fuel in the neighbourhood of the camp had thinned the bush and made our frantic task a possibility. With perspiration streaming from our faces and the roaring and crackling of the fire-fiend coming steadily closer, in a fury of choking smoke and flying cinders, the natives and I worked grimly against hope and against time.

The fire burned itself out only after it had climbed the hill directly north of my tent, within a very few yards, and just on the edge of the railway line to the south. We had a thanksgiving Christmas feast when danger was over. Dhalberdiggin ran away with his woman along the line, and dared not approach Kabbarli for many moons, although I had no intention of reproaching him.

A little while later the drought broke, after nearly eight years. On a day of scorching wind, 106 degrees in my tent, I looked out upon the amazing phenomena of a great grey mountain range moving slowly towards me across the Plain, a cloud range hundreds of feet high with many clefts and crevices, blue and glacial or dark and cavernous, with outjutting ridges exactly like weather-worn granite. The contours never changed, although within it a ground wind whirled and spiralled horizontally. The natives were terrified at this moving mountain.

Suddenly it was upon us. The mountain became a whirling mass of sand and wind and rain. I clung to the ridge-pole and shut my eyes in a tornado of blowing canvas and lashing branches and corrugated iron, while the thousand and one water-vessels beat about me in pandemonium.

There followed many gusty showers, and after the parched years, a vision beautiful. Green returned to earth, and the world was filled with the sweet fresh scent of herbage. On my way from the Siding, I now gathered armfuls of flowers, the slight rare glories of that barren bush.

One day, in the heat of April, there appeared before my tent a naked woman and her crippled son. They had walked for a thousand miles, from Mingana Water, beyond the border of Western and South Australia, after having been abandoned in the desert by a mob of thirty wild cannibals. The woman's husband was dead, and her name was Nabbari. She had a firestick, a wooden scoop for digging out animal burrows, and her digging-stick, pointed at one end. Her boy, Marburning, carried a broken spear to help him in his lameness, but Nabbari had carried him most of the way.

Following the tracks, as the mobs had turned hither and thither in their search of food and water, so Nabbari zigzagged with the boy, often forced to retrace her steps. Four seasons, each with its own special foods, had passed in her travels and never in all that time was her firestick allowed to go out; for it is forbidden to women to make fires.

Day after day small fires were lighted to cook snakes and rabbits and bandicoots, lizards and iguanas, and every living thing that provided a mouthful. They killed many dingoes, and even their pet puppies, but the little boy clung lovingly to the last one. When meat supplies failed, they lived upon edible grubs and honey, ants, and beetles, and *wong-unu* (a grass), the seeds of which Nabbari masticated before she cooked them when there was no water. In the arid areas she found moisture in the mallee-roots, and shook the heavy dew-drops into her *weera* from the small bushes and herbage so that she and her boy throve on the long journey.

Many times they came upon the scene of old fights, or the hidden places of the manhood ceremonies—of these they would make a wide detour—or an orphan water where, after she had drunk of it, Nabbari would set up her death-wail. But the live tracks of her relatives who had preceded her were always visible, and from them she gained courage to follow.

From the spinifex country the two travellers passed

into the sand-hill country. Marburning was carried on
Nabbari's shoulders or across her back when his lameness became acute, and the dingo puppy hunted game,
and was taught by Nabbari to share his kill. Soon they
were in the wallaby country. Next they came upon the
swamps, dried up but still affording some kinds of food,
and here the tracks of her relations became fresher and
more numerous.

At last they came to the jumble of hills in the hollow
of which lies Yooldil-gabbi. From one of these Nabbari
looked down upon Gondiri—the Plain, the home of the
great man-eating snake—the transcontinental train. The
little white dots on the edge of the railway-line that were
the houses of the white settlers had no meaning for her,
but knowing that she was near the camp of her own people, she made a little fire and made a "woman smoke"
signal. Mindari and others at once went out in answer
to the smoke, and as Mindari was the first to reach her,
she became his woman. So that when Nabbari, naked,
with bright red seeds fastened in the strands of her hair
and hanging over her eyes like a fly-swish, came to my
camp over the last hill, Mindari was not far away. With
due regard for dramatic effect, he had sent Nabbari and
Marburning to make their own acquaintance with Kabbarli the Grandmother. No questions were asked on this
our first meeting. Food and clothing and a welcome were
given: the big happy sigh that came from Nabbari was
eloquent of the joy and relief at her long journey's
ending.

For the special observance of Christmas and Empire
Day I always managed to save up and shepherd supplies,
a more than usually generous provision of flour, tea, sugar
and jam, with all the new clothing I could muster. This
year big fires were made, and there was an Empire Day
procession of Kabbarli and the men, carrying bags of
flour on their heads, women and children following, in
new clothes, eager for the division of food, tobacco and
sweets.

Special invitations were issued some three weeks previously so that some crude idea of what "The Day"

meant to these aboriginal wards of the Empire might be grasped by them. It was not "Kijmij," for Christmas feasting comes in the summer. Then what was "Embai-de"? There were several among them who had acted in the native display for the Prince at Cook, and as during that short period there was "lashin's and lavin's" of food, and the young "King-King" by his gentle manner and bearing had made a lasting and vivid impression upon them, it was easy to connect His Royal Highness with Empire Day, and to bring its aboriginal meaning to them.

Empire Day was the King's feast day. White people and black people belonged to the King. A long time ago, when the white man first came over the sea to his country the King said to them: "Look out for all the *waddi, koong-ga* and *gijjara* (men, women and children) and tell them the King's law; they are not to kill the white men and the white men must not kill them." And the King said: "Good food and clothing to all the black people when they are hungry, and old, and sick!" By and by the King's people said: "We will have one Empire Day every winter-time, and on that day every man, woman and child must have bread and meat, as much as they can eat, so that they will always speak of that day as the King's Day, and a day of happy feasting." Our King sits down far away over the sea, but he tells all his Governments to look out for his black people on Empire Day, and so Kabbarli was going to do what her King wished, and everybody in camp was to come—not before sunrise—and make big fires, and Kabbarli would give them flour to make dampers and tea, and sugar as much as they all could eat and drink, because it was Empire Day, and the King would be glad to know that his black children had feasted.

During my sixteen years at Ooldea camp the procedure varied little. Long before sunrise the camp was astir, could hear the low murmur of voices in the still dawn air and long before I had prepared and eaten my breakfast and tidied my tent, the procession could be seen filing along the hill-top to the valley beside the tent, where the feast was to be held.

Each family made its own big fire for the damper- and tea-making, so that there were many fires, round each of which its own family group sat and waited. The young bachelors made a special little yard for themselves within which their fire was lighted and their billies tended by a young sister. The breakwind of bushes made their enclosure temporarily sacred from all except the children, who played unchecked round about all the fires.

Presently, to the cries of *"Kabbarli na! Kabbarli na!"*[1] I went to see if all my guests were assembled.

"Where's Karrimu?"

"At the camp."

"Call him, tell him to come and get Empire Day bread."

Ensued a great shouting across the valley. Karrimu is a widower, self-made. Before he arrived at my camp in 1921, he had clubbed his two women "for talking too much," distributed their cooked bodies, and then travelled with his son, daughter and nephew along the track blazed by his relatives into civilization.

Yagguin, a young initiate, being in Coventry through an unlawful love-affair, was not called, a sign or two from the men giving me the facts of his crime and isolation. Jajjala, another young bachelor, lay prostrate with the white man's disease, contracted somewhere along the line. Separate food was taken to these two solitary folk.

The dampers were made on bags, no dish being considered large enough for the occasion. All had their billies and pannikins in readiness, and presently all filed over to the flour bags beside the tent, and stood round while Kabbarli asked them to repeat after her, "God Save the King," which we all said three times. Then each representative of the families was given flour until they cried, *Alle jeega"* (Enough). The billies were already boiling, and hither and thither Kabbarli moved with her tins of tea and sugar under each arm. How they love sugar! And how they beamed when it was helped in cupfuls, and not with a spoon as on ordinary days. All dampers were

[1] "Hurrah, Grandma."

spread large and wide and thin over the ashes, so that
they should be cooked more quickly. Gaiety and laughter
and the play of children all about made the occasion a
special one. There was abundance for all, and so there
was no lingering thought among the women feasters that
this or that portion must be reserved for brother, son,
father or nephew. They ate, and ate in full content.

Forty pounds of meat, bought from the "sugar train,"
was kept hidden from the men, and was cooked *miri
mawgoon* (human meat) fashion. A deep hole had been
dug in my open fire-place, and a big fire made therein.
Cinders and ashes were partly raked out, and the meat
was placed in the hollow oven, covered with the hot
ashes and cinders, and left to cook for many hours. Little
groups of two and three women, and the only two old
men in camp, came along at frequent intervals and a huge
portion of steak or well-covered meat-bone was cut off
for them. This they devoured in quick secrecy. The men
and boys had been given bullocks' and sheep's heads, legs,
"arms" and entrails by the kindly sugar-train butcher
and so I had no qualms of conscience in reserving my
Empire Day meat gift for the women. Jam was bought
for the children and was also hidden from brothers, sons
and fathers. Only those who live and work for years in
native camps can realize the daily struggle of the poor
women for the barest subsistence. They come behind the
dogs in the economy of camp life.

Empire Day was made an all-day feast for every guest.
Breakfast continued till dinner-time, and dinner till supper, and there was even a surplus for next morning (unless it was eaten during the night). When the children
were filled—literally—we played an aboriginal adaptio
of "Here we go round the mulberry bush," which I ha
arranged "Not without some little fevers of the brow,"
as Mr. Sapsea remarked, being rather hampered by al
original linguistic deficiencies in translation. "Ring-a-ring
a-roses" followed, and then two of their own games—
sort of "hide-and-seek," and a drama of impersonatio
of women wailing for the newly dead. The guests sat en

joying that "satisfaction of fullness," and then, in their usual family group order, they filed back over the hill towards their *ngooras,* calling out *"Balya, Kabbarli"* as they passed.

Chapter XX

INTERLUDE

DURING ALL THESE YEARS THE CONSCIENCE OF AUS-tralia had been slowly but surely awakening to the tre-mendous human problem of the aborigines throughout the continent in the rapid dwindling of the native groups in all settled areas and the inevitable conflict as colo-nization extended. The desire of both State and Federal Governments was to preserve and foster the race, and to temper justice with mercy in their dealings with the native offender. The system of Police patrols, protectorships and Christian mission organizations could offer no satisfactory solution. Beyond the pale of civilization in the great Northern Territory there was unending trouble, cattle killing, tribal murder, the murder of white prospectors and the massacre of Japanese and Malay pearling-crews who entered new country. This was brought to a climax early in 1933 by the tragic death of Mounted-Constable McColl, speared by wild blacks at Woodah Island in the Gulf of Carpentaria in the course of a police patrol sent out to apprehend certain Caledon Bay natives guilty of the murder of five Japanese, who had beached their lug-gers on those sandy shores the year before.

Such was the revulsion of feeling of white colonists in the Territory at the death of the young policeman that a "punitive expedition" was mooted, an unfortunate choice of words reminiscent of past horrors that set the whole of Australia up in arms. Loath to sanction such a prim-

itive revenge, and eager to give the savage in his naked-
ness a fair and just hearing according to the tenets of
British law—of which he knows nothing—the Commonwealth Governor called for practical advice on the subject
from all qualified to give it, and was immediately inun-
dated with conflicting counsel from all corners of the
continent.

From my thirty-five years of closest association with
the natives, and a comprehensive knowledge of their
logics and their temperament, their actions and reactions
and such of their own laws as in their universal tribal
break-down still abide with them, I offered to travel to
the remote native stronghold of Arnhem Land to investi-
gate the matter in the same way in which I had investi-
gated similar matters in Western Australia, officially and
unofficially. In August, 1933, I received a telegram from
the Minister of the Interior inviting me to visit Canberra
immediately to place my plans for the proposed northward journey before Cabinet.

In haste I left my camp on the next passing express,
and two days later enjoyed the first bath worthy of the
name in twelve years—three quarts of water in a kerosene "bucket" cut lengthwise being the most luxurious
that Ooldea, at its best, could provide.

My return to civilization was tinctured with a deep
sadness. Gone were the Australia and the Australians I
had known. In my brief and hurried glimpse of the now
mature and graceful cities of Adelaide, Melbourne and
Sydney, quite alone and in my old-world garb, I felt a
stranger and an anachronism. New South Wales, that I
had seen in the making in the eighties, had a brand-new
and synthetic city to show me, a city strangely free of
the multitudes of men.

It was desired that I should meet all the Ministers in a
friendly informal way, and such was my meeting with
the Prime Minister himself. The Ministers knew the
results of my work, both in Western and South Australia
and their only fear was for the state of my health in an
undertaking arduous in the extreme. I assured them of
my abundant vigour and vitality, being fully restored t

both in the holiday joy of unaccustomed comfort and good living, but their decision, as duly reported to me, was that the difficulties of such a journey into the unexplored wilds of the north, the rigours of the climate of Arnhem Land, the complete isolation of that dark corner of the world, and the possible dangers—though I would have none of them—precluded them from the selection of a woman, and a woman of seventy-four years of age, to carry out the commission.

I returned to Ooldea regretfully, but thoroughly stimulated and rejuvenated in mind and body from that brief but happy sojourn in civilization, as the guest of the Commonwealth Government, with all the luxuries and amenities of life at my command, the pleasant intellectual association of my kind, so long denied me, and a ramble in flowery places.

Quietly I took up the old life, tending the poor fragments of black humanity around me, slipping back once more into the aboriginal languages after that brief but stimulating airing of my almost-forgotten English.

It was at the following Christmastide, following our modest celebration of the festive season, with giant dampers and billy cans full of good cheer, that I received news by telegraph, transmitted to the nearest station at Cook by the supply train and brought to my camp by the ganger, that my name was included in the New Year Honours. The Order of Commander of the British Empire had been conferred upon me. This recognition from our beloved Sovereign, coming as it did when my little camp was almost empty of provender and my heart of hope, has been the full reward of my life's service.

I often asked my natives why they did not return to their own waters.

"No," they said, "we can't go back, we would be talked and killed by the relations of those we killed and ate on our way to Ooldea Water. We are safe here with you, but if we went back we would kill and eat our own people again, and when those whose brothers and fathers we killed and ate came to Yooldil gabbi, you 'look out'

Kabbarli, and you don't let them eat us or let us eat them and so we can all sit down with you, but in our own country we must kill and eat our kind, *beegaringu*[1] always."[2]

When a white settlement was established in these areas, the natives from places far north, south, east and west came in to "sit down" beside the whites. In the rush and glamour of those days the natives reaped a dreadful harvest. As fast as their women died from prostitution they sought recruits to fill their places and made "wives" of their own mothers, sisters, daughters, and as these passed out in agony they fought amongst their own peoples for the women so that life became a dreadful nightmare of quarrelling, spearing, clubbing and every native kind of war.

Among all the little groups that have come to my Ooldea camp from that great Central Reserve during my sixteen years' residence there, there is the same promiscuity. A man is killed and eaten during their trek to Ooldea. His women and children are annexed by the eaters. Another man is killed and his women are again divided. The actual killer may try to keep the women, but the fights and the end are always the same and while the poor derelicts live, these conditions will more or less continue in their Great Reserves. They were able to live without tragedy at my camp, but there was no possibility of any straightening out of the promiscuous tangle they got into through the years. And so, to make their passing easy and keep them from conflict with the white man's laws, a benevolent watchfulness was the most one could give, plus one's own daily and hourly example which was so meticulously watched by them. Feed and help, encourage and advise, study and learn quietly while helping them always, without distinctions of persons or groups, bad or good.

[1] Faction fighting.
[2] A notorious instance of a group "running amok" was furnished by the so-called Laverton mob (Western Australia), in reality collection of derelicts from the fringes of civilization in the gold fields area.

The little factional mobs continued to come out of their hunting-grounds and put themselves under my protection and new little groups were hurried to me, so that I should be the first to greet and feed and restrain them from killing, and I was to sit down always with them.

When I mentioned my own passing, they talked with each other and later said that my grave[1] should be in the bough shed I had built—and near the spot where they had brought the snake effigy and raised it up for me to see. "The little shed belongs to Kabbarli," they said.

Chapter XXI

BIRTH AND DEATH, HEALING ARTS AND JUSTICE

MY HEALING AND MY KABBARLI WISDOM WERE THE source of all my power. My sympathy and magnetism as drew the evil out of their bodies, carefully placing it on the fire when my hands had closed upon it, and throwing the smoke of its passing away from the sufferer; my clairvoyance, practised on malingerers now and then; my thunder—and rain—and fire-magic—the knowledge and intuition supernatural in their eyes, helped me through the years in ministering to their ailments and in ministering a code of laws that was my own and theirs. My methods of treatment were derived from experience only, without regard to medical theory. Their systems, their foods, their native remedies, their simple ailments, their own ways and lives, their reaction to white things and people, white social housing and hospital conditions, all

[1] *Kardal.*

these had to be studied and met and made helpful with my very simple remedies.

I left them in their sandy and grassy beds and shelters, which they could change when they wished or when odours compelled them. I never submitted them to the ordeal of soap and hot water, but used clean olive oil to remove rank smells, but when their odour became objectionable to themselves, they anointed themselves with fresh fat from bird, animal, or reptile.

Only the commonest of our foods are good foods to them, for bowel disorders usually resulted from the white man's made dishes, but my own plain diet that kept me healthy made them healthy too. They loved a potato or onion or apple hot from the ashes, cooked a little, part eaten, and again cooked to prolong the pleasure. Their teeth were kept strong and clean through eating the ashes on their cooked foods. Their own varieties of vegetable and root foods were extensive, nutritive and sustaining when droughts limited meat foods, but they were essentially meat-eaters and however plentiful vegetable foods might be, their systems craved strong meat, and quarrels and killings took place.

The sick must be kept tranquil in familiar environment with their own people about them, seeing the dark faces, hearing the familiar speech, and lying on the only bed that their body can adjust itself upon. First and last their old ways were studied, and so these times of sickness were spent in tranquillity, and they passed over in peace among their kind. My old-fashioned remedies were particularly successful, making me rejoice that I was of Ireland, where bone-setters and wise women could cure all and sundry. My grandmother's cough-mixture, the simple recipe of six ingredients that she dispensed to coughing children for fifty miles round—honey, brandy, lemon, olive oil, powdered candy and vinegar (a tablespoon of each)—was most popular, and they desired to continue it long after the cough had gone.

When Gooburdi fell from her mother's lap into the small fire and both little arms were cruelly burned, carron oil and wadding and white bandages covered with stock ings to hide them from the white people's eyes were made delightful to Gooburdi in a playful way, as I made the tops of the stockings "pocketi" for biscuit or lollie or sweet cake after the dressings were over. I pretended that these came of themselves by Kabbarli's magic, if Gooburdi would let the little arms rest.

Dhambilgna's scald from groin to foot, when Dhalberdiggin emptied a billy-can of boiling tea over her and the half-caste child she brought back to Ooldea, was healed in three weeks, with three daily tendings in her sandy bed, Jinnaweeli and Nyeedura, her two mothers-in-law, and their dozen puppies filling the space left for the healer. When I cured Nyeedura's favourite dog of a broken leg, I received more gratitude and laudation from all camps than when I redeemed a human from the brink of death.

There was gratitude, though there is no native term for it. When I carried poor paralyzed Banyarda pickaback to my camp in a heat of 114 degrees that I might sleep beside her to calm her fear, two of the men saw me labouring. "We will carry her, Kabbarli," they said—the first and only time they had ever offered to relieve me of a human burden or to offer to carry a woman.

There was poor old Banyurda from Koorunda Water, deserted by her group at the siding, whom I carried pickaback to my camp and built her shelter near me, stilling her long wailing with little comforts. But no sooner was she recovered than the men of her group returned, the snake men of two wild and savage groups who had made their first entry into civilization clad in chaff-bags given them somewhere by white men, and they made her crawl to the siding when the trains came, or her pitiable appearance made her an excellent "draw."

As new mobs came from the great Government Reserves, and mingled with those already within civilization, there were many quarrels. I gave food to the victor to share with the vanquished and doctored the wounds. Soft white ash was an excellent substitute for boracic powder. Rool, the sacred kingfisher, gave Yirgilia a broken thigh—the tree from which he fell was only

Rool's agent. Yirgilia refused to sleep in splints. Day after day we played splinting and unsplinting, but I was able to persuade him to lie quietly, and adjusted the soft sand to the lie of the broken bones until we sent him to Albany, where he recovered.

The few cases of gonorrhœa they brought back with them from their treks along the Bight's edge and the civilized places were "healed by first intention." This disease shamed them, and no native sorcerer could cure them. It was visible to their kind, and to the women, and their anger rose and swelled and they beat their women in fury.

If I had a fortune to spend upon them, I should not build one hospital or sick-room, but would repeat and extend my services, keeping them in their own environment. As I myself would shrink from illness under a tree in the open, surrounded by dogs and unwashed humans, with grub and lizard to regale me, so does the wild native suffer in the white man's beds and bedding and discipline and confinement. My system was primitive. So were my patients. I allowed them to live their own lives and die happy.

Motherhood came easily to them. Birth had no pangs for the young mother. She knelt down, rested her buttocks on her heels, pressed her breath, and the baby was born, so easily, so free from pain or obstruction, that there was rarely a cry. The operation performed upon young girls and their initiation to womanhood at an early age tends to this painless birth. The baby is left on the ground, a mother or elder sister will snip the umbilical cord with her strong and long nails, leaving two or three inches on the navel. This is tied in a loose knot and flattened down, and later, when it dries and falls off, hair netted about it in a little ring, to be hung round the baby's neck and left there for weeks and months. It supposed to contain part of the child's spirit existence and when it withers off the baby has absorbed the spirit. The baby is massaged tenderly with soft ashes and charcoal. The pink new-born colour has often given me a pang, lest it should prove to be a dreaded half-caste until I learned that all new-born black babies are of that special pink colour.[1]

On the day of the child's birth, the mother may go on a journey of thirty miles if the group is travelling, but throughout this period she must keep apart from the men. She is not punished if she elects to kill and eat the baby, and returns to camp with or without it to resume her work of vegetable food-gathering. A fire is always made over the spot where the birth took place.

Early in my work I had frequent occasion to study and compare British justice with native law. My first studies were, happily for me, conducted amongst the two most law-abiding people in Western Australia—the Bibbulmun of the South-West and the Broome groups of the North-West. From the remnants of these I learned the admirable native system, based wholly on legend and tradition, and implicitly obeyed without authority or overlord laws, which made for morality and amity.

A man who killed another gave himself up to the dead man's brothers to be killed. Breaches of the totemic and marriage laws among the law-abiding groups were capital crimes. Theft had been unknown, because individual ownership was unknown, and there was never transgression of group boundaries.

In all offences, whether against the white man or the black, I followed their own simple systems throughout, reconciling them with the British according to their lights. Such became their decadence, as civilization spread, that during the last thirty years, among the lawless central groups, I have had to rely more and more upon a clear, straight interpretation of "King's law," especially where white and black philosophies are at variance, in murder, robbery and the killing of cattle and sheep. A subject

---

[1] On two occasions, in 1920 and 1934, I found white-haired children among a group that came to me out of the wild areas on the border of Central and Western Australia, of different parentage, yet having an ashy-grey skin, straight features, thin lips, European head, and white straight hair. I wondered if they might provide an elucidation of the mystery of the lost explorer Leichardt and his men.

would be discussed sometimes for weeks and months before they fully comprehended that they must no longer take the law into their hands. When I had an object lesson among white wrong-doers to show them, the simplicity of these "King's laws" and their impartiality were brought home to the wildest and most primitive among them.

The only system that can be followed today is the British system, with a sprinkling of such few native rules as have survived our settlement in Australia. By careful inquiry into all complaints and misdemeanours, and by fair play always, I have been able to keep the groups, with which I have contacted through thirty-five years, quiet and law-abiding. There has been no tragedy in my camps.

Cruelty to women has been age-long, and this, too, had to be met by our own British law, suiting the punishment to the native's conception of punishment, and thereby stopping the practice of breaking wrist-bone or ankle. Sending them "to Coventry" was my chief punishment, and its results would interest the psychologists of today if they studied its gradual but certain effect on the sinner. And my heart always rejoices when I think that there were no half-castes begotten in any of my camps.

As I saw the effect, year after year, of my dealing out of the King's laws to these primitive, lawless creatures, I began to think of the wonderful easing of their inevitable passing, that would follow the appointment of a King's High Commissioner over these declining people, from north to south, from east to west, of this continent with no limitation to his discretionary powers, no political or religious dominance to shadow his authority, the co-ordination of all missions, settlements and institutions under such a man, and his benevolent supervision of all the derelicts. Their very primitiveness claims our highest.

This thought and hope inspired all my service. I have voiced the desire to many a Minister and many a Ministry, and perhaps before I pass on may see the appoint-

ment of such a universal friend. It is to me the one broad
solution of the whole sorrowful problem.

Amongst these decadents to-day no intricate anthropological study of social laws is necessary, only the administration of British rule, founded on our highest and best
traditions. Anthropology can be given its due place,
though in the breakdown of all their old tribal laws
through contact with civilization it is scarcely necessary.
What they need most is the governance and fatherhood
of the Empire-makers, men of the sterling British type
that brought India and Africa into our Commonwealth
of Nations—a Havelock, a Raffles, a Lugard, a Nichol-
son, a Lawrence of Arabia.

Epilogue

LEAVE-TAKING

I HAD THOUGHT TO SPEND MY LAST DAYS AT OOLDEA, earning my modest living with my pen, ministering, as ever, to those who might need me, faithful to the end of my life's loyalties. But at last a day came that brought me hope, hope of reducing all my hoarded manuscripts to some sort of order, and an opportunity, not of renouncing my life's devotion, but of consummating it.

For the great work to which, in the enthusiasm of early days, I had set my hand—the interpretation of the mind and soul of the Australian aborigine—was as yet untouched.

The ceaseless garnering of thirty-five years of intensive study had been jealously guarded at great personal cost and trouble through all my wanderings. My voluminous notes had been scribbled anyhow and anywhere, on white paper and brown, diaries and notebooks and fragments, illegible and unintelligible to any save me, packed into any receptacle that would hold them in my eight by ten tent, where they became inextricably mixed and were in constant peril of destruction. Now and again I had taken a bulging bundle, trying to reduce it to lucidity, but with the hot winds and sandstorms and the constant demands upon my time and my mercies by the pitiable specimens of humanity about me had only made the ethnological confusion worse confounded.

I had passed the allotted span of life by five long years. My step was as light and my heart as gay as they had been in youth, but I could no longer shut my eyes to the fact that if I were to accomplish my work for Australia and its lost people, I must lose no time.

206

The hope was qualified with regret, for now I must bid farewell to that little tent home patched with a hundred patches, ragged and empty and devoid of comfort, yet so full of loving memories; Kabbarli must take leave of her grandchildren.

The last few days were unforgettable. I had kept my departure a secret, yet in some mysterious way they sensed that something was toward. "Kabbarli!" came the call all day long at the breakwind, to make sure that I was still there, and now when I went up to the station for my mail the children would be all about me, singing the rain-song that I had brought to them from the far North-West:

Ngoona weeli-weeli burniji ngoona—

waving their branches to the plaintive little tune, song and tune coming from the far-off Ashburton areas. Time and again I sat with them on the Kooli hill near my tent, the hill where we had so often been together, scanning the horizon for the smoke of the fires at Boonja Water many miles away, waiting for the coming of the new groups from the thousands of miles north and north-west, doubling and re-doubling in their tracks for weeks and months, fighting and killing and eating on the way.

One day came the news that old Gooyama was lying ill at a camp five miles away, wanting to see Kabbarli. With the extraordinary prevision of the dying, he had come 100 miles from Fowler's Bay in a buggy with Yarrijuna and Stuttering Yarri. He was past food, but it was a pleasure to give some to those who were with him, and near by I found Ardana, frantic in the belief that his old enemy Jinnabullain had sent magic into his liver. This necessitated a second journey for medicine and magic healing—a twenty-mile walk for me all told—and before I left, Ardana was on his way to fight Jinnabullain by magic or spear.

Old Jinnawillie and Nganamana were lying together in another camp. I bandaged Nganamana's bitten breast, but Jinnawillie, so little and so fierce, was obviously nearing her end. Her hand and tongue were against everyone but her giant son Dhalberdiggin, for whom she would fight, beg, steal and kill, and for whom she starved her tiny body throughout his life. I think that her poor face changed and softened only for her son and me. I told her that my Father would look out for her in the country she was passing to, but, as she had room only for her son in her life, she feared. *"Kabbarli mallingga yanning!"* (Grandmother will come soon after you) I comforted Jinnawillie. Not very long after I learned that she was dead.

I had managed for sixteen years to secrete from keen native eyes the totem board of my own initiation and the sacred *eenma* of the dead groups that I had been entrusted to keep "alive." I now brought these from their hiding-place to pack them for transport, and called the men to help me. We sat down at each side of the *eenma,* out of sight and hearing of the women. As I turned one long board face upwards, Yalli-yalla revently touched it, then placed his hand upon my breast and then on his own. It was the curlew totem of his fathers that he had never seen since his own young manhood. He knew that the spirit of totems was within my breast.

Thirteen men came to help me with the manuscripts cases and boxes, seven heavy loads for us to carry by means of rope handles to the siding. I had always strictly reserved one 40-gallon tank of rain-water, to be broached only in my own extremity. We anticipated Empire Day and used it up in a farewell feast. I told them that they might make their dampers at my fire, for the first and last time, for I must leave them. The warm tent and the breakwind must be kept sacred to the memory of Kabbarli. Her magic and kindness would dwell there for them always.

Jubilee day found us early awake. We cleared the tent of its scanty furnishings, and these, with my beloved set of Dickens, solace of so many lonely hours, I sent to the home of a little white girl at the Siding. My grandsons squatted on the slope above me, and I proceeded to shed my working clothes, pushing the garments piecemeal beneath the closed tent flap for eager black hands to grasp. When I emerged it was to find Yalli-yalla glorious in my white dust-coat and Gindigi resplendent in a mackintosh. Being my oldest grandsons, they had confiscated the most dashing raiment, and proudly they strutted in Kabbarli's magic garb. The others divided the shirts and skirts to give to their women.

Crooning and crying, they gathered round me on the slope of the sand-hill. A few strangers were among them, new arrivals from the desert, who had come to this Kabbarli of whom they had heard so much to say hail and farewell. We made a queer procession to the Siding, walking slowly and in single file, as we had so often walked to the sacred ceremonies. Yalli-yalla and Gindigi strode close beside me, their bare feet kicking aside the stone and twigs that my shoes should not be cut.

Because I had the sacred totem boards in my possession, the women dared not approach, but stood away on the north side of the line. Farewell to each one of them and then the little white girl approached. With her, as I sat upon my luggage, I recited the old well-known hymn of childhood, "Now the day is over." In the quiet evenings I have sung it alone to the stars for many a year.

The train came in. My shabby old hold-all that had been my wardrobe since 1909 and still carried my personal possessions for old sake's sake was hoisted aboard.

The last I saw was the soft strained farewell in my natives' eyes. I gave them shillings for the first time, calling each by his native name, with a few words of native nonsense to ease my feelings.

It seemed a dream that the old life was over, the old life of eternal wind and sand, the long, long droughts that take ten years to come and go, the so meagre yet so crowded years that I had spent in such strange company.

There was not an hour of my time wasted in all those years. I did what I set out to do—to make their passing easier and to keep the dreaded half-caste menace from our great continent. I know that I hold a place in their hearts, and that my memory and my magic will keep them *balya,* lest Kabbarli should know, and be *koordudu yooril* (heart crying).

I have tried to tell of their being and their ending and the cause of their decline. Nothing is ever lost in this world and if the slightest impression of anything I have said or done, by example or in devotion, remains with them in comfort for the past or hope for the future, I shall be content.

LEGEND OF HOW THE EAGLE-HAWK BROUGHT THE WATER TO YURIA GABBI

IN DREAMTIMES THE EAGLE-HAWK BROUGHT WATER TO Yuria Burnda (rock) from the far, far west and put it down at the foot of the rock, and sat down beside it with Weeloo his curlew wife. He looked about and saw plenty meat and vegetable food, and every day he went out hunting for meat while Weeloo gathered roots and fruit and ants and lizards. They were living very happily together until one day, when Walja had gone to Moonaba Water to spear an emu, Koongara, the little hawk, stole up to the hut where Weeloo was sitting preparing the supper and took Weeloo away with him to be his wife. When Walja returned with his food he found his ashes cold, and no Weeloo to be seen anywhere. He looked round his hut, and saw the tracks of Koongara, where he had stolen up behind Weeloo. The tracks went south, and when Walja saw them he said, "I will follow them up and kill Koongara and I will beat Weeloo for letting him take her away." The he lighted a little fire on top of the rock and sat down beside it to straighten his spear, and make it strong and hard and sharp. The Kaan'ga (crows) were uncles to Walja, and they had seen Koongara come and steal Weeloo away, but they did not interfere. They now sat near Walja and mocked him, and sang:

> Kaa! Kaa! yamba yuri yarru warranu.
> Kaa! Kaa! yamba yuri yarru warranu.

("Ah! ah! they have gone to a far-away camp; listen, hear them go along the road.")

Walja said nothing, only made his spear more sharp, and when it was ready he got up from the rock where he had been sitting, and he left the mark of the fire, the spear and his knees where he had pressed the spear on the rock for the crows to see, and there they remain to this day—the little fire, the spear and Walja's knees on the hard rock.

Koongara already had a wife, Yanguna, the white cockatoo, but Koongara liked Weeloo better, for Weeloo built her hut in the little hollows of stony places, just as he did, and Yanguna always wanted to have her shelter on leafy places.

Koongara fled with Weeloo to Koorijilla, and he made a deep hollow into which he crept, with Weeloo on top, so that if Walja came while he slept Weeloo would be speared first, and he might have time to get away. Walja was very angry with Weeloo for going away, with Koongara for stealing her, and with Kaan'ga for mocking him, and he made great, great rain come. He gathered all the big rain-clouds from the west, and they came swift and fast to make the rain for him. Koongara saw them coming and he said, "Oh, there's *gabbi* coming to Koo'luna," but while he spoke they came fast and fast and covered all the sky, and the *gabbi* fell from them so heavily that Koongara could not find a dry place to sit down at Koorijilla. Then he and Weeloo went on to Wal-dhabbi, but the *gabbi* followed them there; then they went to Kureeng'-gabbi, where Koongara's hut was, but the *gabbi* followed them up, making a big creek all the way. Koongara was very tired, for there was no place for him to rest in, and when he came to Kureeng'gabbi *burnda* he sat down on top of the rock, with Weeloo beside him. Walja was behind the rain-clouds, and when Koongara sat down Walja came up and speared him, and the marks of the blood and the feet of Koongara are on Kureeng'gabbi rock. Walja took Weeloo back to Yuria so that the crows should see her there, and no more have cause to mock him, and he beat Weeloo with his club, beat her so hard, so hard, that she picked up her digging-stick and hit Walja, crying, "Weeloo, weeloo," all the time, and that is why she has to cry "weeloo" always. Weeloo still lives at Yuria, and in the still nights she sends forth the same cry that she uttered while Walja beat her. Walja also lives at Yuria Gabbi, but he is only a bird now for the dream eagle-hawks have all gone.

That is the legend of Yuria Water.

Index

215